MAGHREB NOIR

WORLDING THE MIDDLE EAST

Maghreb Noir

THE MILITANT-ARTISTS OF NORTH AFRICA AND THE STRUGGLE FOR A PAN-AFRICAN, POSTCOLONIAL FUTURE

Paraska Tolan-Szkilnik

STANFORD UNIVERSITY PRESS
STANFORD, CALIFORNIA

Stanford University Press
Stanford, California

Printed in the United States of America on acid-free, archival-quality paper

Library of Congress Cataloging-in-Publication Data
Names: Tolan-Szkilnik, Paraska, author.
Title: Maghreb noir : the militant-artists of North Africa and the struggle for a Pan-African, postcolonial future / Paraska Tolan-Szkilnik.
Other titles: Worlding the Middle East.
Description: Stanford, California : Stanford University Press, 2023. | Series: Worlding the Middle East | Includes bibliographical references and index.
Identifiers: LCCN 2022046081 (print) | LCCN 2022046082 (ebook) | ISBN 9781503634824 (cloth) | ISBN 9781503635913 (paperback) | ISBN 9781503635920 (epub)
Subjects: LCSH: Arts—Political aspects—Africa, North—History—20th century. | Anti-imperialist movements—Africa, North—History—20th century. | Pan-Africanism—History—20th century. | Arts, Black—Africa, North—20th century. | Arts, North African—20th century.
Classification: LCC NX180.P64 T65 2023 (print) | LCC NX180.P64 (ebook) | DDC 709.61—dc23/eng/20230210
LC record available at https://lccn.loc.gov/2022046081
LC ebook record available at https://lccn.loc.gov/2022046082

Cover design: Alex Robbins
Cover art: Homage to the William Klein movie poster *The Pan-African Festival of Algiers*.
Typeset by Elliott Beard in Arno Pro 11/14

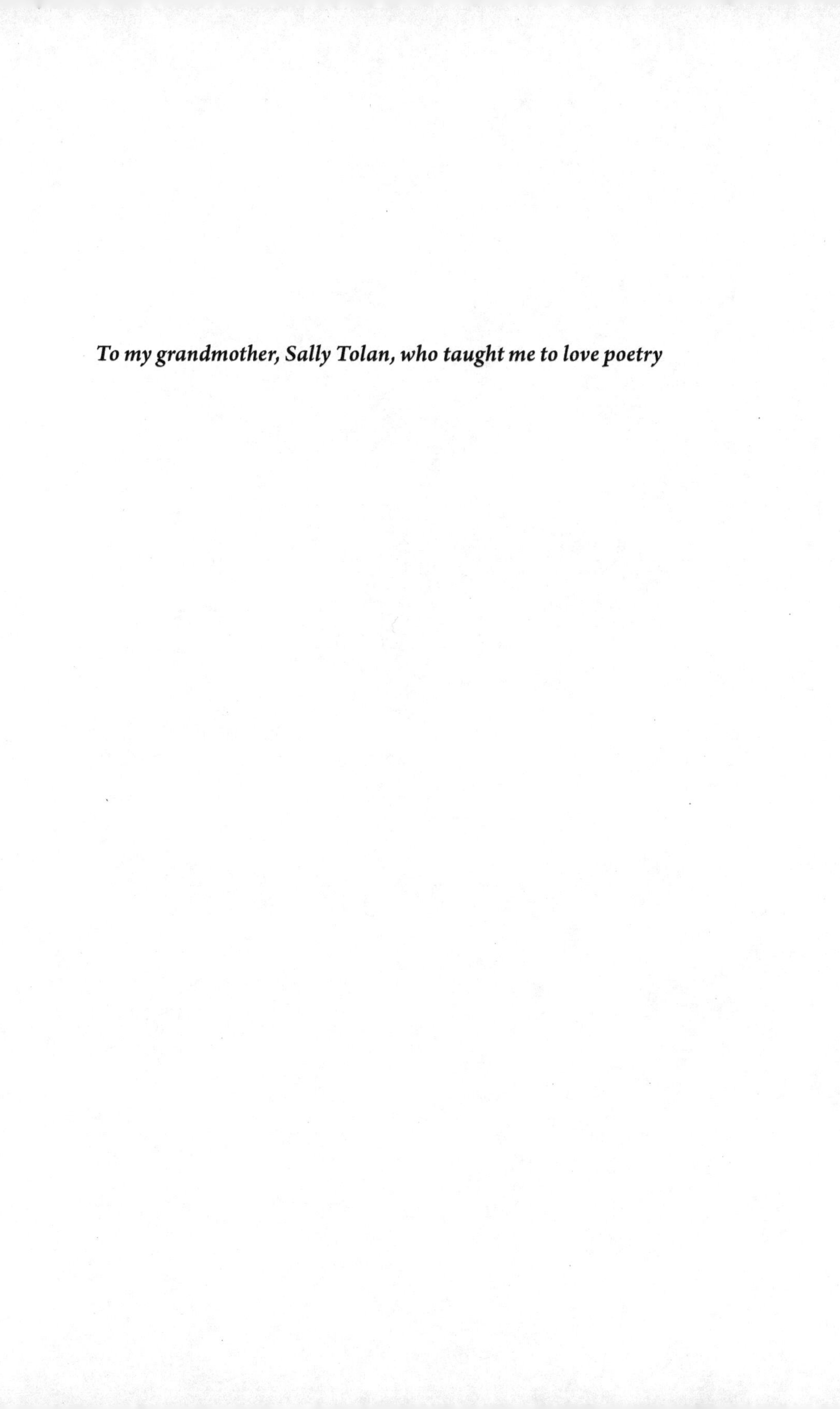

To my grandmother, Sally Tolan, who taught me to love poetry

CONTENTS

CAST OF CHARACTERS

MARIO DE ANDRADE (1928–1990): Angolan poet and founder of the Movimento Popular de Libertação de Angola (MPLA); partner of Sarah Maldoror, father of Anouchka and Henda de Andrade.

NÉJIB AYED (1953–2019): Tunisian film critic, secretary-general then president of the Federation Tunisienne des Cinés-Clubs (FTCC) from 1973 to 1988; executive director of the Journées Cinématographiques de Carthage (JCC) in 2017 and 2018.

FARID BELKAHIA (1934–2014): Moroccan visual artist from Marrakech, member of the Casablanca school and contributor to *Souffles/Anfas.*

ABDELLATIF BEN AMAR (1943–): Tunisian filmmaker, known for *Une si simple histoire* and *Sejnane,* among others.

MEHDI BEN BARKA (1920–1965): Moroccan politician, head of the left-wing Union Nationale des Forces Populaires (UNFP); was a strong opponent of French imperialism and King Hassan II's authoritarianism; murdered in Paris in 1965.

AHMED BEN BELLA (1916–2012): Algerian politicians, soldier, and leader in the Front de Libération Nationale (FLN); first president of Algeria between 1962 and 1965.

TAHAR BEN JELLOUN (1947–): Moroccan writer and poet; published his first poem, "L'aube des dalles," in *Souffles/Anfas.*

FÉRID BOUGHEDIR (1944–): Tunisian filmmaker, film critic, and cinema professor; known for *Un été à la Goulette* and *Halfaouine,* among others.

HOUARI BOUMÉDIÈNE (1932–1978): Algerian nationalist, politician, and army colonel; seized power from his predecessor, Ahmed Ben Bella, in a bloodless coup in 1965.

HABIB BOURGUIBA (1903–2000): Tunisian nationalist leader and statesman; first president of independent Tunisia from 1957 to 1987.

AQUINO DE BRAGANÇA (1924–1986): Goan writer and political activist; leading political and intellectual figure in the fight for Mozambican independence.

AMÍLCAR CABRAL (1924–1973): Militant, poet, and thinker from Cape Verde and Guinea-Bissau; assassinated in 1973.

AIMÉ CÉSAIRE (1913–2008): Martinican poet and politician; one of the founding members of the *négritude* movement and author of the book-length poem *Cahier d'un retour au pays natal* (1939).

MOHAMMED CHABÂA (1935–2013): Moroccan visual artist; member of the Casablanca school and contributor to *Souffles/Anfas.*

MOHAMMED CHALLOUF (1957–): Tunisian filmmaker, known for *Tahar Cheriaa: à l'ombre du baobab.*

TAHAR CHERIAA (1927–2010): Tunisian founder of the Journées Cinématographiques de Carthage, known as the "father of Tunisian and African film"; father of Kaiser Cheriaa.

ELDRIDGE CLEAVER (1935–1988): Black American writer and political activist; headed the international division of the Black Panther Party in Algiers; former husband of Kathleen Cleaver.

KATHLEEN CLEAVER (1945–): Black American law professor, writer, and political activist; headed the international division of the Black Panther Party in Algiers; former wife of Eldridge Cleaver.

HASSAN DALDOUL (1942–): Tunisian director and producer.

LÉON-GONTRAN DAMAS (1912–1978): French poet and politician from French Guiana; founding member of the *négritude* movement.

RENÉ DEPESTRE (1926–): Haitian poet and militant; known for *Hadriana dans tous mes rêves.*

ALIOUNE DIOP (1910–1980): Senegalese writer and editor; founding member of the intellectual and cultural journal *Présence africaine.*

NOURREDINE DJOUDI (1934–): Algerian ambassador to South Africa.

MARCELINO DOS SANTOS (1929–2020): Mozambican poet, militant, and founder of the Fronte de Libertação de Moçambique (FRELIMO).

FRANTZ FANON (1925–1961): Martinican psychiatrist and political philosopher; supporter of the Algerian struggle for independence and writer of the notorious *The Wretched of the Earth* (1961).

MARIA AMÁLIA LOPES FONSECA (1928–?): Born to an influential Cape Verdean family, Fonseca moved to Rabat in 1960 and became director of the administrative department of the permanent secretary of the Conferência das Organizações Nacionalistas das Colónias Portuguesas (CONCP).

JELILA HAFSIA (1927–): Tunisian journalist, writer, and director of the cultural club Tahar Haddad.

HASSAN II (1929–1999): King of Morocco from 1961 until his death in 1999; son of Muhammed V and father of Mohammed VI, the present king.

MED HONDO (1936–2019): Franco-Mauritanian actor, filmmaker, and producer; known for *Soleil Ô* and *Les bicots-nègres vos voisins.*

TED JOANS (1928–2003): Black American painter, beat poet, and militant; known for *A Black Pow-Wow of Jazz Poems* (1969) and *Afrodisia* (1970).

MOHAMMED KHAÏR-EDDINE (1941–1995): Moroccan Berber poet from Tafraout; cofounder of *Souffles/Anfas*; exiled to France in 1965.

ABDELLATIF LAÂBI (1942–): Moroccan poet, militant, and founder of *Souffles/Anfas*; imprisoned for many years in Morocco, currently living in France; husband of Jocelyne Laâbi.

JOCELYNE LAÂBI (1943–): Born in Lyon but raised in Morocco; published several children's books based on Moroccan culture and traditions and her memoir, *La liqueur d'aloès* (2005); wife of Abdellatif Laâbi.

ANDRÉ LAUDE (1936–1995): French writer, poet, and journalist; friend of Med Hondo and *Souffles/Anfas.*

SARAH MALDOROR (1938–2022): Guadeloupean filmmaker (known for *Monamgambee* and *Sambizanga,* among others); partner of Mario de Andrade, mother of Anouchka and Henda de Andrade.

TONI MARAINI (1941–): Italian writer, art historian, and member of the *Souffles/Anfas* team; wife of Mohamed Melehi.

DENIS MARTINEZ (1941–): Algerian painter, friend of Jean Sénac, and founder of the Aouchem painting movement.

MOHAMED MELEHI (1936–): Moroccan painter and designer of the *Black Sun of Renewal* on the *Souffles* cover; husband of Toni Maraini.

MOHAMMED V (1909–1961): Sultan of Morocco from 1927 to 1953, then king of the independent Kingdom of Morocco from 1957 until his death in 1961; father of Hassan II.

ELAINE MOKHTEFI (1928–): American writer and militant; organized the American contingent of the Festival Culturel Pan-Africain d'Alger (PANAF) in 1969; published her memoir *Algiers: Third World Capital* in 2018.

BITTY MORO (1939–2019): Actor and theater director from the Ivory Coast; attended the Festival Culturel Pan-Africain d'Alger.

AGOSTINHO NETO (1922–1979): Angolan politician and poet; member of the "Cabral generation"; leader of the MPLA and first president of independent Angola from 1975 to 1979.

MOSTAFA NISSABOURY (1943–): Moroccan poet and cofounder of *Souffles/Anfas.*

OUSMANE SEMBÈNE (1923–2007): Senegalese writer, filmmaker, and militant; known for *La noire de . . .* (1966), which was the first African film exhibited at the Journées Cinématographiques de Carthage.

JEAN SÉNAC (1926–1973): Algerian writer and militant for Algerian independence; creator of the militant-poet radio show *Poésie sur tous les fronts;* assassinated in his apartment in August 1973.

LÉOPOLD SÉDAR SENGHOR (1906–2001): First Senegalese president from 1960 to 1980; poet and founding member of the *négritude* movement.

ABRAHAM SERFATY (1926–2010): Moroccan writer and opponent of King Hassan II; contributed to *Souffles/Anfas*; lived in hiding for two years and then was imprisoned for seventeen years before moving to France.

ARCHIE SHEPP (1937–): Black American saxophonist; attended the Festival Culturel Pan-Africain d'Alger, where he performed with poet Ted Joans and a group of Touareg musicians.

HOCINE TANDJAOUI (1949–): Algerian writer, writer, and disenchanted youth in Boumédiène's Algeria.

ACRONYMS

ALN: Armée de Libération Nationale

ANC: African National Congress

CEI: Casa dos Estudantes do Império

CNC: Centre National de la Cinématographie

COMACICO: Compagnie Africaine Cinématographique Industrielle et Commerciale

CONCP: Conferência das Organizações Nacionalistas das Colónias Portuguesas

FEPACI: Fédération Panafricaine des Cinéastes

FESPACO: Festival Panafricain du Cinéma et de la Télévision de Ouagadougou

FLN: Front de Libération Nationale

FRELIMO: Frente de Libertação de Moçambique

FTCC: Fédération Tunisienne des Ciné-Clubs

JCC: Journées Cinématographiques de Carthage

MAC: Movimento Anti-colonial

MLSTP: Movimento de Libertação de São Tomé e Príncipe

MNA: Mouvement National Algérien

MPLA: Movimento Popular de Libertação de Angola

OAS: Organisation Armée Secrète

OAU: Organization of African Unity

PAIGC: Partido Africano da Independência da Guiné e Cabo Verde

PANAF: Pan-African Festival of Algiers (Festival Culturel Pan-Africain d'Alger)

SECMA: Society d'Exploitation Cinématographique Africaine

SNED: Société Nationale d'Édition et de Diffusion

UDMA: Union Démocratique du Manifeste Algérien

UGET: Union Générale des Étudiants de Tunisie

UMT: Union Marocaine du Travail

UN: United Nations

UNESCO: United Nations Educational, Scientific, and Cultural Organization

UNFP: Union Nationale des Forces Populaires (Morocco)

MAGHREB NOIR

INTRODUCTION

ON A BLISTERING SUMMER DAY in July 1969, a car packed with Moroccan poets and painters, including writer Tahar Ben Jelloun, poet Abdellatif Laâbi, and militant Abraham Serfaty, drove into Algiers for the Pan-African Festival of Algiers (PANAF). At the festival, the young Moroccans joined thousands of militant-artists from across the African continent, Europe, Asia, and the Americas. Hotels were overflowing with official delegations from newly independent states, so Ben Jelloun and other non-official attendees had to sleep in schools, in gymnasiums, and even under bridges. During the PANAF, Ben Jelloun met and interviewed Senegalese film director Ousmane Sembène, whose work he loved. To Ben Jelloun, Sembène's 1968 film *Le mandat* was the African continent's first cinematic manifesto because it balked at the harsh realities of life under postcolonial authoritarian regimes. During the interview, Ben Jelloun asked Sembène, "How should African cinema define itself in contrast with Western culture?" Sembène responded categorically: "Let us not talk about the West. Let's talk about us."[1] The conversation then turned to the role of the artist in Africa. "For me he [the artist] is a politician," Sembène professed; "he is a man completely engaged in perpetual dissent. His role is to be a militant, a fighter."[2] For Sembène there was only one valid form of art in postcolonial Africa: militant art.

Ben Jelloun and Sembène were debating the role of African artists amid one of the biggest celebrations of revolutionary culture on the African continent, the PANAF. Funded by the Algerian state and the Organization of African Unity (OAU), the PANAF consecrated political art through a series of parades, concerts, poetry readings, and visual art exhibits. "The occidental idea of culture has gone a long way and has favored a thesis according to which culture is a luxury of the 'over-developed,'" read one of the PANAF's pamphlets.[3] The artists at the PANAF aimed to do away with this unacceptable distinction between art and life. Culture in postcolonial Africa, claimed Algerian president Houari Boumédiène in the PANAF's opening speech, was a crucial "weapon in the struggle for liberation."[4]

In the first years of postindependence, the Algerian Front de Libération Nationale (National Liberation Front; FLN), one of several nationalist organizations that fought for Algeria's independence from France, appropriated the revolution the Algerian people led against the colonial powers.[5] The FLN created an independence narrative that glorified the party's leaders as anticolonial heroes and celebrated them through state-commissioned art. Monopolizing postcolonial cultural production, the Algerian government propagated the idea of freedom as a collective, Pan-African liberation from foreign rule.[6] Pan-Africanism appealed to the Algerian government because, as it was organized around a loose federation of African states, it did not undermine the FLN's authority. Furthermore, by focusing on Pan-Africanism as a state ideology, Algerian leaders hoped that anticolonial agitators would continue to channel their anger outward, toward the former colonial powers, rather than inwards, toward their increasingly authoritarian leaders.

Given the publicized goal of the PANAF, Ben Jelloun and Sembène could have felt right at home in the boisterous streets of 1969 Algiers. But they and their peers were not fooled by the Algerian government's attempt at controlling the Pan-African conversation, for they understood that freedom extended well beyond the postcolonial states' infrastructures.[7] They viewed the festival as co-opting the power and potential of revolutionary art, transforming it into a state project that served to uphold a corrupt postcolonial government. And so, outside major state-sponsored events such as the PANAF, Ben Jelloun, Sembène, and their peers met around kitchen tables, in dimly lit bars, and in the leafy cafés of the Algerian capital to talk about what *they* thought the role of the artist was in postcolonial Africa. Like Sembène, they concluded that the role of the artist was to dissent.

In the decade or so after independence, two different forms of Pan-

Africanism collided in the Maghreb. The first was a state-level project staged for all to see at events such as the PANAF. The other was a state-skeptical project led by a fluctuating group of militant-artists who created a Pan-African culture, dissenting from both the enduring legacies of European colonialism and the authoritarianism of the postcolonial states.[8] Because of the Maghrebi governments' largely successful attempts at monopolizing postcolonial Pan-African culture, we must look outside the state, its people and infrastructures, to find that dissenting Pan-Africanism in alternative sites of political engagement such as the radio airwaves, the pages of magazines, festival gatherings, and the intimate spaces of bedrooms.

Maghreb Noir tunes in on these conversations of dissent among militant-artists of what I have termed the Maghreb Generation because of the central role the Maghreb played in their political and artistic evolution.[9] The capital cities of the Maghreb (Rabat, Algiers, Tunis) were points of convergence for militant-artists; spaces to write, paint, print zines, film, train militarily, laugh, make love, and debate the future of postcolonial Africa. *Maghreb Noir* is the story of the Maghreb's alternative sites of Pan-African engagement and the militant-artists who inhabited these spaces.

PAN-AFRICANISM AND RACE IN THE MAGHREB

The numerous migratory crises that Europe has faced in the past ten years have made the Maghreb the epicenter of Europe's immigration anxieties. Indeed, the Maghreb has become, for many Africans, an entryway into Europe—a place of passage, a liminal space in which to wait for visas or boats. In the Maghreb, too, the increase in the Black and migrant population has revived many debates on the Maghreb's relationship to the rest of Africa.[10] The 2011 Tunisian Revolution cast a spotlight on the conditions of Black Tunisians.[11] To understand the demands of Black Maghrebis and the lived reality of Black migrants in the Maghreb, it is imperative to write the history of relations between the Maghreb and the rest of Africa.

Despite its location on the Mediterranean and its long history as a crossroads between the Middle East, Africa, and Europe, North Africa has remained marginal to the historiographies of all those regions. The Sahara still acts as a dividing line between the Maghreb and the rest of the African continent. A new generation of historians, geographers, and anthropologists have started to break down this construct by revealing the dynamic movement of people, goods, and ideas across Africa in the precolonial and colonial eras.[12] More recently, a few scholars have foregrounded the Maghreb as a Pan-African political and cultural hub in the postcolonial era.[13] These scholars are writing against decades of French colonial dictates and policies that attempted to sever the Maghreb from the rest of Africa. Indeed, the French imperial government was terrified that transcontinental solidarity would develop between their territories and breed anti-French sentiment and revolutionary anticolonialism. To maintain their empire, the French drew a line in the sand between what they saw as Arab Africa and Black Africa, exploiting linguistic and cultural differences between Black, Berber, and Arab inhabitants of the Maghreb.[14]

Stories about Pan-Africanism and the Black Atlantic also rarely include North Africa,[15] despite the fact that many Black American writers, intellectuals, and artists not only reflected on the plight of North Africans in Europe but also traveled to North Africa.[16] American performer Josephine Baker, adored internationally by both Black and white audiences, spent much of World War II leading the French resistance efforts from Morocco and providing Moroccan passports to Jews fleeing Nazi persecution.[17] The Black American writers James Baldwin, Claude McKay, Jessie Redmon Fauset, and William Gardner Smith, while residing in Paris, traveled to the Maghreb, and expressed their solidarity with the Algerian struggle for independence.[18] In 1972, Baldwin wrote, "He [the Algerian], and his brothers were, in fact, being murdered by my hosts [the French]. And Algeria, after all, is a part of Africa, and France, after all, is a part of Europe. The Algerian and I were both, alike, victims of this history, and I was still a part of Africa, even though I had been carried out of it nearly four hundred years before."[19]

Maghreb Noir turns to the role that the Maghreb played in the development of a postcolonial Pan-Africanism. First, I argue that the Maghreb Generation's definition of Blackness was political rather than just racial.[20] With their capacious understanding of Blackness, the members of the Maghreb Generation included all colonized, formerly colonized, or otherwise marginalized peoples from across the globe within the Pan-African community. Second, because the ideas of Pan-Africanism were no longer limited exclusively to Black people, a multitude of Black, Arab, White, and Amazigh militants living in the Maghreb during the 1950s, 1960s, and 1970s, took up the project of Pan-Africanism and radically transformed it into a multilingual, multiracial, militant-artistic project.

Indeed, the encounters in North Africa between Black and Maghrebi artists challenged the foundations on which many believed Pan-African solidarities were based. Before traveling to the Maghreb, poets such as the Angolan Mario de Andrade, Haitian René Depestre, and American Ted Joans articulated their ideas along the lines of racial and national solidarity. They were inspired by the political Pan-Africanism of their forefathers, who had fought to free African people through anticolonial struggles and a series of Pan-African congresses.[21] They were stirred by the poetry of the *négritude* movement; they read the works of Léopold Sédar Senghor, Aimé Césaire, and Léon-Gontran Damas, and, throughout the 1950s, they searched for their own Blackness.[22] Often this involved the pursuit of a nationally specific *négritude,* an Angolan, Haitian, or American Black identity.

But as the 1950s became the 1960s, the leaders of the new Black nations became increasingly autocratic. The *négritude*-rendered policies of Senghor in Senegal and Papa Doc Duvalier in Haiti became repulsive to these militant-artists. As Depestre, Joans, and Andrade traveled in the Maghreb, they met Maghrebi poets such as the Moroccan Abdellatif Laâbi and Algerian Jean Sénac, who were equally disenchanted with the new leaders of the postcolonial world. From Algiers, Rabat, and Tunis, they started declaring that rigid racial solidarity was obsolete. In 1966, Depestre published an essay in the Moroccan literary journal *Souffles,* arguing that "separated from the historical context of the revolution in the Third-World, *négritude* became an unacceptable 'black Zionism' which kept the Black people away from their duty to do the revolution."[23] Joans, who by 1966 had been living in the Maghreb for six years, wrote to his friend, French poet André Breton, that he would not go to Dakar for what he called "Senghor's *merde noire*" (Senghor's Black shit), otherwise known as the First World Festival of Black Arts (1966), because he did not want to participate in an event where artists and poets would be "held up (financially) . . . by Senghor's black bourgeoisie gangsters assisted by the U.S.A. fat-black-pussy-cat officials."[24] He boycotted Dakar in his "own sweet way," he continued, by "crossing the Sahara" to Oran, Algeria.[25]

This is not to say that the language of race was absent from the discourse of postcolonial Pan-Africanism; after all, members of the Maghreb Generation were still careful to distinguish themselves from white Europeans and Americans. Eager not to be confused with the white poets, beatniks, hippies, or "hairy marijuana dealers" of Paris and San Francisco, these poets made clear that they were no mere "marchers of war and peace."[26] Their intention was not to beat the "tam-tams of victory,"[27] or to loll in the comforts of folklore and exoticism, but rather to "dynamite the rotten halls of the old humanisms."[28] The militant-artists of the Maghreb Generation pushed beyond the global color line imposed by the former colonial powers, and in so doing they discursively colored all colonized and formerly colonized people, all those who resisted neocolonialism and authoritarianism.[29] The Pan-African community, hence, extended beyond the boundaries of the continent, or even of the Diaspora, to all those who sought a third way between the former colonial powers and the new postcolonial states. At the center of that community was the African continent. This book expands the horizons of Black Internationalism by introducing a new hub of Black thought, after Black London, Black Paris, Black New York: Black Tunis, Black Rabat, and Black Algiers—the cities of the *Maghreb Noir*.[30]

THE CHALLENGES AND DELIGHTS OF A MULTILINGUAL, GLOBAL SOURCE BASE

This project uncovers a history of postcolonial collaboration between militant-artists from across the globe. To write a narrative of artistic activism, I traveled to the Maghreb, France, and the United States. I conducted interviews and scoured through militant-artists' personal papers, putting together a rich archive of letters, pamphlets, and memorabilia donated by my interviewees. This archive was interdisciplinary in nature: it included poetry, film, and drawings, as well as the more typical historical sources such as newspapers and correspondence. It was also a multilingual archive: I've used sources in English, French, Portuguese, Italian, Spanish, and Arabic. Because of the diversity of primary source materials, I have made the choice to focus the narrative of this book exclusively on primary materials and to engage with secondary sources in the endnotes. This is by no means a dismissal of the excellent scholarship that has guided me through researching and writing this book; rather, it is a stylistic choice predicated on my desire to tell a compelling story.

Because of the nature of the contemporary Maghrebi regimes, I was unable to access state archives, either because I was not authorized to do so or because these archives seemingly did not exist. Only in Tunisia was I able to examine documents in the National Archive, but these were few and far between. Most of the JCC (Journées Cinématographiques de Carthage) archives, it seems, have not been classified by the Tunisian Ministry of Culture. However, state-sponsored newspapers and presses followed events such as the PANAF and the JCC closely, publishing play-by-plays of the performances and debates. Much of that plentiful literature is now housed in the Maghrebi national libraries and is thus relatively accessible.

Because the state-sponsored newspapers did not give me a sense of what was going on in the hallways of the Maghrebi governments between state officials, I relied on sources from the French Diplomatic Archives in Nantes to better understand the political context behind the Algerian, Moroccan, and Tunisian regimes' various Pan-African projects. The French were active and worried observers of any sort of anti-imperial rapprochement between the Maghreb and other African governments. The French embassies wrote extensive reports to the French Ministry of Foreign Affairs concerning Morocco's involvement in arms trades with the Lusophone militants, tensions arising at the PANAF, and movie projections at the JCC. They commented, with some relief it seems, on the disagreements among Maghrebi states and between the Maghreb and other regions of Africa. At the same time, they continued to play a large part in those divisions, leveraging their technical, economic, and cultural cooperation to promote pro-French politics on the African continent. All these divisive dynamics are visible in the documents from the Diplomatic Archives, masquerading under the guise of cultural reporting on the events in the Maghreb.

Collections of personal papers, such as the Jean Sénac archives in Marseille and Algiers, the René Depestre archives in Limoges, and the Ted Joans archive in Berkeley, have allowed me to delve into the lives of a few of the characters in this project. These archives were rich in terms of what they revealed about the interior lives of the Maghreb Generation, although the peripatetic nature of these characters' lives meant that there were significant gaps in the documentation—papers were lost, forgotten, or destroyed during moves, forced exiles, or after their death. The Ted Joans archives housed at the Bancroft Library in Berkeley consist of 19 1/2 linear feet of artwork, poetry, and newspaper clippings, among other things. Perusing Joans's archive was a joyful and at times overwhelming affair: he was an avid notetaker and doodler, and printouts of his poems often included a dense transcript of notes and sexually explicit drawings. Jean Sénac's archives, housed at both the Mediterranean Literary Archives in Marseille and the National Library in Algeria, were also abundant, though the collection in Algeria was not always in a good state. Like Joans, Sénac kept a plethora of records of his intimate life, from romantic letters to half-smoked cigarettes on which he had scribbled a line of poetry. Both men were essentially hoarders, and I say this as a happy historian lucky enough to sift through their papers.[31]

Another major source of written archival material comes directly from the protagonists of this book. When I interviewed people such as Kaiser Cheriaa, Hassan Daldoul, Sarah Maldoror, and others, they generously allowed me to copy documents that they had in their possession. These documents complemented the interviews I conducted with them and filled some of the gaps in the state archives. Of course, they were also only a portion of the materials produced during the 1960s and 1970s and thus only reflect what some people thought it was important to keep.

In addition to written sources, between 2018 and 2019 I conducted thirty-three oral history interviews in France, Tunisia, Algeria, Morocco, and the United States, in Arabic, French, and English, some in a mix of French and Arabic or French and English. Though I interviewed in Morocco and Algeria, most of the interviews I conducted were with Tunisian filmmakers and film critics. Because archival documentation was sparse when it came to the JCC, oral interviews provided most of the information for the Tunisian section of the project. Most of my interviewees, the Tunisian filmmakers as well as those I interviewed in Algeria, Morocco, France, and the United States, had been interviewed before. This meant that many of them were familiar with the interview setting and had fixed some of their memories by retelling them over and over. When I brought up information that I had found in the archive or asked questions about their relationships with specific people, I was sometimes able to break the repetition of a fixed narrative and bring up recollections that did not always fit into their well-worn stories. Because many of my interviewees were committed to narrating a specific political project, informed by contemporary concerns and by a general nostalgia for a period of African history that they saw as brighter, they often overlooked tensions, ignoring or even disputing the influence of racial prejudice in various Pan-African projects.

My method of interviewing was semi-structured. I often began with a few questions but then generally let my narrators direct the interview themselves, which led to some unintended conversations, including one theme that came up again and again: sex and women's sexual liberation. Of the thirty-three people I interviewed, only nine were women. None of the women discussed sex or intimacy with me, and in fact, when I asked Sarah Maldoror about her partner Mario de Andrade, she responded with: "That is my private business, Ma'am."[32] The men I interviewed, however, brought up sexual fantasies and sexual encounters frequently, revealing the many ways in which these encounters challenged or cemented their racial perceptions of themselves and others. Chapter 4 emerged from these uncomfortable but revealing encounters.

My interest in the intersection of art and politics began in 2011, when I wrote an honors undergraduate thesis about the visual arts in postrevolutionary Iran. In 2014, I traveled to Tunisia to do research for my master's thesis, which I was writing at the École des Hautes Études en Sciences Sociales in Paris. I spent three weeks darting around Tunis and its vicinity interviewing Tunisian painters. In Tunis in 2014, and then again as I conducted the interviews for this project, I benefited from my position as a young French white woman. My interviewees were overwhelmingly kind and gracious; they opened their archives to me and sent me off with books and snacks. They never questioned my motives, never seemed suspicious. On the contrary, my interviewees often let down their guard in ways that I imagine they might not have had I been a foreign man, or possibly more suspicious, a local.

I completed most of my elementary and secondary education in Nantes, France. Even before the French parliament adopted the 2005 law stipulating that schools needed to teach "the positive sides of colonialism," the history textbooks that I grew up with tended to treat colonialism as a mostly positive enterprise that helped African countries develop the exploitation of their national resources and build up their infrastructure, thus concealing much of the violence and profiteering of colonialism.[33] My own interests in the history of Africa and the Maghreb stem from the gaps in my French secondary education, but also, more generally, from the lack of a public reckoning with the histories of France's racial, linguistic, and religious diversity. Working on *Maghreb Noir* for the past eight years has been a process of unlearning. *Maghreb Noir* focuses on telling the stories my French school curriculum did not include—stories that are essential in order for everyone, not just French citizens, to grasp the world of the twenty-first century.

STRUCTURE OF THE BOOK

Maghreb Noir moves chronologically and geographically from late 1950s Rabat, through late 1960s Algiers, and to early 1970s Tunis. Each chapter focuses on a case study of a specific transnational encounter between the militant-artists of the Maghreb Generation. Beginning in Morocco, Chapter 1 follows the peregrinations of a group of Luso-African poets and militants from Lisbon to Paris to Rabat. Starting in the late 1950s, these young militant-artists used Rabat as a home base for anticolonial activism in the Portuguese colonies. Morocco served as a liberated space on the African continent, where they could imagine what one could be in the wake of empire. There, they met young Moroccan writers who were haunted by similar concerns over their role in the postcolonial world, among them the poet Abdellatif Laâbi, founder of the Moroccan literary journal *Souffles*. Chapter 2 centers on the editorial group of *Souffles*. Over the course of seven years, from 1966 to 1973, *Souffles* took off from being a small Moroccan literary journal to become a paper caucus through which writers from across the African continent and the Diaspora called for an African cultural revolution.

Maghreb Noir's third and fourth chapters turn to Algeria's role in shaping Pan-African thought. By the mid-1960s, Algiers was teeming with revolutionaries from across Africa, the Americas, and Asia, leading the famous militant Amílcar Cabral to call Algiers the "Mecca of Revolutionaries." Not everyone in Algiers, however, was an enthusiastic supporter of the Algerian government's bid for Pan-African leadership. Chapter 3 gives voice to poets and artists from Algeria and all over the world who viewed the festival as a façade erected to conceal the decaying ideals that had once sustained the Algerian Revolution. Chapter 4 offers a window onto the carnal underbelly of Algiers's status as the Mecca of Revolutionaries by looking at sexual and romantic interactions between artists of the Maghreb Generation during the PANAF in 1969. Finally, Chapter 5 turns to Tunisia's attempt to match Moroccan and Algerian Pan-African leadership. The Tunisian Cultural Ministry, determined to become a key player in the African cultural scene, created the JCC in 1966. Under the joint leadership of the Tunisian intellectual Tahar Cheriaa and the Senegalese novelist and director Ousmane Sembène, the biennale transcended the Tunisian state's original intent and became a hub for members of the Maghreb Generation to continue creating a Pan-Africanism of dissent.

Maghreb Noir takes the reader from Rabat through Algiers to Tunis. Making use of primary sources, historical analysis, and, I hope, some good old storytelling, this book reconstructs the Maghreb Generation's moves, their friendships, their intimate relationships, and their artistic production. Weaving together micro- and macrohistories, *Maghreb Noir* makes the case for a history of the Maghreb that includes the entire African continent and that situates the region as a center of intellectual and cultural production in the second half of the twentieth century.

ONE

REVOLT RESPECTS NO BORDERS

Luso-African Revolutionaries in Rabat

My cry of revolt echoes in the longest valleys of the Earth. . . . It respects no borders / My cry of revolt vibrates in the chests of all Men.

AMÍLCAR CABRAL, 1966

"**THERE IS ONE FACT I** want to emphasize," insisted Noureddine Djoudi in a 2018 interview at the hotel Saint-George in Algiers; "Morocco did not assist African liberation movements like Algeria. They are making all this noise now, organizing conferences, but they did not help, not really."[1] Djoudi, an Algerian who grew up in Morocco, was postcolonial Algeria's primary government spokesperson in Africa. In the late 1950s, Djoudi trained in an Algerian national liberation camp near the Moroccan city of Oujda. When Algeria gained its independence from France in 1962, Djoudi served as the Algerian ambassador to almost a dozen African countries until the 1980s.[2] Two days after our initial interview, as we drove to Zeralda to meet Nelson Mandela's grandson, Djoudi reiterated that I should make sure to "get the story straight."[3] Djoudi was determined to rectify what he perceived as a budding and problematic historical narrative. "Morocco did not play a central role in helping liberation movements," he repeated for the umpteenth time.[4]

Djoudi's insistence is a testament to the enduring competition and strife between Morocco and Algeria, which extended from their involvement in

Pan-African politics to questions of their desert borders.[5] Above all, however, his emphasis is a response to the rise in scholarly and public attention to the part that the Maghreb played in the 1960s and 1970s in hosting revolutionary movements and training freedom fighters from across Africa. Scholars have fostered a narrative of Algeria, in particular, as a hub of revolutionary activity and a key player in determining the ideology and composition of the Third World and Pan-African communities.[6] Algeria notably hosted and trained the so-called *pieds-rouges* (red feet), a babel of leftists, revolutionaries, and other idealists from around the globe drawn there by the country's reputation as the Mecca of Revolutionaries.[7]

When it comes to the history of Pan-Africanism, the scholarship on Algeria completely overshadows that on Morocco. Scholars have ignored the fact that before Algeria had even attained its independence, the Kingdom of Morocco served as a staging ground and provided money and weapons to *pieds-rouges* from around the world.[8] The Algerian freedom fighters were themselves trained in Moroccan camps, such as the one near Oujda where Noureddine Djoudi sojourned. From the late 1950s into the mid-1960s, Morocco took a front-row seat in the deliberations over the future of Africa, toeing a revolutionary and anti-imperial line that many scholars have overlooked.

In the early years of Moroccan independence, for the militant-artists of the Maghreb Generation, Rabat was the place to be, vibrant and multicultural; the city was a crossroads between the Arab world, Europe, and Africa. Thanks to both its strategic location on the shores of the Mediterranean and the welcoming policies of Moroccan king Mohammed V, Rabat attracted dozens of exiled militants from Portugal's colonies in Africa who yearned to return to the African continent. From 1957 to 1966, Goan Aquino de Bragança, Mozambican Marcelino dos Santos, Cape Verdean Amílcar Cabral, and Angolan Mario Pinto de Andrade, all Luso-African militants and poets, made the Moroccan capital their home. Their presence attracted even more young Luso-African revolutionaries to Rabat. And so, by 1961, Rabat had become a hub for militants from the Portuguese colonies. The Moroccan government provided room and board, as well as military training. Rabat was the birthplace of the transnational network of revolutionaries I refer to as the Maghreb Generation—a network that expanded, at first with the help of the Moroccan state and later in direct defiance of it.

Before their move to Rabat, Cabral, dos Santos, Andrade, and Bragança met in the colonial capitals of Lisbon and Paris. In the hallways of the Casa dos Estudantes do Império and the back room of the Parisian editing house Présence Africaine, these young Luso-Africans fraternized with many eminent African and Black intellectuals, including the founders of the *négritude* movement.[9] At first it was their passion for poetry and literature that politicized them. In the late 1950s, spurred by their meetings with and readings of Frantz Fanon, these men broke from the *négritude* generation and instead began to emphasize material concerns and their connection with non-elite, rural, and poor Africans. As Cabral famously said in 1966 at the Tricontinental Conference in Havana—a conference that both he and Andrade attended—"it is not by screaming or writing bad words against imperialism that we will defeat it."[10]

In addition to emphasizing material concerns, these young Luso-African militant-poets moved away from the more nationalist preoccupations of their predecessors. The decision to move to Rabat demonstrates their transnational inclination. In Morocco, they developed contacts with militant-artists from across Africa and the Diaspora, spent time on the premises of the Union Marocaine du Travail (Moroccan Workers' Union; UMT), trained with soldiers from the royal army, met anti-apartheid leader Nelson Mandela, and worked to create a transnational grassroots movement that did not hesitate to challenge the postcolonial nation-state when it became authoritarian. They cultivated a revolutionary rhetoric that accounts for their moving in and out of favor with the Moroccan government. If independent nationhood was central to their rhetoric, they were unwilling to sacrifice their ideals for any government, or so they claimed. For many of these African anticolonialists, there was no contradiction between nationalism and Pan-Africanism or Third-Worldism. Just as these militants were strategically fighting for national independence, they were imagining themselves as part of a much larger struggle; they understood that nationalism was a useful stage on the journey toward the much grander goal of freedom that they envisioned for the postcolonial world.[11] Blending poetry and politics, the young Luso-African militant-artists built a transnational support network from their home base in Rabat.

But as Morocco settled into political independence, the royal government's political alliances started to shift. When King Mohammed V died in early 1961, his son and successor, Hassan II, started to retract his government's financial and rhetorical support for such movements and isolated

Morocco from many of its revolutionary African allies. Hassan II turned instead toward a staunchly anticommunist axis, striking a strong friendship with Zairean leader Mobutu Sese Seko and initiating a very different kind of Pan-Africanism.[12] This explains, in part, the current oblivion about Morocco's history of support for international revolutionaries. By 1962, the newly independent Algeria had filled the vacuum created by Morocco's abandonment of the revolutionary cause. It seems that Noureddine Djoudi was right, albeit with a caveat: *after* 1962, Algeria's official support of African liberation struggles was much more significant than Morocco's. The increasingly repressive attitudes of the young King Hassan II motivated Mario de Andrade, Marcelino dos Santos, and Aquino de Bragança to move their base to Algiers and to disentangle themselves from a Moroccan government that was now sinking into right-wing authoritarianism.

LISBON AND PARIS: ANTICOLONIAL METROPOLISES IN EUROPE

The Portuguese government created the Casa dos Estudantes do Império (CEI) in 1944 to supervise students from Portugal's African colonies studying in Lisbon.[13] The government's stated intent was to prepare their overseas subjects for imperial duties and develop their sense of dedication, patriotism, and goodwill.[14] Instead, to the dismay of its founders, the CEI became a space for anticolonial socialization. Young men and women from across the Portuguese Empire met in the hallways of the CEI, wrote poetry, and organized their respective countries' liberation struggles. It was in the halls of the CEI that Mario de Andrade first met Amílcar Cabral and was inspired to abandon his studies and commit himself fully to the liberation of Angola.

Mario Pinto de Andrade, born in Golungo-Alto, Angola, in 1928, moved to Lisbon in 1948 to study Latin and Greek at the University of Lisbon.[15] Amílcar Cabral, born in Bafatá, then Portuguese Guinea, in 1924, moved from Cape Verde in 1945 to study at the Higher Institute of Agronomy of the Technical University of Lisbon.[16] At their first meeting, Andrade remembered feeling a sort of bubbling under his skin: "Of course something was bubbling in our heads, not in a precise manner, not very well formulated—but we were in the process of formulating it, there was a collective subconscious being born."[17] After Cabral, Andrade met the Angolan militant-poet

Agostinho Neto and Mozambican militant-poet Marcelino dos Santos.[18] The four of them formed the core of what scholars have in turn called the "Generation of 50," the "Generation of 48," or as Andrade himself preferred, "the Cabral Generation," named after the man Andrade considered the group's most illustrious member.

After meeting Cabral and Neto, Andrade turned away from his classical studies; Greek and Latin seemed increasingly irrelevant. Eager to find a space in which they could learn about Africa, as well as educate their peers on the issues facing the continent, the four men created the Center of African Studies in the living room of their friends the Espirito Santo family. They still used the CEI to recruit new members, but they did not feel that they could fully develop their "Africanity" in a setting that included the sons and daughters of colonizers who, as Andrade noted, "were not particularly interested in discovering their *négritude*."[19] At the new Center of African Studies, Cabral would give presentations about African agriculture, Neto would discuss African history, and Andrade would talk about African literature, oral traditions, and African languages.[20] They wrote for the literary journal *Mensagem* and read the Martinican poet Aimé Césaire, the Senegalese poet Léopold Sédar Senghor, the Black American poet Langston Hughes and novelist Richard Wright, the Cuban poet Nicolas Guillén, and the Brazilian writer Jorge Amado. When they couldn't find Portuguese translations, they translated the works themselves.

> We recited poems by Nicolas Guillén—it was obligatory, it was part of our patrimony, of the intellectual baggage of the progressive African, in Lisbon at the time: he [the progressive African] must have read Senghor's *Anthology of Black and Malgache Literature*—my copy which had been through everyone's hands: I had lent it . . . to Agostinho Neto, and of course to Amílcar Cabral; I lost it later.[21]

Andrade noted that the Portuguese literary scene was relatively impoverished when it came to Marxist texts. In the Portuguese system, he bemoaned, "we had to learn Portuguese manuals by heart, . . . it was literally mimetic teaching, that one had to do in order to pass the exams."[22] So, they would fill the voids left by the Portuguese education system by turning to what came out of Brazil. Brazil, at the time, was much more progressive, and Brazilians would translate the Russians, such as Nicolas Gogol, or the Black Americans, such as Langston Hughes.

They could recite French philosopher Jean-Paul Sartre's introduction to Senghor's *Anthology* by heart. They read and exchanged worn copies of the Pan-African quarterly cultural, political, and literary magazine *Présence africaine,* which they received through two women who worked in the Buchholz Library, rumored to be two Nazi refugees in Portugal. They all read the same books, such as *Os negros da America,* about the struggle of Black Americans, and Mao Zedong's *The Long March.*[23] The more they read, the more they developed their African consciousness, Andrade noted, for these texts were not simply cultural, they were political. When they read Alioune Diop's editorials in *Présence africaine,* Andrade explained, it was like hearing a battle cry.[24] In fact, Andrade revealed, they used literature to recruit young African scholars to their group. They would draw people in with conversations about literature and poetry readings, and then identify the *éléments conscients* (politically conscious individuals) and agitate them to see how far they would be willing to go in their political resistance.[25]

The poets of the *négritude* movement inflamed the passions of Mario de Andrade and his cohort of poets and friends; they were on a quest to find their Luso-African *négritude.* In 1953 Andrade and his friend from São Tomé, Francisco Tenreiro, published the zine *Poesía negra de expressão portuguesa* to add their cries to the chorus of Black voices from the French Antilles and French West Africa. Inspired by Senegalese poet Léopold Sédar Senghor's *Anthologie de la nouvelle poésie nègre et malgache,* Andrade's anthology included seven poets who wove Kibundu and Portuguese together in their poems, thus articulating their duality, their Luso-Africanness.[26] The booklet opens with a manifesto for finding one's *négritude,* illustrated by the Portuguese surrealist painter António Pimentel Domingues, which inexplicably shows a women offering her breasts to the reader, perhaps as an illustration of the fountain of *négritude.* Every member of the Cabral Generation, in Lisbon or Luanda, went through the discovery of their *négritude,* explained Andrade: "It was our rupture with assimilation. We had to rediscover everything. Not just Angola, but Africa and the world, which the colonial administration had hidden, obscured from us."[27]

While the Center of African Studies had been a haven for the members of the Cabral Generation in the early 1950s, by the mid-1950s, Lisbon was rapidly becoming a dangerous place for anticolonial activists in which to live and organize. Neto was in and out of jail for political activism, and the Portuguese police repeatedly disrupted the Center of African Stud-

POESIA NEGRA

DE EXPRESSÃO PORTUGUESA

NO limiar do primeiro caderno de poesia negro-africana de expressão portuguesa, ocorrem-nos algumas considerações forçosamente breves sobre as características essenciais da poesia negra. Poesia negra, não já sòmente aquela que é produto do negro indígena da África, mas também a das Américas e esta que surge hoje como fruto amadurecido duma nova consciência dos problemas africanos, elaborada com a ajuda técnica das tradições culturais da Europa.

Na África Negra, a poesia tradicional não vive por si, como um dado de existência própria, mas apenas quando as palavras são essenciais à música, e a música e as palavras à dança. É uma forma sempre interessada e integrada numa expressão estética mais larga e complexa — o drama ritual. Toda a poesia está expressa nas canções, vinculadas aos acontecimentos da comunidade: nas cerimónias de nascimento, iniciação, casamento, caça ou funeral, quando há necessidade de os jóvens exercerem a sua influência sobre a amada, de as mães educarem ou embalarem os filhos, de os velhos perpetuarem a tradição da comunidade, de os chefes religiosos ou civis conservarem a obediência dos seus súbditos, de os guerreiros despertarem a coragem durante o combate e inspirarem temor ao inimigo, enfim, canções religiosas de feitiçaria e maldição, canções invocando os benefícios da natureza, canções executadas pelos trabalhadores e tudo o mais que seja peculiar ao grupo. E a servir estas canções, as línguas e dialectos veiculares nativos, duma notável expressividade e concisão, tal como os ritmos de tam-tam ...

Um pouco por toda a África Negra se mantém ainda esta poesia, mais viva numas regiões, mais esbatida noutras. Assinalemos o caso da África do Sul, paralelamente ao caso doutras regiões africanas sob dominação belga e inglesa, onde se nota uma conservação dos valores culturais africanos, recriados de forma dinâmica, graças ao esforço de superar o condicionamento opressivo da segregação.

Mas as artes dos Negro-Africanos estão ameaçadas. Com efeito, desde o séc. XV que o contacto de uma certa Europa com a África vem realizando nos corpos sociais do então chamado continente negro, um amolecimento da sua força gregária, até mesmo a sua destruição, destribalizando os homens, negando os seus valores culturais, desgastando as forças aborígenes em proveito da formação dum novo continente. E nem por isso essa Europa, velho continente tão orgulhoso das luzes da sua civilização e cultura, quis ceder um pouco da sua claridade, para uma tomada de contacto com as «sombras» das civilizações e culturas da África Negra, um tanto entregues à sua marginalidade pessoal. «Sombras» que só muito tarde, no princípio deste século, entrariam a iluminar os salões da Europa com a «harmoniosa fealdade» das suas artes plásticas. E deste facto — da Europa se negar em estabelecer diálogo com a África, reduzir a nada os valores negros, impor a sua civilização e só ela, fazer dos homens negros, homens à sua imagem e semelhança e só à sua imagem e semelhança — nasceu o «évolué», o desenraizado, sem quaisquer tradições autênticas, quer europeias quer africanas. Um tipo de homem, de novo marginal e transitório que se diluiu na mentalidade europeia, pressentindo vagamente as suas origens africanas. Assim é que a poesia negra mais enraizada no complexo social africano se afigura hoje ao negro de formação europeia, particularmente ao de língua francesa e portuguesa, como um processo longínquo e mesmo incompreensível, nas sua forma linguística nativa.

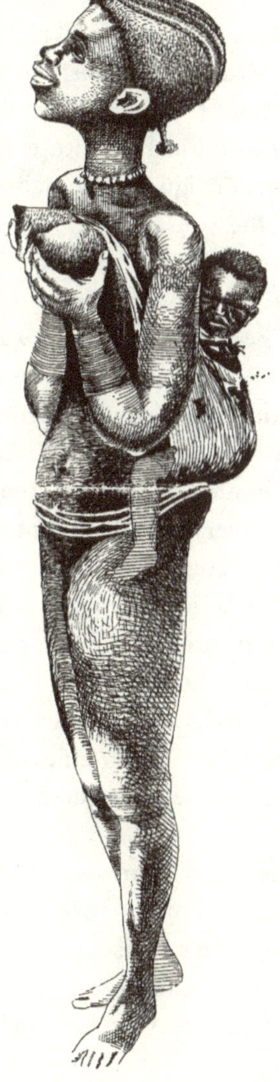

Entretanto, abre-se um novo caminho de reconquista dos valores perdidos. O negro-africano ocidentalizado, «consumidor de civilização branca», exprime uma atitude, num movimento formalmente cultural — a «negritude». Agora é o novo negro que surge entre duas guerras, consciente dos problemas da sua particular alienação, a alienação colonial e reivindica o seu lugar nos quadros da vida económica, social e política. Sinceramente interessado na preparação duma síntese de civilizações, dum justo e equilibrado diálogo Europa-África, Léopold Sédar Senghor, poeta do Senegal, fiel representante da negritude, põe o problema: Porque não unir as nossas duas claridades a fim de suprimir todas as sombras? Ou, para empregar uma imagem familiar, porque razão: cultivando o nosso jardim, não enxertar o rebento europeu sobre o nosso rebento selvagem? Virtude das civilizações mestiças ...

Mas como essa síntese ainda vem longe, o problema actual reside na conquista duma personalização, numa reabilitação de valores. A poesia do negro ocidentalizado provém duma necessidade imperiosa e angustiante de reencontrar os valores nativos destruídos, necessidade de se readaptar ao seu ambiente, necessidade de gritar a sua presença no mundo.

Aimé Césaire não se cansa de afirmar na sua forma poética tão penetrante:

(...) Et nous sommes debout maintenant,
mon pays et moi, les cheveux dans le
vent, ma main petite maintenant dans
son poing énorme et la force n'est pas
en nous, mais au-dessus de nous, dans
une voix qui vrille la nuit et l'audience
comme la pénétrance d'une guêpe
apocalyptique.
Et la voix prononce que l'Europe nous
a pendant des siècles gavés de mensonges
et gonflés de pestilences,
car il n'est point vrai que l'œuvre de
l'homme est finie
que nous n'avons rien à faire au monde
que nous parasitons le monde
qu'il suffit que nous nous mettions au
pas du monde

mais l'œuvre de l'homme vient seulement
de commencer
et il reste à l'homme à conquérir toute
interdiction immobilisée aux coins de
sa ferveur
et aucune race ne possède le monopole
de la beauté, de l'intelligence, de la
force
et il est place pour tous au rendez-vous
de la conquête et nous savons maintenant
que le soleil tourne autour de
notre terre éclairant la parcelle qu'a
fixée notre volonté seule et que toute
étoile chute le ciel en terre à notre
commandement sans limite.

(CONTINUA NA PÁGINA 2)

FIGURE 1. The first page of the *Anthology of Black Poetry of Portuguese Expression*, put together by Francisco Tenreiro and Mario de Andrade, published in May 1953, with art by António Domingues. Reprint courtesy of Annouchka de Andrade and Henda Ducados.

ies' meetings.[28] Cabral decided to return to Cape Verde in 1952, and in the summer of 1954 Andrade moved to Paris. A typical product of the urban upper class of Angola, Andrade could easily have returned to Luanda and taken his place in the colonial hierarchy, enjoying the relative privileges with which that position came. Instead, he joined the vanguard of national liberation in Lisbon, and along with his friends and colleagues at the CEI, began struggling against the colonial hierarchy, eventually moving to Paris to continue the fight.[29] In Andrade's mind Paris represented a great intellectual and political adventure; there, he hoped, he would be able to speak out against Portuguese colonialism more loudly and freely.[30]

In the summer of 1954, when Andrade arrived in Paris, the French Empire was in turmoil. The First Indochina War had just ended; the partisans of Moroccan king Mohammed V were leading violent riots in Fez and Khenifra; and Tunisia was poised to conduct negotiations for its independence. The empire was crumbling.[31] Andrade arrived in Paris penniless with the intention of working at *Présence africaine*. Following the recommendation of his friend Marcelino dos Santos, Andrade headed straight to No. 1 boulevard Jourdan, the Maison du Maroc (Morocco House) at the Cité Universitaire. Dos Santos was not there, but the Goan Aquino de Bragança welcomed Andrade. They chatted all night, aided by a bottle of port that Andrade had brought in his meager luggage. Andrade immediately had "the conviction, which was typical of our youth, that something permanent was being created in the relationship."[32] For a few months Bragança and dos Santos let Andrade sleep clandestinely in their room. In Paris, Andrade widened the circle of influence of the Cabral Generation and translated the struggle of the Portuguese colonies to the anticolonial intellectual scene in Paris.

The story of Paris as center stage for an ebullient debate on anticolonialism and anti-imperialism has already been told many times. The historiography of Black Paris is dedicated entirely to exploring the role of Paris as an anticolonial metropolis, to examining the connections between Black Africans and Black Americans in the Latin Quarter, dissecting the early years of the *négritude* literary movement, and explaining why so many Black Americans found Paris a friendlier place than New York.[33] Still, the importance of Paris as a place of encounter between militant-artists from across Africa and the Third World cannot be overstated. Moroccan poet Abdellatif Laâbi describes the social scene in post-1945 Paris:

> They all came through here, brothers and enemies, geniuses and originals of all genres, visionaries and analysts, prophets and architects, generals and popes, and everyone added their poem to dethrone the other poems. . . . Here we sit at the table, we are brought into the competition, the race of the clocks, the mythical stomach of the Absolute megalopolis. Speak or die![34]

To Mario de Andrade, Paris felt like an African capital. "It was in Paris that I felt I was moving to an African rhythm," he remembered, "to the rhythm of Africa in its entirety, Africa spread out in its globality—for all the struggles, on all fronts, be they political or cultural, were reverberating in Paris."[35]

In Paris, dos Santos, Andrade, and Bragança broadened their already significant politico-literary education. In permanent contact with writers and thinkers from around the world, they met the writers they had avidly read in Lisbon, including Senegalese poet Léopold Sédar Senghor, Martinican poet Aimé Césaire, Senegalese historian Cheikh Anta Diop, and French philosopher Jean-Paul Sartre. They met with members of the French working class to familiarize themselves with the struggles of the European proletariat. They were friendly with the French Communist Party, though most of them never formally joined because their residency in France was already tenuous and they did not want to draw any more suspicion from the French authorities. In any case, they resented the fact that members of the Communist Party often refused their calls for racial solidarity, claiming that this distracted from the proletarian revolution.[36] They debated *négritude* and the decolonization of the mind, as well as writing poetry and prose and taking part in countless political demonstrations. Andrade participated in the First International Congress of Black Writers and Artists in 1956 and met poets and militants from across the francophone and anglophone worlds. Dos Santos and Andrade wrote for *Présence africaine,* through which they made several crucial contacts with other radical writers, among them Moroccan poet Abdellatif Laâbi and Algerian poet Jean Sénac, one of the first Algerians Andrade met, who became a close friend.[37]

These encounters in Paris were a crucial first step in the creation of the transnational networks of liberation that went on to blossom in the Maghreb. A significant number of Maghrebi students and activists lived in Paris, which had not been the case in Lisbon. At Présence Africaine, at the Cité Universitaire, and in the cafés of the Latin Quarter, dos Santos, Andrade, and Bragança mingled and exchanged ideas with these students, whose familiar experiences of colonialism inspired similar revolutionary ideals. One of the causes that most preoccupied them, Andrade remembered, was the Algerian War of Independence. They felt very close to what was happening in Algeria. "I can't say we were thinking of an armed struggle already," recalled Andrade, "but we saw the similarities: a settler-colony, a big European presence."[38] In their minds, they compared the Algerian conflict to their struggle as Angolans and Mozambicans, and Algeria's victories invigorated them.

At the Cité Universitaire's Maison du Maroc, the three men established tight links with the anticolonial Moroccan community based in France, including the Moroccan nationalist leader Mehdi Ben Barka and other members of the monarchist and anticolonialist party of the Istiqlal.[39] They participated in anticolonial protests, sometimes serving as proxies for their Moroccan friends who risked being arrested or interrogated by the French police.[40] As Dos Santos remembered:

> There were demonstrations for the return of the king to Morocco. . . . The police invaded the Cité Universitaire, which was forbidden; we demonstrated, shouting, "Guillaume assassin, Guillaume assassin!" It was General Guillaume who had been placed in Morocco as a big chief of the country. And we were shouting there "OUT!" Many of our colleagues, Moroccan, would not go out on the road to demonstrate.[41]

Mohammed V, the first king of Morocco, was a source of inspiration to many of the young militants from the African continent. His triumphant return to Rabat on November 16, 1955, and his proclamation of Moroccan independence were filmed and broadcast across Africa and Europe. To Andrade, Bragança, and dos Santos, the return of the king would be one of the first victories in their two-decades-long struggle against colonialism. When the king finally arrived in Morocco and declared it independent, Bragança "immediately jumped to Morocco," remembered dos Santos.[42] Bragança settled in Rabat in 1957and began writing for the Moroccan journal *Al-Istiqlal*, in addition to his work as personal secretary to Ben Barka.[43] He also started weaving together a network of comrades and militants and preparing the groundwork for his two friends to join him a few years later.

By the late 1950s, dos Santos's and Andrade's time in Paris was drawing to a close. While Paris had seemed like a haven in the mid-1950s, by the end of the decade things were becoming increasingly unsafe. In November

1957, the three friends met with Amílcar Cabral in dos Santos's apartment and resolved to create a political organization to fight Portuguese colonialism: the Movimento Anti-colonial (MAC). Demonstrating the impact of the struggles in the Maghreb on these men's minds, the MAC's manifesto opened thus: "The heroic struggle of the people of Algeria is proving that any oppressed African people can resist and fight victoriously against the colonist oppressors—and is an example and a fountain of inspiration for the movements of national liberation in Africa and the whole world."[44] Shortly following this meeting, the police expelled dos Santos from France. They also interrogated Andrade, but Alioune Diop and Léopold Sédar Senghor both intervened in Andrade's favor. In the end, Andrade was permitted to stay in Paris; nevertheless, his name and those of his peers were on a list at the Direction de la Sûreté du Territoire, where they were suspected of being communists. "Paris was becoming a dangerous place," Andrade remembered; "not exactly the ideal place to lead a clandestine political organization for the liberation of the Portuguese colonies, at the very moment in which France was engaged in the war in Algeria and was an ally of the Portuguese government."[45] Indeed, between 1956 and 1957 France was leading a brutal campaign of political repression in Algeria, torturing and disappearing members of the rebel FLN.[46]

As Paris, the anticolonial metropolis, became a hotbed for police violence and repression, like Lisbon before it, militants started looking for other options. In 1959, writers from across the African continent gathered in Rome for the Second Congress of Negro Writers and Artists, where Andrade met the Martinican philosopher and psychiatrist Frantz Fanon for the second time. The two men had crossed paths before, in 1956, at the Paris-based First International Congress of Black Writers and Artists; by 1959 Fanon no longer worked for the French government but instead had responsibilities within the FLN. He had become counselor of the provisional government of Algeria, and he was tasked with enlarging the FLN's anti-imperialist camp to include Angolan and Mozambican militants. Fanon explained to Andrade that the FLN had the means to provide military training for young activists from Angola and Mozambique and would gladly welcome them in Tunisia, on one of its bases.[47]

This meeting with Fanon and the example set by Algeria, Andrade explained, defined the path forward for the colonized intellectual. Fanon's contribution to the congress was titled "Reciprocal Foundations for National Culture and the Struggle for Liberation." For the first time, as Andrade remembered, Fanon revealed to an African and international public the "revolutionary mutation from cultural discourse to armed struggle for national liberation,"[48] a development that was missing from the concept of the cultural problem as formulated by the previous generation of African intellectuals. It was only in 1959, when Fanon delivered his remarks in Rome, that Andrade and his peers understood that struggling for the universal recognition of Blackness was obsolete. Andrade, who had been an avid reader of Senghor and Césaire, concluded that *négritude*'s power had been exhausted.

On a more personal level, meeting Fanon and hearing his remarks at the symposium had a profound impact on Andrade's vision of the future. "This meeting with Fanon reinforced in each one of us an important decision," explained Andrade. "We had to go back to Africa. We couldn't stay spread out all over Europe; Europe was a middle passage for Africa."[49] To Andrade, the "middle passage" was a process of self-creation; having acquired a sharp political consciousness in Lisbon and Paris, he was ready to return to Africa and mobilize the Maghreb Generation.[50] At the end of 1959, according to Andrade, Cabral also declared: "Enough with Europe, children. To Africa one and all!"[51]

"TO AFRICA ONE AND ALL": THE BIRTH OF THE MAGHREB GENERATION IN RABAT

In January 1960, militants from five of the Portuguese colonies met at the Second All-African Peoples' Conference in Tunis and decided to establish a more inclusive and permanent office for the liberation of the Portuguese colonies. And Bragança's presence in Morocco made Rabat the obvious choice for its headquarters. In April 1961, the Conference of the Nationalist Organizations of the Portuguese Colonies (CONCP) arranged, with the Moroccan government's assistance, a conference in Casablanca.[52] This symposium brought together the Partido Africano da Independência da Guiné e Cabo Verde (PAIGC), Movimento Popular de Libertação de Angola (MPLA), Frente de Libertação de Moçambique (FRELIMO), and Movimento de Libertação de São Tomé e Príncipe (MLSTP) to condemn Portuguese colonialism and call for support from the already independent African nations. The conference drew two more Lusophone militants to

Rabat: Maria Amália Lopes Fonseca of the PAIGC and Marcelino dos Santos representing the MPLA. Andrade was elected president of the CONCP and started traveling back and forth regularly between Conakry, the capital of Guinea, and Rabat. He eventually moved to Rabat in 1963 with his partner, filmmaker Sarah Maldoror, and their two daughters, Anouchka and Henda.[53]

Maria Amália Lopes Fonseca, the only woman of the group, performed much of the organization's secretarial duties, sending countless letters and telegrams to militants across Africa and Europe. According to dos Santos, Fonseca had the particularly useful qualification of being able "to write and type, in Portuguese, English, and French."[54] Despite her indispensability to the organization, Fonseca appears mostly in the margins of the organization's archives. She was born on the island of São Nicolau, Cape Verde, in 1928, to an influential Cape Verdean family.[55] Her first experience of colonial violence was in the Portuguese colony of São Tomé in Príncipe, where she lived as a teenager, when she witnessed a *colono* (settler) slapping her landlord in the face. In an interview she gave the Angolan Associação Tchiweka de Documentação, Fonseca describes the emotional impact this experience had on her: "These are the types of things that no matter how long I live I will never forget."[56] Fonseca lived in Paris in 1960, where doubtless she met other Luso-African militants, and she joined the struggle against Portuguese colonialism in a revolt against the many acts of colonial violence she had witnessed as a teenager in São Tomé. In 1961, Fonseca moved to Morocco to pursue a guerilla training course and meet other comrades of the CONCP. She ended up staying in Rabat and became the director of the administrative department of the permanent secretary of the CONCP.

The militants of the CONCP did not choose Morocco randomly. The newly independent kingdom was strategically located close to Portugal—an easy transit center between the African continent and Europe. Andrade, dos Santos, and Bragança had waged their first political battles with their Moroccan peers at the Cité Universitaire in Paris. Morocco was an appealing place, a symbol of political victory and of their hopes for the future of the Portuguese colonies. On a practical level, many of their old comrades from the Maison du Maroc now held important positions in the Moroccan government and could help them obtain military and financial support. Morocco's aid did not come without a cost, however: according to Mario de Andrade, the Moroccan government requested the liberation

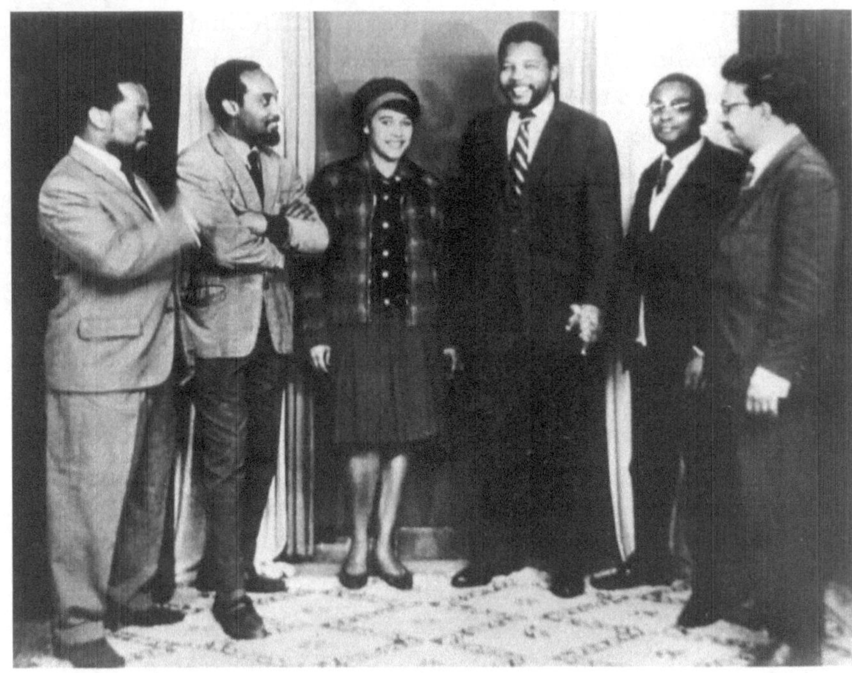

FIGURE 2. From left to right: Rabat Kesha (ANC), Marcelino dos Santos (CONCP, FRELIMO), Maria Amália Lopes Fonseca (CONCP, PAIGC), Nelson Mandela (ANC), Mario Pinto de Andrade (CONCP, MPLA), and Aquino de Bragança (CONCP) in Rabat in March 1962. Reprint courtesy of Annouchka de Andrade and Henda Ducados.

groups' support for the Moroccan claim to Mauritania—support they only gave reluctantly, afraid it would seem as if they were condemning another member country of the UN (United Nations).[57]

The CONCP was the embodiment of the type of political organization that dos Santos, Andrade, Cabral, Neto, and their peers had yearned for. While the CONCP consisted of an alliance of nationalist organizations, its primary cause was to unify the African masses to defeat Portuguese colonialism. This unity, the CONCP argued, would "be forged in direct action against colonialism."[58] The CONCP published individual resolutions for each country but also provided a game plan for liquidating Portuguese colonialism on all fronts. Appealing for funds from all African countries, the CONCP set itself up as a strategic hub through which funds would be distributed to the various national conflicts. But the CONCP organizers did not find nationalism to be a particularly appealing solution for the long term. In a speech before the second meeting of the Union of Black African Students (UGEAN), held in Rabat in August 1963, Cabral explained to the young African students that they were divided. "Why?" he asked. "Because some of you want your actions in foreign lands to be organic, and others want national unions, be they created in Parisian cafés or the cold streets of Moscow." The reality, claimed Cabral, is that they would be stronger if they were united, "if you hold hands solidly, in our fight against Portuguese colonialism and for progress."[59]

The choice of Morocco demonstrated the transnational predilection of the CONCP's members. Practically every speech given at the CONCP's Casablanca conference pointed to the similarities between the Moroccan people and the people under Portuguese colonial rule. The representative of the Moroccan Mouvement Populaire, Mohammed Darbani, proclaimed, "It is a happy omen that this conference is being held at the very place where Portuguese colonialism was so badly defeated," for, he explained, "the Moroccan people were the first to fight against Portuguese colonialism."[60] The CONCP was eager to make its case to the world and to the Moroccan people in particular. Most speeches were delivered in French; when a delegate could not speak French, they expressed their regret: "Unfortunately, the fifty hours I have spent in [Morocco] are not enough for me to be able to speak to you in Arabic or French," apologized Adelino Gwambe, president of the National Democratic Union of Mozambique of Mozambique.[61] By all accounts, the first conference of the CONCP was a resounding success.

While the CONCP's first conference had taken place in Casablanca, it is in Rabat that the members of the CONCP settled. After all, the palace was funding the CONCP, thereby providing its members with offices and places to live in the political capital. Photographs from the early 1960s show Mario Pinto de Andrade grinning in the sunlight and overgrown courtyard of his house in Rabat and Amílcar Cabral's young daughter starting at the camera on the balcony of her parents' apartment.[62] In Rabat, dos Santos, Fonseca, Andrade, and Bragança reunited and worked in concert to kindle international support for the CONCP. After Lisbon and Paris, Rabat became the new center of Pan-African intellectual and cultural life. Rabat also had a distinct advantage over Paris: it was not the metropole of a colonial empire but a liberated African city. The streets of Rabat in the early 1960s were teeming with students sitting in cafés, drinking Stork Beer, and talking about the revolution.[63]

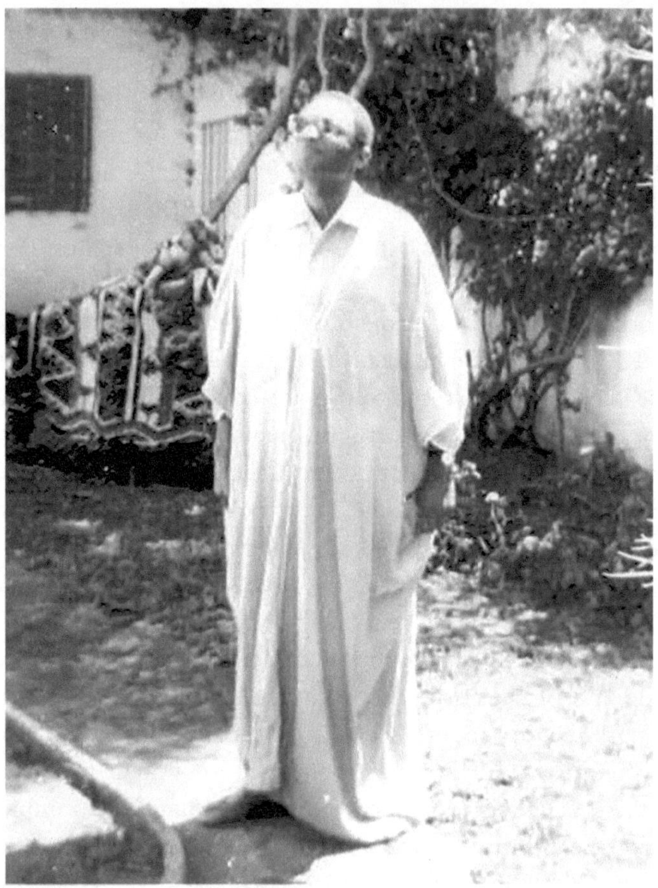

FIGURE 3. Mario Pinto de Andrade, Rabat, 1964. Fundo Mario Pinto de Andrade, Fundação Mário Soares, http://casacomum.org/cc/visualizador?pasta=07223.002.038; reprint courtesy of Annouchka de Andrade and Henda Ducados.

The energy that had animated these young militant-artists in Paris found a direction in Morocco, where the government gave them all the fixings of a budding state: money, legitimacy, weapons, and military training. In Rabat, they were no longer dependent on "French hospitality," no longer students in the colonial capitals but spokespersons for their own states, representatives of their people on the international stage. While in Paris and Lisbon the militant-artists had merely been able to discuss their radical ideas, in Rabat they found the actual material means to carry them out. The return to the African continent made it possible for them to lead and train other militants and to broaden the ranks of the Maghreb Generation. As Andrade acknowledged in a Rabat press conference, by December 1961 Morocco had become the hub of the nationalists from the Portuguese colonies, providing room and board as well as military training to dozens of young men from the Portuguese colonies."[64] And so, with the sponsorship of the Moroccan king, Rabat became the first home of the Maghreb Generation.

Immediately after the conference in Casablanca, at the end of April 1961, Marcelino dos Santos wrote to King Hassan II thanking him for his aid in organizing the conference, a "support that will forever stay engraved in the memory of our children."[65] Counting on Hassan II's continued support, dos Santos asked if the king could provide a monthly stipend of 5,000 dirham for an office, a residence for the secretary-general, and general office supplies, as well as Moroccan passports for the militants who would need them. Dos Santos also requested money for publishing brochures about the CONCP in English, French, Arabic, and Portuguese, as well as access to Moroccan radio to broadcast the CONCP's call to arms to Moroccan, African, and European audiences.

A couple of months later, in a June 1961 letter to João Cabral, the assistant secretary-general of the CONCP, dos Santos explained that henceforth any refugee of a Portuguese colony was welcome in Morocco: "They will only have to declare that they are political refugees of the Portuguese colonies!"[66] He complained, however, that the Moroccan government still had not approved the money for the CONCP brochure or access to Moroccan radio; he hoped these issues would be fixed soon. "Inchah Allah," he idiomatically ended his letter. Through his usage of this classic Arabic expression—an invocation of God—dos Santos showed the imprint of his stay in Morocco.[67]

Dos Santos did not limit his call for support to the Moroccan government, however; he also petitioned various Moroccan political parties and syndicates for money, appealing to their sense of Pan-African brotherhood.[68] The UMT was particularly supportive. In February 1960, MPLA member Lucio Lara wrote to Amílcar Cabral, who had by then assumed the pseudonym Abel Djassi, assuring him that their Moroccan friends had kept their promises and that Lara and his friends were comfortably settled in the UMT house. Lara vowed that the Moroccan labor unions would support Cabral's cause, for they are "men of action, who don't waste much time on vague things, like so many of the political organizations that we know."[69] Cabral, who was traveling in and out of Morocco regularly, always stayed at the UMT headquarters.[70] The UMT's journal, *L'avant garde,* regularly published articles and reports in Arabic, French, and Portuguese from the CONCP.[71] When the CONCP's relationship with the Moroccan government deteriorated a few years later, members of Moroccan labor unions continued to support the liberation groups.[72]

By December 1961, the CONCP was finally able to both print out a regular bulletin and make pronouncements on Moroccan radio. The bulletin informed readers on the happenings in the Portuguese colonies and demonstrated the CONCP's support for other liberation struggles, such as that of the Algerian people. This publication, written in French, addressed the Portuguese subjects and referred to the Moroccan people as "Moroccan brothers."[73]

Along with the ability to broadcast their message, the CONCP received military assistance from the Moroccan army. According to the first commander of the Exército Popular de Libertação de Angola, the first contingent of eighty MPLA fighters conducted their training in Morocco—fighters who constituted the "embryo" of the guerilla. They took the oath of service in Rabat in the presence of Agostinho Neto and Mario de Andrade. Several other guerilla members trained in three different camps across Morocco and went on to become generals and leading members of the liberation movements.[74] Cabral organized the training of many guerilla members in Morocco. In spring 1962, he headed a contingent of about twenty Guineans to Morocco. The men's military schooling was extensive, including exercises in sabotage, acts of terrorism, ways of setting traps, and ways of avoiding capture.[75] These trainees were equipped with everything they could need, dos Santos assured Cabral, even cigarettes.[76] Not only did the Moroccan government furnish provisions to trainees in Morocco, but they also shipped supplies to fighters in the Portuguese colonies. On January 29, 1963, the *Indus,* hailing from Casablanca, arrived in the port of Conakry carrying in its hull 1,380 boxes of milk, 490 boxes of sardines, one table, one stool, and one old couch, all destined for the fighters in Guinea-Bissau.[77]

While the Moroccan government had responded positively to dos Santos's request to assist the Lusophone militants, over the course of the early 1960s Moroccan support grew increasingly tepid. Particularly revealing of this trend is a series of exchanges following dos Santos's visit to Rabat in July 1963. By 1963, dos Santos had made the move out of Rabat but came back regularly in his function as secretary-general of the CONCP. In Rabat

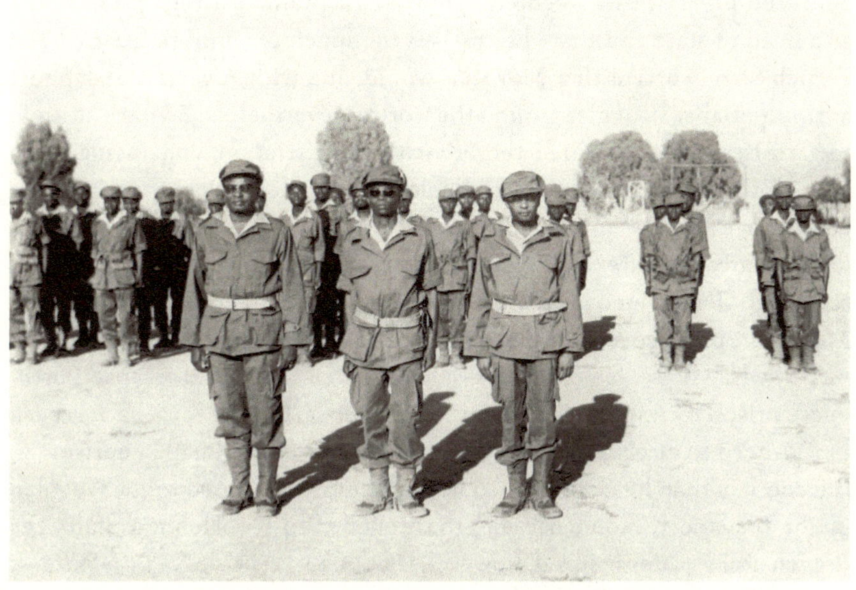

FIGURE 4. Military training in Morocco. Agostinho Neto, Africano Neto, and Mario de Andrade at the border in June 1962. Reprint courtesy of Annouchka de Andrade and Henda Ducados.

on July 1, 1963, in front of representatives from African embassies, Algeria, and China, dos Santos thanked the Moroccan people, the king, and the government not only for their moral support but also for their assistance in money and arms.[78] This speech, reported by a few liberal French journalists, worried members of the French embassy in Morocco. Jacques Tiné, the French chargé d'affaires of the Ministry of Foreign Affairs, immediately asked M. Zentar, the director of political affairs at the Moroccan Ministry of Foreign Affairs, about dos Santos's allusions to the Moroccan assistance in providing armaments. Zentar promised Tiné that he had no idea what dos Santos was talking about and that the official Moroccan services had no knowledge of these deliveries. He also reminded Tiné that there were no longer any training camps for Angolan nationalists in Morocco; they had all been transferred to Algeria. Tiné, perhaps in an attempt to reassure his superiors in the French administration, noted that at the OAU summit in Addis Ababa in May 1963, Zentar seemed critical of the attitude of Algeria's president, Ahmed Ben Bella. Zentar had complained that Ben Bella confused his past as a freedom fighter and agitator with his present role as a head of state and that "he smelled too much of [gun] powder."[79] The French were worried that Morocco would side with Algeria and support anti-imperialist struggles around the world. Nevertheless, Zentar's attitude toward Ben Bella reassured the French administration, convincing them that Moroccan officials were less ideologically inclined than their Algerian counterparts.

Similarly, in a letter dated June 1963, the French ambassador to Morocco, seemingly determined to reassure the French government, claimed that the Moroccan press coverage of Agostinho Neto's 1963 visit to Morocco was merely white noise. Neto, then president of the MPLA, had escaped Portuguese prison by jumping on a boat to Tangiers.[80] In June 1963, he was back in Morocco to celebrate the second anniversary of the Luanda uprising in the country that, he claimed, had been the most dedicated to the Angolan plight. In his correspondence with the French minister of foreign affairs, the French ambassador insisted, however, that Neto's visit was of little interest to most Moroccans, despite the Moroccan journal *Nation africaine*'s claim that "every Moroccan citizen feels concerned with this cause and ideal."[81]

Despite France's determination to see Morocco as an ally and a less radical partner than neighboring Algeria, and despite Morocco's efforts to conceal their support for the Luso-African militant groups, the French administration could not deny absolutely that the Moroccan government was involved in what they considered suspicious business. A number of confidential exchanges from the early 1960s disclose French confusion as to what the Moroccans were up to. Some investigation was necessary: an August 1962 letter from the French consul revealed that there was indeed a camp for Black soldiers in Ksiba, soldiers of uncertain origin.[82] A confidential letter from the French minister of foreign affairs dated September 8, 1962, noted that the Moroccan government had welcomed sixteen Angolan students collected from a boat off the coast of Casablanca. These students claimed that the Portuguese police were determined to arrest them because of their affiliations with the Angolan liberation movement and that they had escaped just as they were about to be captured. The French minister of foreign affairs included a list of names, birthdates, and marital status.[83] A confidential letter from members of the French embassy to the Portuguese embassy in Morocco, dated September 21, 1962, reported that forty tons of armament intended for the MPLA were sitting in the port of

Casablanca. This was certainly just the tip of the iceberg, the French feared; Morocco was probably at the crux of an arms trafficking ring serving Kenya and Angola.[84] The French embassy in Dar Es Salaam informed the French foreign minister that Morocco had welcomed three hundred militants of FRELIMO for guerilla training, eighty-six of whom had already received training from the Moroccan government.[85]

French administrators had been in denial concerning the extent of Morocco's involvement in the training and assisting of anti-Portuguese liberation movements. Moroccan officials were also increasingly unwilling to acknowledge Moroccan support for African liberation movements and feigned ignorance when questioned by their French counterparts. A change in policy spurred by Mohammed V's death in February 1961 and the ascent to power of Hassan II, his pro-Western son, gradually tempered Morocco's anti-neocolonial rhetoric. Moroccan officials did not hesitate to criticize their Algerian peers, hoping to endear themselves to a French administration still wounded by the Algerian War of Independence. The Moroccan government no longer touted its position as a hub for *pieds-rouges,* and indeed, by 1966, Aquino de Bragança, Marcelino dos Santos, and Mario de Andrade had all deserted Rabat for Algiers.

THE MAGHREB GENERATION MIGRATES TO ALGIERS

By 1963, Aquino de Bragança was convinced that Algeria was to become the new revolutionary hotspot. According to Mario de Andrade, the leaders in Rabat were unhappy with this change of allegiance, particularly when rumors spread that Angolans and Mozambicans were fighting on the Algerian side in the 1963 War of the Sands, a series of desert skirmishes on the border between Algeria and Morocco.[86] Although these rumors were later disproven, the Moroccan government ended up cutting off any direct aid to the Luso-African liberation movements, despite having been their first and most important source of financial, material, and military support.[87] This did not mean, however, as Andrade noted, that the Moroccan government or the Moroccan people did not endorse the movements' actions. The end of the financial subsidies had less to do with the liberation movements and more with growing tensions and competition between Morocco and Algeria and the looming conflict in the western Sahara. In 1963, when the War of the Sands ended, Amílcar Cabral wrote to King Hassan II, expressing his joy that the conflict between Morocco and Algeria had been resolved and emphasizing the importance of a peaceful, brotherly relationship between the two Maghrebi countries for all the liberation struggles in Africa and for African unity.[88]

If the leaders in Rabat were unhappy with the Luso-Africans' strong allegiance to the Algerians, the latter were increasingly discontented with a Moroccan government that was steadily descending into repression. Early on, in 1961, a political crisis caused by a disagreement between the minister of African affairs, Abdelkrim Al-Khatib, and King Hassan II had paralyzed the workings of the CONCP in Rabat. Dos Santos expressed his worry and eagerness for the crisis to be resolved, since it was blocking the arrival of a new boatload of trainees from Conakry.[89] In 1963, Mehdi Ben Barka, Hassan II's chief political opponent, sent Cabral two letters concerning the trial of 103 members of the Union Nationale des Forces Populaires (UNFP), accused by Hassan II of instigating a coup.[90] In these letters, Ben Barka denounced the "feudal-neocolonialist Moroccan royalty," which left unchecked, he claimed, could have dire consequences for the entire African continent.[91] In the envelope, along with his plea to Cabral, Ben Barka slipped the resolution of the Afro-Asiatic Solidarity Committee, an organization created after the 1957 Cairo conference that reaffirmed the Bandung principles against colonialism and neocolonialism:[92] "We reaffirm the message of solidarity of the Afro-Asiatic people against this cruel and pernicious form of neocolonialism, which empties our independences of their true meaning, to perpetuate instead capitalist interests, and our exploitation at the hands of foreigners, with the help of a handful of Moroccan turncoats.[93] Though it is unclear whether Cabral ever answered these letters (on one of the letters he wrote, "I received this late; it would be difficult for me to . . . respond"), it is clear that Ben Barka had developed a relationship with the members of the CONCP based in Rabat and was counting on their support against the Moroccan monarchy.

Despite their move to Algiers, the Luso-African militants did not break off contact with their Moroccan friends and fellow activists. Mario de Andrade and Marcelino dos Santos continued to travel to Morocco regularly, and the Luso-Africans reunited with several of their Moroccan peers and friends at the PANAF in July 1969.[94] Andrade continued to use his Moroccan passport until 1966 and kept strong ties with many Moroccan friends, including young Moroccan poet and militant Abdellatif Laâbi, and journalist Zakya Daoud, founder of the Moroccan journal *Lamalif*.[95]

More important still than the individual relationships knitting together the Moroccans and the Mozambicans was the precedent people such dos Santos, Cabral, and Andrade set: resistance to imperialism, colonialism, or neocolonialism had to be organized transnationally and had to make use of both culture *and* arms. A previous generation of Black poets had used poetry as a form of self-assertion, to regain a sense of dignity, as a way of claiming the colonizer's language, and, as Léopold Sédar Senghor put it, to bring Blacks into the "universal civilization."[96] But these Luso-African poet-politicians took *négritude*'s battles one step further. They did not intend to limit their poetry to delineating their identity; instead, they hoped to create a new identity. With poetry, they planned to overhaul the universal, not join it. They were interested in the aesthetic only if it had an impact on the practical and the militant. Poetry would work in the service of liberty and true decolonization, not as a tool of national unification deployed by new African governments. It was in this dual capacity, as artists and militants, that they inspired an entire generation of Moroccan poets, disillusioned with the poetry of their predecessors, to take a political stance and transform the postcolonial world well beyond Morocco. It is this vision that inspired the birth of journals such as the Moroccan literary magazine *Souffles*—the story that is at the center of this book's second chapter.

TWO

A CONTINENT IN ITS TOTALITY

Moroccan Literary Journal Souffles *Turns to Angola*

I turn around. A continent. I see it in its totality and beyond. Looted, empty. Petrified birds. No trace, life. As in the beginning.

ABDELLATIF LAÂBI, 2003

IN 1976, MOROCCAN POET Abdellatif Laâbi wrote a letter from prison to his friend Angolan poet Mario de Andrade. The letter was affectionate and melancholic; Laâbi had by then been in prison for four years. Yet Laâbi had not lost the will to struggle, for, as he told Andrade, the fight "for liberation is not limited to territory: it is the fight for men and women; it is the fight to throw, into the same trash can of history, colonialism, and racism; and it is based in the power of the people."[1]

If in the late 1950s and early 1960s Rabat had been a welcoming place for left-leaning African revolutionaries such as Marcelino dos Santos, Mario de Andrade, and Amália Fonseca, by the mid-1960s the Moroccan government had switched its allegiances and cut off funding to the CONCP. Disenchanted, the Luso-Africans moved out of Rabat. Hassan II began a campaign of retraditionalization, revitalizing Morocco's Arab identity and its relationship to Islam, organizing religious festivals (*mawasim*), and building mosques across Africa in an effort to become commander of the African faithful.[2] This move toward retraditionalization motivated Hassan II to strengthen Morocco's relationship with France and reactionary regimes across Africa, thus bringing Morocco firmly into the Western camp of the Cold War. The Moroccan government's time as a champion of the Maghreb Generation was over.

Domestically, the monarchy cemented its absolute control. Police officers started surveilling high schools, the government prohibited all left-wing parties, and the chief Moroccan dissident voice, the Third-Worldist militant Mehdi Ben Barka, "disappeared" (i.e., was assassinated) in Paris in October 1965.[3] In March 1965, the National Union of Students of Morocco called for high school students to march against new educational measures that would block access to higher education for Moroccans over sixteen, thus stifling hopes of social progress for many young Moroccans from the working class and rural areas.[4] As students took to the streets, Casablancans joined them in protest. The repression was swift: Hassan II deployed tanks, and his generals, particularly General Oufkir (who later kidnapped dissident Mehdi Ben Barka in Paris), fired on the crowd, killing hundreds and arresting thousands. In a televised speech following the massacre, Hassan II reprimanded the students: "Allow me to tell you that there is no greater danger to the State than a so-called intellectual. It would have been better if you were all illiterate."[5]

In June, the king dissolved parliament and declared a state of emergency, which lasted until 1970 and then was quickly followed by two attempted coups, plunging Morocco into a state of repression and social turmoil. Hassan II began to reign with absolute power and clamped down on any dissent.[6] It was the beginning of the so-called Years of Lead, a period of roughly forty years in which Hassan II attempted to suffocate Moroccan civil society by curtailing political participation and cultural production.[7] According to the Equity and Reconciliation Commission, established by King Mohammed VI in 2004, 325 Moroccans died during the Years of Lead as a result of "public forces' disproportionate use of force"; during protests between 1965 and 1990, Moroccans were arbitrarily detained and tortured with sleep deprivation, threatened, burned with cigarettes, and forced to sit on bottles.[8]

Disenchanted with their postindependence lives, Moroccan youth started looking to the international stage for inspiration in their struggle against authoritarianism at home. The world around these young Moroccans indeed seemed ready to change: Cuba and Algeria had led successful and widely broadcast revolutions; the Vietnam War was inspiring anticapitalist movements around the world; students were leading protests from Paris to Tunis; and the Palestinian freedom movement was stirring up support across Africa and the Arab world. In response to both the increased authoritarianism of the Moroccan state and the international movements of protest, several Marxist-leaning young Moroccans created political organizations dedicated to the struggle for democracy in postindependence Morocco. Moroccan Marxist-Leninist groups placed class struggle at the center of their project to overthrow Hassan II's regime, which they saw as conspiring with transnational capitalism and neocolonial interests.[9]

At the center of these political organizations were the cultural journals through which Marxist-Leninists recruited and communicated. Historians have overlooked the importance of culture and the arts as tools for recruitment, ways of enflaming the passions of political organizations' base, and tools of mass consciousness-raising. Several literary journals served this function in Morocco, two of the most important being *Lamalif* and *Souffles* (and its later Arabic-language version *Anfas*). Journalist Zakya Daoud and her husband Mohamed Loghlam started *Lamalif* in March 1966; concurrently, Abdellatif Laâbi, Mostafa Nissaboury, and Mohammed Khaïr-Eddine founded *Souffles*. Though both avant-garde journals became platforms for Morroco's Marxist-Leninist movement, they had different methods. *Lamalif* preferred an information-oriented approach that allowed the journal to survive until 1988. *Souffles,* which started as a Maghreb-focused journal in French, took a radical turn through the editorial team's contact with Luso-African poets and the arrival of new members on the editorial team, including Moroccan Abraham Serfaty. As early as 1967, *Souffles* opted for more direct critiques of the government—an approach that landed many of the *Souffles* editorial team either in prison or in exile by 1971.[10]

There is excellent scholarship on the role that *Souffles* played in the Moroccan literary and political scenes, as well as on *Souffles'* international interests, particularly when it comes to the question of Palestine.[11] But few scholars have looked to *Souffles'* engagement with African and Pan-African thought. If the Moroccan government no longer offered Marcelino dos Santos, Agostinho Neto, Amílcar Cabral, Mario de Andrade, and their Luso-African peers a physical home in Rabat, these militant-poets found shelter within the pages of *Souffles.*[12] Not only did they contribute texts to the journal, but the editorial team of *Souffles* engaged with the Luso-

Africans' poetry and with the work of the Pan-Africanist thinkers who had inspired the Luso-Africans. *Souffles* was a second home, in Morocco, for the Maghreb Generation and a node in the creation of a dissenting form of Pan-Africanism.

THE BIRTH OF *SOUFFLES*

"We wanted to do something that grappled with what culture would be in the aftermath of independence," remembered Mostafa Nissaboury in a Casablanca café in February 2018. "The government wasn't interested in culture," he continued. "There was a cultural affairs department, but what was that? There was a little museum, a few archaeological sites. . . . When there was an international cultural event, they would send along a little delegation of erudites. But we wanted to shake things up." Nissaboury grew up in Casablanca's medina, the old city, in a family of anticolonial resistance fighters. When he first met Abdellatif Laâbi in 1966, something sparked between them. Laâbi, who was born in Fes but raised in Casablanca, was living in Rabat with his wife, Jocelyne Laâbi, and their child. According to Nissaboury, Rabat bored Laâbi. Its proximity to the palace attracted political and intellectual personalities but also required participation in high-society events and all the social niceties this entailed. Nissaboury introduced Laâbi to Moroccan Amazigh poet Mohammed Khaïr-Eddine, with whom Nissaboury had founded the journal *Poésie toute* in 1964. Together the three men started thinking of ways to build a community, outside the government's official circles, in which to discuss the role of the artist in postcolonial Morocco.

In January 1966, the three poets visited an exhibition in Rabat at the Mohammed V National Theater organized by three young Moroccan artists, Mohamed Melehi, Mohamed Chabâa, and Farid Belkahia, in concert with Italian art historian Toni Maraini, who wrote the exhibition's introductory texts. This was the Casablanca school's first exhibition, and none of the art was for sale because, as Melehi put it, young students had to understand "that art is a message, an idea, not a product to be sold," not a luxury, as it too often was for the bourgeoisie.[13] The Casablanca school rejected the West's notion that art was a luxury, and through their use of bright colors and geometric shapes they grounded the school's aesthetic in traditional Moroccan forms of art such as rug-weaving and pottery.

Inspired by their meeting with the artists of the Casablanca school, Laâbi, Khaïr-Eddine, and Nissaboury created *Souffles* as a space for young Moroccans who were discontented with Moroccan artistic institutions. The first edition of *Souffles*, published in early 1966, was only about thirty pages long. It sported a minimalist cover designed by Mohamed Melehi, a black circle described by Toni Maraini as the "Black sun of Renewal."[14] *Souffles* was "like a family," remembered Moroccan writer Tahar Ben Jelloun, whose first published poem, "L'aube des dalles," appeared in the journal's twelfth issue in 1968.[15]

Toni Maraini, Mohamed Melehi's wife, and Jocelyne Laâbi, Abdellatif's wife, were the only women in the group. Maraini was an Italian art history professor who had moved to Casablanca to teach at the Casablanca Fine Arts School, where she overhauled the art history program. "In 1964 when

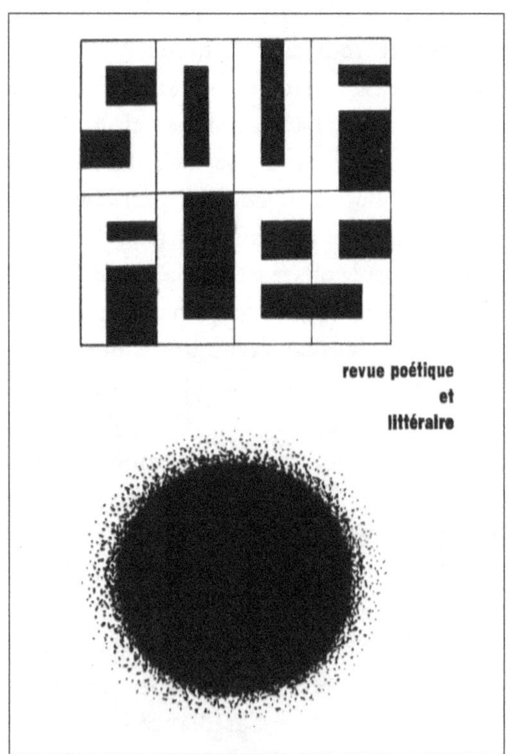

FIGURE 5. The first issue of *Souffles* with Mohamed Melehi's "Black Sun of Renewal," 1966. Reprint courtesy of Abdellatif Laâbi.

I got to Casablanca," remembered Maraini in 2018, "there had never been a class on the arts of Morocco, and even less on the arts of Africa, something the students ignored even the existence of. So, my first class started with Africa—not arbitrarily divided like during the colonial period between White and Black Africa—but seen instead, since the fertile prehistoric Sahara, as one body, a thousand-year crossroads."[16] Maraini traveled with the *Souffles* group to the PANAF in 1969 and wrote much of the introductory material for the visual artists of the *Souffles* group. She often wrote texts without signing them, "either because [she] was transcribing discussions that we had had *as a group*, or because, as a foreign woman, it was better to merge with the group."[17] Writer and translator Jocelyne Laâbi, Abdellatif's wife, was responsible for most of the practical aspects of the journal, typing up many of the journal's early editions.

Soon the editorial team of *Souffles* grew to include artists and writers from all over Morocco, Algeria, Africa, and the rest of the world. The editors started sending the journal to subscribers in France, Germany, Czechoslovakia, and the United States.[18] Gradually, what had started as a small Moroccan cultural journal blossomed to become a hub for dissident Pan-African thought. Just as their Luso-African peers had been politicized by their participation in poetry journals in Lisbon and Paris, *Souffles* became a recruiting tool for young activists in Morocco and beyond—they came for the poetry and stayed for the politics. At the core of *Souffles*' mission was the belief that decolonization was not finished, that continued vigilance was necessary to combat neocolonialism and truly achieve political and cultural independence. "The immense majority of formerly colonized peoples have not yet regained a sense of self, of their existential sovereignty, of their right to speak," wrote Laâbi in 1967. "And most of their intellectuals (who are the people's spokesmen), who think of themselves as free, are unknowingly fighting with very subtle forms of alienation."[19]

The *Souffles*' team was participating in an emerging discourse about the role of the intellectual and artist in postindependence Africa.[20] They were inspired by Moroccan Third-Worldist intellectual Mehdi Ben Barka, who thought it necessary to the take stock of what had happened since the fervent moment of African independence and to evaluate whether "all these liberations were obtained through a victory over the colonizer or in collaboration with him."[21] The *Souffles* group broke from an earlier generation of intellectuals—namely, those *négritude* intellectuals who had found their voice in Paris or Lisbon, those for whom the Bible was still "Socrates-Aristotle and Marx-Lenin-Sartre,"[22] those who, just as they were supposedly speaking out fiercely for decolonization, were so inspired by European humanism and universalism that they constantly sought out European approval.[23] The writers in *Souffles* no longer wished to be introduced by European intellectuals; in fact, Europeans were no longer their interlocutors—the militant-artists of the Maghreb Generation were. They turned away from Europe and its abstract humanism, "injected in strong doses in the culture of the former colonizer,"[24] and chose instead "extremism," as Laâbi called it: "a refusal of contingencies and easy friendships, a permanent anxiety of being, to be complete without artificial or spare limbs."[25] Extremism meant becoming a poet of the people and refusing easy friendships with the Moroccan intellectual or political elite.[26]

From the beginning, *Souffles* adopted a transnational perspective. "Something is brewing in Africa," wrote Laâbi in his 1966 manifesto-like prologue. "*Souffles* does not limit itself to one niche or minaret, nor does it recognize any borders; our Maghrebi, African, European, and other friends are all invited to participate in our modest enterprise," urged Laâbi.[27] Because of their disagreements with the Moroccan political and intellectual elite, *Souffles* turned to Africa and the Black Diaspora for support in their fight against neocolonialism, French and American imperialism, and their own government's oppressive behavior. As the *Souffles* writers witnessed and wrote about the political upheavals around the world, they started feeling that poetry alone could not rectify the extreme power imbalances between Europe and the rest of the world, which mirrored Luso-African revolutionaries' own realization that culture would not be enough to bring about revolutionary change.

Indeed, as I argue, the revolutionary and Pan-African bent that *Souffles* took in its last three years was largely due to the editorial board's encounter with intellectuals and militants from the Lusophone world—intellectuals such as Mario de Andrade, Amílcar Cabral, Marcelino dos Santos, Agostinho Neto, and Aquino de Bragança.[28] Abdellatif Laâbi, who had met them in the early 1960s in Rabat through the official circles of the palace, maintained strong ties with poets from the Lusophone world and started including their work in the spring of 1968. The Luso-Africans inspired Laâbi and the rest of the *Souffles* editorial team to look beyond the Moroccan cultural and political landscape. Between 1968 and 1971, they became active members of a transnational network of revolutionary artists and intellectuals, all decidedly anticapitalist, anticolonial, and anti-imperialist, and all concerned with how to use poetry as a weapon in a continuous revolution. Along with the journal, many of its members were active in Moroccan Marxist groups and publicly denounced the repressive Moroccan government, which eventually led to the groups' arrest and imprisonment at the hands of the regime.

SOUFFLES AND THE PAN-AFRICAN PHILOSOPHERS

Much like their Luso-African peers, one of the first political and cultural movements that the *Souffles* group had to contend with was *négritude.* While Andrade's initial approach to *négritude* was to emulate Senghor's *Anthologie de la poésie nègre et malgache,* the *Souffles* team almost immediately dismissed *négritude* as obsolete and infantilizing. Andrade may have found solace in the recovery of Black dignity, but the concept of *négritude* did not speak to the *Souffles* group. To Laâbi the proponents of *négritude* were "electronic monkeys," wind-up toys with which Europeans could play: "Thank you daddy Senghor Uncle négricultivator thanks for introducing me exposing me undressing me strip-teasing me in my natural state my collective memory my unconscious-nightmare my moral-wisdom," Laâbi wrote in his 1969 poem "Windup Monkey."[29] To Laâbi, Senghor was farming "negroes" for the West to use as it pleased. With a language steeped in European racial tropes, Laâbi denounced *négritude* as apish.

Anti-Senghor rhetoric was common throughout the journal's existence; the Senegalese president was regularly designated as corrupt, naive, and a Europhile. He was the figurehead of a racial ideology that made the members of *Souffles* deeply uncomfortable. When, in April 1966, Senghor opened the Festival Mondial des Arts Nègres (First World Festival of Black Arts) in Dakar, Moroccan journalist Abdallah Stouky, *Souffles*' envoy at the festival, dubbed Senghor a "greco-latin Negro," in ironic reference to Senghor's distinction between Greco-Latin and Black cultures. "Using, as one must, all of the modern means of propaganda," mocked Stouky, "a grand Senegalese chief, . . . surrounded by sad ethnologists and false champions of decolonization and emancipation, will call for the gathering of all Black forces in the world."[30] Stouky was not impressed by the festival, the apogee of exoticism, as he claimed, with its sad museums and its dapper audience "whistling at the sight of breasts, as in any other strip-tease show in Pigalle."[31]

While Andrade and his peers had turned away from *négritude* toward a form of racialized revolutionary ideology, they still respected the steps that *négritude* had allowed them to take in the process of building self-awareness.[32] Laâbi and his peers, however, could not get past Senghor's manipulation of *négritude*. Both groups agreed, however, that in the 1960s, *négritude* was no longer an appropriate ideology. "In 1966," asked Stouky, "what can *négritude* possibly mean? Does the Negro even still exist? Are we still at a point where we need to racialize thought?"[33] For Stouky, not only was *négritude* anachronistic, but Blacks themselves no longer existed, replaced instead by the proletariat. "The Negro no longer exists. The African has taken his place," Stouky explained. "We should not forget that 'questions of race are but a superstructure, a mantle, an obscure ideological emanation concealing an economic reality.'"[34] According to Stouky and his peers at *Souffles*, the search for a racial identity that characterized the *négritude* movement was a false issue, a veil obscuring the realities of economic underdevelopment. For the members of *Souffles*, of whom many were Marxist-Leninist, Senghor's *négritude* conflicted with the ideas of class-based liberation.

Mostafa Nissaboury explained in our 2018 interview that, unlike Senghor and Césaire, he was not in search of his identity: "Moroccans were the only ones in all of Africa who could talk about their own history. For the Ottoman Empire stopped at our doors. Cooking, language, literature—all those have no Ottoman influences. We are an exception compared to all the other Arab and African countries." These, he claimed, were the reasons *négritude* did not resonate with many of the members of *Souffles*. "I had too many identities and cultures; I didn't need to go searching for any of them," he insisted.[35] This is the same reason Berber or Amazigh identities and political claims appear practically nowhere in *Souffles'* political project. Moroccan Marxist-Leninists were interested in class and paid little attention to questions of identity or cultural diversity.

Martinican poet Aimé Césaire, cofounder of the *négritude* movement and member of the French Communist Party and thus much more class-conscious than Senghor, was much more to *Souffles'* liking than Senghor.[36] Césaire was both a source of inspiration and a forefather with whom to contend. In an article titled "Préface à un procès à la *négritude*," published in the third edition of the journal in the fall of 1966, French poet André Laude sought to figure out if "*négritude*, which has a past, can claim a future."[37] The *négritude* intellectuals, Laude explained, detached from their own culture, had nothing with which to counter the colonial invasion of the mind but the memory of having been something other than a rootless person. To Laude, Césaire alone had managed to clear a passage, with the help of surrealism, the "miraculous weapon," capable of killing the white cadaver nailed inside him. Young African writers were no longer convinced by Senghor's *négritude* or his African socialism. While many members of the African bourgeoisie may have seized upon these concepts, argued Laude, "it seems that many of the young generations are in opposition to any form of theory . . . that does not offer viable solutions to the crucial problems of the postindependence world."[38]

The editors of *Souffles* much preferred the concrete ideas of Frantz Fanon. Though Frantz Fanon had been dead for five years by the time the first issue of *Souffles* was published, his philosophy had reached its apogee in the mid-1960s; he was quoted at length by the Black Panthers and translated into Swedish and Arabic.[39] His seminal text, *The Wretched of the Earth,* was first published in 1961 and quickly became a must-read for all young, politically minded Africans. A diagnosis of the dehumanizing effects of colonization, *The Wretched of the Earth* was above all a concrete road map for achieving political, social, and cultural decolonization. Fanon's articulation of violent insurgency and the devastating psychological effects of colonialism resonated with the members of *Souffles,* many of whom were trained philosophers; Fanon's text was theirs to claim. The first time Laâbi read Fanon's work, as a student in Rabat, he felt he was reading his own story and that of his people. Fanon's text, he said later, "opened my eyes to my social body and my past and present memory; it had me spell out my identity, deeply stirred my roots, inoculated my fury to be, to demand, and to refuse."[40]

If Fanon had influenced the Luso-African poets to return to the African continent, Laâbi and his peers also heeded his call to leave Europe behind.[41] Fanon's philosophy permeated *Souffles*' understanding of the role of culture in Africa, the Maghreb, and the Third World. The journal was steeped in Fanon's analyses and writings, as the main topics of the journal demonstrate: the decolonization of culture, the role of the Third World intellectual, the persistence of the colonial system in the cultural arena, and the necessity to highlight popular culture.[42] Thirteen authors cited Fanon over the course of the journal's tenure, second only to Karl Marx (cited by sixteen writers).[43] The contributors used his expressions and fragments of his wording, which they wove through their own analyses, constructing a tight-knit tapestry of both new and borrowed postcolonial theory. They used Fanon as a justification for a certain number of their positions on the use of violence, as well as on the question of language. In response to critics calling him a sellout for writing in French, Laâbi retorted, "Frantz Fanon wrote *Les damnés de la terre* (as much of a theoretical work as a literary one) in French. We do not think that the militants of Francophonie can take pride in his work!"[44]

The Wretched of the Earth provided a clear layout of the phases of development of the "colonized intellectual." Fanon first presented his paper "On National Culture" at the Second Congress of Negro Writers and Artists in Rome in 1959, in front of such militant-poets as Mario de Andrade. Through this paper, Fanon delivered the first death blow to the *négritude* movement, just a year before Léopold Sédar Senghor became Senegal's first president. Delineating the ways to achieve a decolonized national culture, Fanon explained that the "colonized writer" naturally traversed three stages. First, the "colonized writer" became so enamored with European culture that he completely assimilated European literary trends: symbolism, surrealism, romanticism, etc.[45] To illustrate this first stage, Fanon cited a poem by Haitian René Depestre, who, while having been close to many of the founding members of the *négritude* movement, had by 1959 moved to Cuba, invited to join the revolution by Che Guevara himself. In the poem, Depestre demonstrates how colonialism infected the mind, took over the body, and starved the soul.

> A fine, upstanding husband
> Who recited Racine and Corneille
> And Voltaire and Rousseau
> And old Hugo and the young Musset
> And Gide and Valery
> And so many others as well . . .
> But to tell the truth he knew nothing
> Because culture does not come without making concessions
> Without conceding your flesh and blood
> Without conceding yourself to others
> A concession worth just as much as
> Classicism or Romanticism
> And all that nurtures our Soul.[46]

After this stage of assimilation, Fanon explained, the colonized writer turned back to his roots. But since the colonized writer was completely disconnected from his people, since he had conceded his very flesh and blood, he could only recall old childhood memories, old legends, and an ancient concept of the world. To Fanon, *négritude* was stuck in this second stage, glorifying a fictitious past, to impress the European colonizer and conform to European perceptions of Africa. Fanon argued that the *négritude* poets still had to transition to the third stage, the combat stage, where "instead of letting the people's lethargy prevail, [the colonized writer] turns into a galvanizer of the people."[47] This is the stage in which *Souffles*, the Luso-Africans, and the Maghreb Generation more generally claimed to be. They were no longer interested in talking to Europeans, in glorifying traditional Arabic poetry or "Negro-African" painting, only in rousing the masses. In the ideological struggle between *négritude* and Fanonism, the Maghreb Generation stood on Fanon's side, committed to the third, militant stage of the revolution.

At first, Abdellatif Laâbi expressed some reservations when it came to Fanon's analysis of the Arab world. In *Souffles*' fourth issue, published in the fall of 1966, Laâbi reminded readers that modes of colonization were different from one country to the other and argued that Fanon excessively conflated his observations of Algeria and the rest of Africa. If some cultures, particularly in "Black Africa," Laâbi wrote, "certainly alive but comparatively closed and not participating in modern society," did not counterbalance colonialism, the Arab Nahda (Awakening) had demonstrated "an ideological and cultural opposition, and a dynamic one."[48] Although Fanon's brand of internationalism inspired the writers of *Souffles*, Laâbi was still not willing in 1966 to concede that the situation in the Maghreb was as bleak as that of other "Black African" countries. It was not necessary, Laâbi asserted, for the postcolonial recovery of Moroccan culture to go through the same stages as the rediscovery of "Black culture." "Moroccan and Arab culture did not need as much exhibitionism to be present. It already existed."[49] For Laâbi, as for Nissaboury, Moroccans did not have to go through as conspicuous a self-discovery as the creators of *négritude*—which indicates how little they knew in 1966 about the cultures of "Black African" countries, having discovered Senegal, for instance, almost exclusively through the writings of Senghor. While they were attracted to the theories of other Pan-African revolutionaries, they knew little of the material and cultural realities of the rest of the continent.

Slowly Laâbi and his peers started to grow more comfortable with Fanon's reading of the effects of colonialism on the African continent, perhaps as they grew more familiar with the lived realities of other Africans, through their friendships with Mario de Andrade, Amílcar Cabral, and others. In December 1970, at a meeting of Arab poets in Beirut, Laâbi explained that, while the Maghrebi poets had a lot in common with Arab poets, in the Maghreb "the colonial rape was much more ambitious, more extreme, and more brutal" than in the rest of the Middle East. In that sense, he explained, the Moroccans and Maghrebis were much closer to the revolutionary movements coming out of Africa and the Antilles:

> The works of one Aimé Césaire, one Frantz Fanon, and, more recently, the writings of René Depestre (Haiti), one Mario de Andrade (Angola), one Cabral (Portuguese Guinea) etc.... rigorously correspond to our own mollifying and restructuring efforts as well as to the necessities of a fight again cultural and ideological domination and for an authentic and revolutionary culture of the laboring masses.[50]

With this statement Laâbi searched for new alliances. Instead of looking to the Levant, he found peers and models in Africa and the African Diaspora. In Laâbi's poetic world, two races of men faced off. On one side was the race of the torturers, the hyenas, the vermin, the vampires, the jackals; on the other side was the Maghreb Generation, "the wretched of the earth," his tribe, his brothers of the rugged hands, those who lived in the "malaria of the streets."[51] These were *Souffles'* peers—a generation, led by Frantz Fanon, that included Maghrebis; Africans from other parts of the continent, such as Andrade and Cabral; and figures of the Black Atlantic, such as Depestre.

Through its engagement with Pan-African thinkers, *Souffles* had made the shift from a small Moroccan literary journal primarily concerned with the state of poetry in the nation to a militant magazine taking part in a worldwide movement to decolonize the mind through poetry, political action, and guerilla warfare. By the late 1960s, the journal was at the center of a worldwide conversation about neocolonialism, imperialism, and Pan-Africanism. Scholars have often situated that conversation in the Americas or in Europe, but the existence of *Souffles* and the reach of its subscribers and contributors showcase the centrality of the African continent and of the Maghreb to this dialogue. Through *Souffles*, Morocco once more became a hub for thinkers and artists from the Americas, Europe, Asia, Africa, and the Middle East to meet, in person or on paper, and to exchange ideas.

WHICH LANGUAGE TO WRITE IN?

One of the fiercest controversies on the pages of *Souffles* was the question of language. This was, of course, at the center of many of the debates among African writers, whether they were francophone, lusophone, anglophone, or arabophone, or spoke Wolof, Kibundu, or Twi. Writers generally fell into three different groups. The first group comprised those who wrote in the colonial tongue and argued that this was either necessary or unproblematic. Algerian writer Kateb Yacine, whose *Polygone étoilé* was reviewed by Laâbi in *Souffles'* fourth issue, famously called the French language Algeria's "spoils of war." The second group included those who used the colonial language but modified its rhythm and syntax or added words to claim it as their own, to "black-ify" it, as was the case with Césaire and Moroccan writer Abdelkebir Kathibi.[52] And finally there was the third group, those who chose to write instead in their Indigenous tongue, such as Kenyan writer Ngũgĩ wa Thiong'o.[53] One of the main problems these writers faced is that not all were capable of writing in the Indigenous tongues of their country. Many urban Angolans, for instance, had only rudimentary understandings of Indigenous languages.[54] The writers of *Souffles,* like many of their African peers, ended up adopting all three of these stances at some point or another. At first, Laâbi and his peers argued against those, such as Tunisian Albert Memmi and Algerian Malek Haddad, who thought Maghrebi francophone literature was doomed.[55] Laâbi was convinced that a decolonized Francophone literature could exist in Morocco, hence *Souffles'* somewhat ironic subtitle (for a French-language journal), *Revue arabe du Maghreb* (Arab journal of the Maghreb). But as the journal came under fire for publishing in French, Laâbi began to argue that their use of French was a weapon in the resistance to neocolonialism. Finally, as the 1960s turned into the 1970s, *Souffles* opted to transition to Arabic, which *Souffles'* members now considered a more authentic expression of Moroccan identity—even though most of the editorial team wrote in French and despite the fact that the Arabic they were using was Fusha (Modern Standard Arabic) and not Darijah (Moroccan Arabic). The switch to Arabic came with a shift of focus away from Africa, toward Pan-Arab nationalism, the

Arab revolution, and an overwhelming focus on the struggle of the Palestinian people.

While a few of the poets in the *Souffles* team asserted their Amazigh identity, including founding member Mohammed Khaïr-Eddine, the idea of writing in Amazigh was never brought up. In fact, in the fourth issue of *Souffles,* Laâbi explained that because in "Black Africa" there were a "multiplicity of Indigenous languages," they had no choice but to write in the colonial language. In the Maghreb, Laâbi argued, things were different: there was "one language of secular culture": Arabic.[56] The option of using the Amazigh languages did not even occur to Laâbi.

In his manifesto-like prologue to the very first issue of *Souffles,* Laâbi explained that the *Souffles* writers were quite aware of the equivocality of writing such a journal in French.[57] But he dismissed this as a "fake problem." The important thing, he clarified, was to match the written language to the poet's interior world, although some might never succeed in this, even in their national language. In *Souffles,* Laâbi explained, the poets expressed their sensual depths through the intermediary of a language "fine-combed by their history, their mythology, their anger, in short their own personality."[58] As *Souffles'* cofounder, Mustafa Nissaboury, explained in a letter also published in the first issue: "Poetry must be nothing other than synonymous with flesh, blood, sweat, and saliva. . . . It must drop all metaphysical and philosophical preoccupations to cling instead to the (hu)man, with his movements, his grimaces, the scream of his entrails."[59] Beauty was not the concern; this group of Moroccan poets were not interested in stylistic devices but in raw emotion.

If in 1966 Laâbi dismissed his use of French as a "fake problem," by 1970 he seemed increasingly defensive about *Souffles'* primary language. The *Souffles* poets, he insisted, refused to be categorized, cloistered by language purity; their use of French did not mean they subscribed to the French or European canon. Despite the poets' use of French, he said, the "coexistence was not pacific."[60] In an article titled "Contemporary Maghrebi Literature and Francophonie," he explained that the usage of French was a middle passage; eventually, the only true way to be decolonized would be to think and write in one's national language, which for Moroccans would be Arabic. Again Laâbi made no mention of Amazigh. In the meantime, however, Laâbi's aim was to create a new literature altogether—a terrorist literature—which would shatter the original logic of the French language at all levels (syntactic, phonetic, morphological, graphical, symbolic, etc.), and infuse the French language with Maghrebi concerns.[61] This form of literature took many forms: for poet Khaïr-Eddine, it was a "linguistic guerilla" in which violence was directed inward, against the language itself, and outward, against the society it criticized.[62]

In the same 1970 issue, in an article titled "About the Trial of Francophone Maghrebi Literature," Laâbi clearly showed irritation toward critics of the journal's choice of language, accusing them of being hypocrites, lovers of French writers Jean-Paul Sartre and Albert Camus and only pseudo-defenders of Arab culture. "They may write in Arabic," he exclaimed, "but in reality, they are neo-imperialists and into European literary fashions and trends."[63] If *Souffles* was unapologetic about its usage of French in the first few issues, as the journal matured and its audience grew, the absence of Arabic became more and more problematic. The journal dedicated its tenth/eleventh issue to Arabic-language poetry from the Maghreb. A couple of other issues also contained a few poems in Arabic, including some by Laâbi himself. But it wasn't until 1971 that *Souffles'* editors decided to launch an Arabic-language branch: *Anfas*.

In December 1971, after a short pause due to lack of funding, the *Souffles* editorial team announced that they could no longer condemn *francophonie* as a tool of neocolonialism while writing exclusively in French. They revealed their creation of *Anfas* in the previous May of 1971. *Anfas'* objective was different, they emphasized. *Souffles* would remain for those Moroccan intellectuals who "due to their complex vis-à-vis Western culture" could not read Arabic, as well as for foreigners who agreed with the *Souffles* team's ideals.[64] Thus, *Souffles* would no longer be a progressive platform, "a forced tribune of *francophonie*, but a journal dedicated to informing and making connections; the usage of French would thus take on a practical and objective role."[65] Like Kenyan writer and intellectual Ngũgĩ Wa Thiong'o, who switched from writing in English to writing exclusively in Gikuyu, the members of *Souffles* wondered how they could address themselves to the lives of the masses if they were writing in a language that the people could not read or even understand. In the same breath, the editorial team explained that *Souffles/Anfas* could no longer publish any materials that were not centered on the Maghreb and the Arab world. "Not that we feel less concerned by the fight in Africa and the Third World, but we believe that others can lead that struggle better than we can," the editors explained.[66] The switch to Arabic occurred just a year after Serfaty and Laâbi created Ilā al-Amām (Forward), the Marxist-Leninist group with which they hoped to lead the struggle against the Moroccan monarchy. The Moroccan revolution was contingent on the Arab revolution for the members of Ilā al-Amām. Thus, switching to Arabic and turning away from the African revolution was part of a political project to lead an Arab revolution from Palestine to Rabat against the Arab bourgeoisie.[67] In Ilā al-Amām's founding text, the writers criticized the Moroccan government for bedding down with international capitalists and imperialists, arguing that it was through the Arab revolution that the Moroccan Left would truly achieve independence from the forces of neocolonialism. Mention of the Arab revolution and its importance appeared fifty-nine times in the organization's compilation of founding texts; the African revolution, however, was not mentioned once.[68]

Souffles/Anfas thus abandoned its Pan-African dimension just as the editorial board decided to publish an Arabic version. The usage of French had permitted *Souffles* to participate in a global network of ideas emerging from a diversity of linguistic, cultural, and geographical locations. It allowed *Souffles* to discursively link Moroccan postcolonial and working-class realities with those same conflicts and struggles involving subaltern populations in Africa, Latin America, the Caribbean, and the United-States.[69] Though *Souffles/Anfas* claimed it would continue in French, its rhetoric had changed: it was no longer participating in a transnational network of revolutionary poets. The continued use of French in 1971 only served to maintain contact with the European "fringe" that supported the struggles of the Arab people.

Anfas did not have much to do with *Souffles'* original intent. Purely political, the editorial board only dedicated two articles over the course of its eight issues to literature and only published a couple poems. *Anfas* was committed to serving a Marxist-Leninist working-class audience by simplifying and adapting its style to the language predominantly spoken by the broadest base of the literate public, though how many people read it is less clear—*Anfas* was published in Modern Standard Arabic, not in Darijah. According to the 1960 census, only 11 percent of the Moroccan population were literate. Of those who could read, 51 percent were literate in Arabic, 40 percent in Arabic and French, and 8 percent in French alone.[70] Thus, though the switch to Arabic would open the journal to a broader base, that audience would still represent, at best, 11 percent of the total Moroccan population. *Anfas* undoubtedly had a much wider circulation than *Souffles*: it was published monthly, rather than quarterly; cost nearly half the price (1.50 dirhams instead of 2.50); and five thousand copies were printed, as opposed to *Souffles'* one thousand copies.[71] *Anfas* contributed significantly to the development of a strong Marxist-Leninist movement in Morocco, becoming the intellectual showcase of the movement. The editorial board of *Anfas* were very outspoken against the Moroccan government and wrote tirelessly about the struggles of the Moroccan working class and those of the Palestinians.

Anfas approached the Palestinian problem head on, dedicating, at minimum, one article per issue to Palestine, a clear reflection of a political turn that situated the Moroccan Marxist-Leninist revolution within the larger Arab revolution. The journal's final issue, dedicated to the resolution of the Palestinian problem, included such subsections as "Workers' Struggles," "National Realities," "Arab Nation," and "Ideological Action."[72] "Literary-Souffles" now took up only ten pages of the journal; the large majority of the journal's articles were focused on the Arab world and on the question of Palestine.

Many of those who have written about *Souffles*, and indeed the members of *Souffles* itself, claim that it was the issue of Palestine that politicized the *Souffles* team. After the devastating losses of the 1967 Six-Day War, the *Souffles* writers could no longer sit by and write poetry. *Souffles'* entire fifteenth issue was dedicated to the Palestinian revolution. The journals' editors opened the issue with the following: "It seems to us after several months that an essentially literary revue could become, possibly, a sort of 'luxury' considering the many shortcomings of the national press." Laâbi testified to the importance of Palestine to his political trajectory: "My political consciousness was born from my adherence to the Palestinian cause. . . . It determined my commitment in the struggles that followed, even those in my own country."[73] To many of the *Souffles* editors, Palestine was an Arab problem, one around which all the revolutionaries and masses of the Arab world could coalesce. The enemy was no longer just the West but the bourgeois nationalists of Jordan and Egypt, who were seemingly capitulating to Zionism and imperialism. As the *Souffles* team wrote in 1970, "A new Arab solidarity was born at the bottom, as a retort to the solidarity at the top which is tainted by all sorts of secondary considerations."[74] After this fifteenth issue, the journal's format changed, forsaking the abstract covers of the first installments for photographs and drawings depicting men carrying Kalashnikovs and a much more explicit Marxist-Leninist tone. Some of *Souffles'* contributors distanced themselves as a result, among them Nissaboury, claiming that the journal had abandoned its original literary intent to tumble wholeheartedly into the arms of the radical Left.

But just as some contributors abandoned the journal, new editors joined. Abraham Serfaty, who joined *Souffles* in 1968, was emblematic of *Souffles'* new message. He and Laâbi had met in early 1968 during political debates about the issue of Palestine. Born in 1926 to a middle-class Jewish family, Serfaty was a mining engineer, a member of both the French and Moroccan Communist Parties, and a lifelong anti-Zionist, Serfaty wrote extensively both for *Souffles* and *Anfas* about the Palestinian question contributing two articles to *Souffles'* special edition on Palestine, "Moroccan Judaism and Zionism" and "Is the Israeli State a Nation?"[75] Under Serfaty's leadership, *Souffles'* poetry section shrank: gone were the poems of Nissaboury and Khaïr-Eddine, replaced by articles about the Arab-Israeli conflict and the link between imperialism and capitalism.[76] Serfaty was particularly inspired by the struggle of Black Americans and fascinated by the Black Panthers, whose Ten-Point Program he republished in *Souffles* in 1969 after meeting them at the PANAF.[77] When, in 1970, he and Laâbi decided, along with other young Moroccans, to pursue a democratic revolution in Morocco, he would often tell his comrades, "We are all Malcolm Xs."[78] In a 1970 piece for *Souffles* titled "African Revolution and the Direction of the Proletariat," Serfaty denounced the co-opting of socialism by African leaders and argued that a proletarian revolution in the Maghreb could only occur within the context of an African revolution.[79]

In its eighth and final issue, *Anfas* published an article titled "A New Palestine in the Sahara," which condemned the Moroccan, Algerian, and Spanish imperialism with respect to the Sahrawi people and voiced the editors' support for Saharan independence.[80] It may very well be this final editorial that set the Moroccan government loose upon the *Souffles/Anfas* editors. For *Anfas* was much more threatening than *Souffles* to the Moroccan political establishment, owing to its use of Arabic and its much wider reach. A month after the publication of *Anfas'* eighth issue, Laâbi and Serfaty were arrested for being "the leader[s] of Moroccan maoists."[81]

SOUFFLES AND THE LUSO-AFRICANS

While many of the scholars studying *Souffles* have argued that it was the conflict in Palestine that politicized the journal's members, *Souffles'* political bent began well before the journal's fifteenth issue. Their politicization was intricately linked to the editors' unflinching admiration of and support for the Luso-African poets Mario de Andrade, Amílcar Cabral, and Marcelino dos Santos, whom they had met in Rabat in the early 1960s. The *Souffles* writers looked to the conflicts in Angola, Mozambique, and all over the Portuguese colonies for inspiration in how to deploy Fanon's theoretical tools to decolonize culture in Africa.

Souffles' ninth issue, published in spring 1968, was dedicated almost entirely to the Cultural Congress of Havana. The congress, organized by the Cuban government in January 1968, brought together militant intellectuals from over seventy countries around the world to garner political support for the fights of the masses against imperialism. *Souffles'* ninth issue included a series of essays, curated by Andrade himself, relaying the anti-*négritude* and Third-Worldist message of the congress to the journal's readership. In a short editorial, the *Souffles* board explained that they had specifically chosen the texts that related to the question of *négritude* to continue their ongoing effort to situate the journal vis-à-vis contemporary debates in the Third World. Their goal was to demonstrate that *Souffles* had transcended *négritude* and perhaps to bring in Black voices like Andrade's to bolster their point.[82]

Indeed, the two essays Andrade presented to *Souffles'* readership were virulent critiques of *négritude* pronounced by Haitian poet René Depestre and the Guinean playwright Condetto Nénékhaly-Camara. Andrade explained that it was of dire importance for all those living in the 1968 postcolonial world to dismiss *négritude* and recognize the importance of political engagement. Andrade's rhetoric had changed since his publication of the *Antologia de la poesia de expressão portuguesa* in 1953. After five years in France, three in Morocco, and two in Algeria, gone was the admiration for the *négritude* movement, replaced by a more action-oriented rhetoric. Andrade's primary concerns were no longer to add one's' "particular tonalities . . . to the great human symphony" or to bring Black voices into the universal chorus.[83] In 1968, Andrade highlighted, they no longer cared if the West understood them—"our differences or our singularities."[84] Andrade contended that what Africa and the Third World ought to add to the great human symphony was the revolution itself. In other words, Andrade was arguing not for enriching humanism but for toppling it.

In "The Revolutionary Intellectual and His Responsibilities toward the Third World," René Depestre claimed that *négritude* "separated from the historical context of the revolution in the Third World became an unacceptable "black Zionism" which kept the Black people away from their duty to make revolution."[85] To Depestre, racial unity and the quasi-religious longing for a precolonial Africa, both pillars of Black Zionism and *négritude,* were mere distractions, mystifying the social realities of race. Once again, Depestre called for a more concrete philosophy than *négritude,* something that could adequately address the economic and social conditions of people in Haiti and Cuba. Like the members of *Souffles,* Depestre was shifting toward a more class-driven analysis than one based on identity or cultural diversity. Condetto Nénékhaly-Camara, on the other hand, proclaimed *négritude* to be a sort of "false narcissism," like one "of those mad dogs spinning on themselves trying to kiss their own tails."[86] How could one believe that the values endorsed by the *négritude* movement had anything to do with the level of melanin in one's skin? he asked. To Nénékhaly-Camara, there was only one condition: that of the human. *Négritude,* he concluded, was isolating Black people from the revolution by convincing them of their singularity. Mario de Andrade ended his dossier on the Congress of Havana with a short piece titled "Culture and Arms." In his typical way, Andrade blended revolutionary rhetoric with excerpts from poetry to argue that the most poetic of acts was to revolt against one's own dispossession, through violence. Other hands will beat the drums of guerilla victory in Guinea, he wrote. In the meantime:

Go tell the Portuguese
To stop scaring us in the bush
For there is new blood
That shoulders the gun
For there is young blood
To defend the homeland
Only fire will make you leave
Oh Portuguese
Only the fire of the gun

Only the finger on the trigger
Will make you leave.[87]

For Andrade, not only was fighting the most poetic of acts, but in the fire of combat new forms of culture would emerge: the poet's language transformed to become accessible to all, intellectuals as well as farmers.

This ninth issue set the tone for the last four years of *Souffles*' tenure as a literary journal: poetry would be a political rallying cry or it would not be published. By giving voice to thinkers such as Andrade, Depestre, and Nénékhaly-Camara, *Souffles* positioned itself as a Maghrebi literary journal that spoke to and for people across Africa, the Black Atlantic, and the Third World. In the tenth and eleventh issues, advertisements started regularly appearing for the radical Cuban journal *Casa de las Américas*, thus confirming *Souffles*' links to the Tricontinentalist movements. After all, one of *Souffles*' political heroes was the Tricontinentalist Mehdi Ben Barka, who was kidnapped and murdered in 1965 just as he was planning the Tricontinental Congress in Havana.[88]

In 1970, for *Souffles*' nineteenth edition, the editors decided to dedicate an entire issue to the struggle in Africa, with a focus on the Portuguese colonies to which Portugal held on "tenaciously."[89] The cover, designed by artist Mohamed Chabâa, was a mosaic of an image of Patrice Lumumba accompanied by a drawing of an armed militant, brought together with winding lines reminiscent of the grooves in a tree trunk. Upon publishing this issue, *Souffles* also printed a poster celebrating the tenth anniversary of February 4, 1960—the day that sparked the MPLA's armed revolt in Angola. The poster, designed by Chabâa as well, depicts a black figure gazing at a bleeding red sun, above a poem by Agostinho Neto titled "The Struggle" in which he evokes the waves of Angolan fighters that will push back the Portuguese bayonets.[90]

Mohamed Chabâa, who with Mohamed Melehi and Farid Belkahia was a founding member of the Casablanca school of painting, was also a graphic designer. Inspired by the study of Amazigh textiles, Chabâa rooted his work in a Moroccan and African modernity.[91] The poster printed with Souffles' nineteenth issue demonstrated that influence with its hard-edged geometric abstractions and an eye that resembles the ancient Egyptian Eye of Horus.

Abraham Serfaty opened the nineteenth issue with a brief homage to

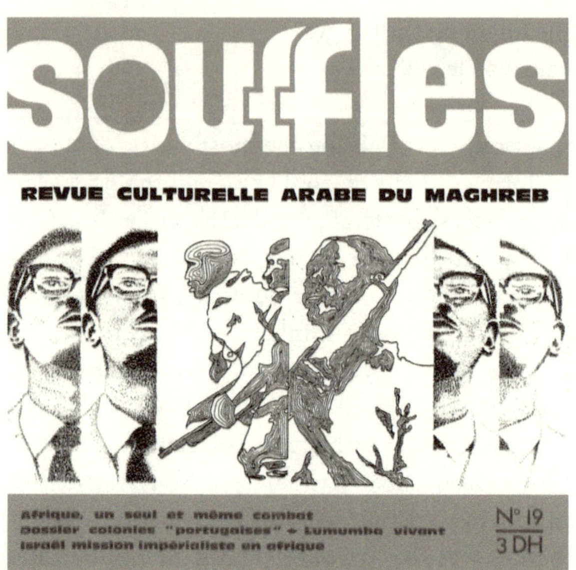

FIGURE 6. **"Afrique, un seul et même combat."** ***Souffles,*** **no. 19 (1970). Reprint courtesy of Abdellatif Laâbi.**

Patrice Lumumba, assassinated ten years prior but who Serfaty claimed lived again through the struggles of Amílcar Cabral and Agostinho Neto. Directed by Andrade and including texts by Cabral, dos Santos, and Neto, the nineteenth issue came complete with a small presentation on each Portuguese colony, poems, and manifestos. Introducing this special issue, the *Souffles* team explained that the fight led by the Mozambican and Angolan militants against Portuguese ultracolonialism was one of the most advanced in Africa. Reflecting on their strategies and realizing that the enemy was the same in Mozambique as in Palestine, Eritrea, or South Africa, *Souffles* decided to title this special issue "Africa: One and the Same Battle." *Souffles* presented the anticolonial struggles in South Africa, Namibia, Zimbabwe, Eritrea, Chad, and the Sahara in addition to their focus on the MPLA and FRELIMO, the whole time underlining the fact that they could only win these battles through inter-African cooperation.

The entire issue was dedicated to making one thing clear: the battles in northern Africa and the rest of Africa were the same and must be waged in tandem if there was any hope of victory. In introducing the struggles in Chad and Eritrea, the *Souffles* team explained that imperialism sought to

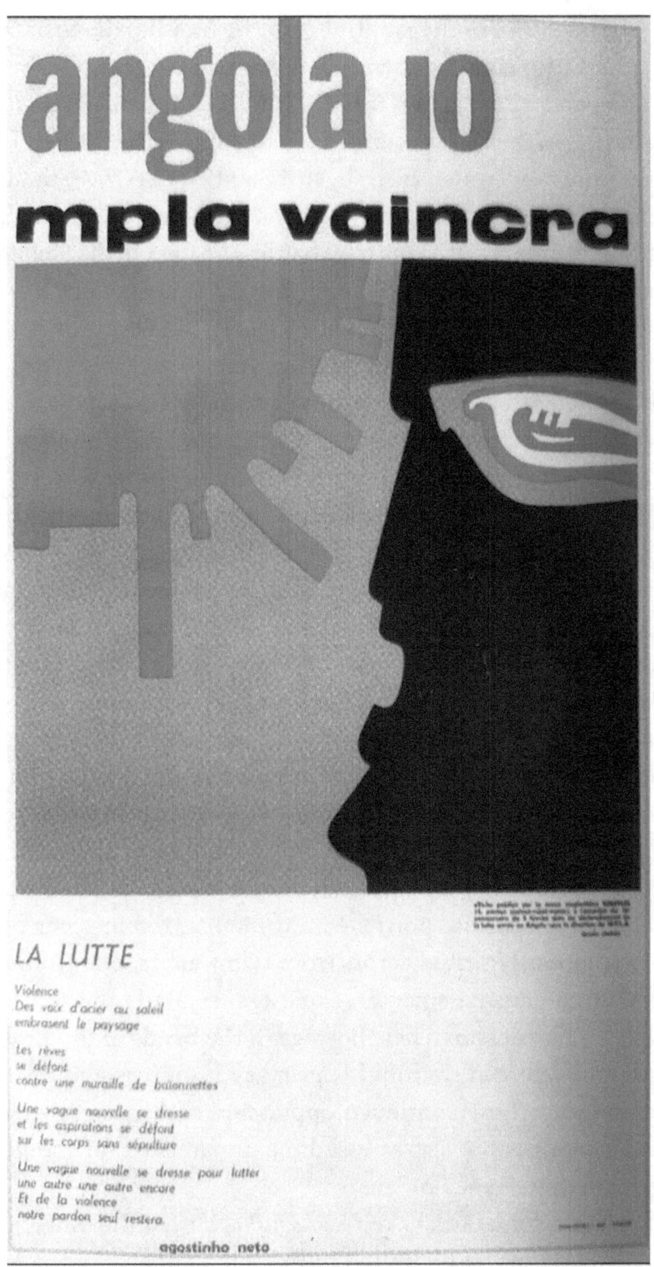

FIGURE 7. "Angola 10: MPLA Will Win." Poster designed by Mohammed Chabâa, including "The Struggle," poem by Agostinho Neto, *Souffles*, no. 19 (1970). Reprint courtesy of Abdellatif Laâbi.

separate Africa into two; the emptiness in the middle, the Sahara, was reserved by the Europeans for themselves, in their endless search for cheap thrills, petrol, and minerals. To this day they still attempt to divide us, the writers decried, with the occasional help of some long-toothed bourgeois nationalists; and now "watch as Arab Africa and Black Africa stand together in the same fight, against the same enemy of the people. And see the emptiness is no longer empty but a common battle."[92] After all, the *Souffles* editors asked, "is Chad in north or sub-Saharan Africa? Is Eritrea Black or Arab?"[93]

In a text titled "We Must Fight until Victory," an excerpt from a speech Agostinho Neto delivered on Radio Tanzanie in January 1968, Neto explained that the MPLA was not leading a racial war; they were not fighting the white man merely because of his whiteness. All those who came to Angola, unarmed, ready to fight, or to help in any other way, he claimed, would never be treated as enemies. "We do not look for support only south of the Sahara, what we call black Africa, where the inhabitants' skin is darker," he insisted. "We also seek help in North Africa, where the people have light skin."[94] Do not confuse your enemies with your friends, he warned his listeners, underscoring once more the necessity of Pan-African partnership and of dissent against repressive national or "Black" regimes.

A rare addition to *Souffles*' artistic vocabulary served to underline the point that the Arab revolution and the African revolution were intertwined—namely, cartoons. The only issue to include cartoons, "Africa One and the Same Battle" sported two drawings, one by French cartoonist Siné (Maurice Sinet) and the other by biologist Jamal Bellakhdar.[95] Siné's whole-page drawing portrayed a capitalist, reminiscent of Charles de Gaulle, pompously seated across from two waiters, one Arab the other Black, serving the businessman an explosive cocktail. The second caricature depicted a businessman held hostage in the hands of the Arab and African revolutions, forced to drop his primary resources and his hat. Both drawings underlined the continued oppression of Africans by white politicians and capitalists but also stressed the urgent need for a joint effort in bringing down these neocolonialists.

Appropriately, for a literary review, *Souffles* closed the nineteenth issue with a FRELIMO report dedicated to the role of poetry in the Mozambican War of Independence. After a short presentation on the history of Mozambican poetry from the nineteenth century to the end of World War II, the authors of the FRELIMO brief explained that any contemporary poet

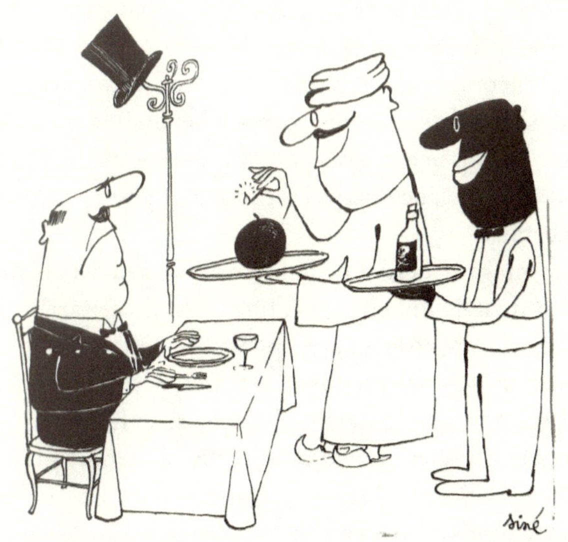

FIGURE 8. Cartoon by Maurice Sinet (Siné). *Souffles*, no. 19 (1970). Reprint courtesy of Abdellatif Laâbi.

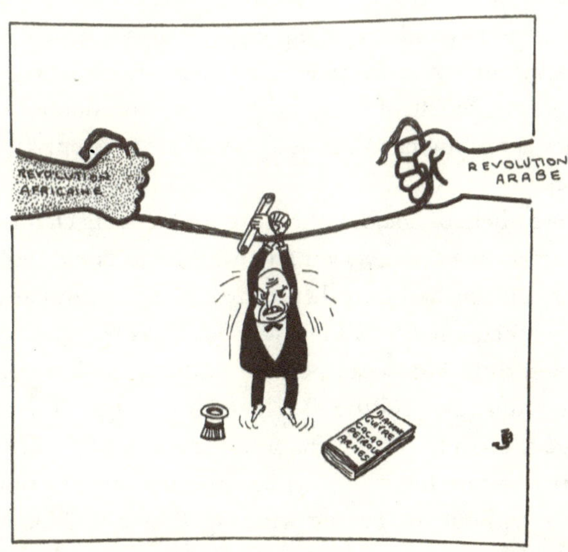

FIGURE 9. Cartoon by Jamal Bellakhdar. *Souffles*, no. 19 (1970). Reprint courtesy of Abdellatif Laâbi.

who did not directly participate in the struggle on the ground was so detached from reality that they knew liberty only by name. Only the revolution could provide poets with essential elements, without which poetry was impartial and incomplete; "only the revolution can substantiate poetry's most outlandish dreams and even go well beyond its dreams."[96] For with the revolution, "words became real, in the literal sense. . . . There is no longer metaphorical dissemblance between the fire of poetry and the fire of grenades and mortars."[97]

New Mozambican poetry, the bulletin explained, was revolutionary because it was intimately linked to life. It was not art for art's sake but art for life's sake. This was the norm in precapitalist societies, the bulletin claimed, but an anomaly in Western capitalist societies, where making art was a job, a specialization, and where viewing art was reserved for an hour or so of a person's day in a museum or theater, with seemingly no relation to the rest of one's life. In the old European world, poetry was an exceptional art for exceptional people. Poetry in the new African world, however, was no longer a specialization; "there is no longer 'the poet' once everyone is a poet. Tomorrow there will be no masters, for everyone will have become master of themselves. This is the lesson of poetry, and it is essential to our revolution."[98] Not only did the revolution entirely transform the nature of poetry and art more generally in Mozambique, but it also liberated the power of speech so that all could become poets. The poems in these pages, the report explained, were just the tip of the iceberg of poetic production in the Portuguese colonies, a testament to the quantity of creative energy liberated by the revolution.

Like the members of *Souffles*, the Lusophone poets claimed to make a non-elitist poetry, one that every man and woman could understand and write: a poetry entrenched in reality, coarse and beautiful as it was. Their material, they all claimed, was life itself. Much as the Casablanca school took inspiration from Moroccan popular culture, the Luso-African poets reread popular and rural culture as a locus of struggle. The new Mozambican poets gave birth to the new nation, named it, named its heroes, and used their art as a rallying cry. "It is because never will I retreat / never, never, never / without my people winning / here in Mozambique," exclaimed Marcelino dos Santos. In this they were all heeding the advice of their hero Frantz Fanon, who in 1959 had explained that during the revolutionary phase "a great many men and women who previously would never have thought of writing, now that they find themselves in exceptional circumstances, in prison, in the resistance or on the eve of their execution, feel the need to proclaim their nation, to portray their people and become the spokesperson of a new reality in action."[99]

Historians have overlooked how crucial the realm of the cultural was in rousing African men and women's sense of political outrage and their desire to take political as well as, at times, violent action against colonialism and neocolonialism.[100] We have too often left the realm of culture to literary critics, ignoring how much poetry and art more generally inflamed militants' political imagination.[101] Yet, again and again in interviews and in their memoires, members of the Maghreb Generation emphasized how central poetry, film, and music were to their politicization. And the relationship between art and politics did not stop there, as demonstrated by the FRELIMO pamphlet above. As men and women became more politically active, they didn't stop making art—instead, the Maghreb Generation weaponized cultural production. As the revolution took hold of the Mozambican and Angolan *maquis*, argued FRELIMO, everyone started writing and composing poetry. Luso-African militant-poets such as Andrade and dos Santos argued that culture should not be treated merely as the handmaiden of politics; rather, making the revolution was a cultural act par excellence.

Throughout the preparation of *Souffles*' nineteenth issue, Laâbi and Andrade were in close correspondence, exchanging notes, requesting edits, and discussing content. The letters, though to the point, bear witness to the intimacy of their relationship through the frequency of the exchanges and the use of *tu* (the familiar "you") and the closing *fraternellement* (fraternally) or *amicalement* (amicably). In July 1970, Andrade even urged Laâbi to travel to Algiers so they could finish the dossier as a team and present with the utmost clarity the political ideology of the various liberation movements.[102] After a frantic back-and-forth, Laâbi wrote to Andrade in October 1970 telling him that the nineteenth issue of *Souffles* on the Portuguese colonies was out with the printer and reassuring him that no matter the limits of this dossier, *Souffles* would not stop with this first round of information about the anti-Portuguese colonial struggle. "In future issues," he averred, "we will attempt (with your help), to give room anytime possible to the liberation struggles in Africa."[103] In fact, as early as February 1971, Laâbi wrote Andrade again asking for help with the twentieth issue of *Souffles*. The *Souffles* team were preparing a report on education, and Laâbi was wondering whether Andrade could send him some information on education in the liberated zones of Angola.[104]

Laâbi was never quite able to make good on his promise to Andrade to include more and more Africa-related content. *Souffles/Anfas* printed another two issues before tragedy struck. On January 27, 1972, the Moroccan government arrested Serfaty and Laâbi in their homes, transported them to the Rabat police headquarters, and immediately began to torture them. The Moroccan government held the two writers in the Laâlou prison, the very same prison in which the French government had held Serfaty some twenty-two years earlier. On February 25, 1972, the police freed Serfaty and Laâbi under the pressure of student protests—students who took to the streets brandishing copies of *Souffles/Anfas*. On March 14, when the police once more raided the two writers' homes, they found Laâbi, but Serfaty had fled to live in hiding and continue the revolution from underground.[105]

Souffles/Anfas' staff had never attempted to conceal its increasingly political bent and its collaboration with the Moroccan Far Left. On the contrary, the journal proclaimed its revolutionary project for all to hear, "without much prudence," wrote Abdellatif Laâbi's wife, Jocelyne, "for prudence was not fashionable, and what could a journal risk? Worst case scenario: a ban, which nobody even thought of!"[106] But two successive military coup attempts, in 1971 and 1972, had left Hassan II's regime feeling shaky and eager to clamp down on any form of dissent. In September 1973, after a lengthy trial, in which the primary piece of evidence presented against Laâbi was a complete collection of *Souffles/Anfas*, the judge handed out a verdict: Abdellatif Laâbi was condemned to ten years in prison for the crime of opinion. "In front of the judge," wrote Jocelyne Laâbi, "the issues of *Souffles* were piled high, undeniable testimonies to Abdellatif's breach of national security. No other proof was brought against him. For all of them, it was books and paper. Nothing but paper."[107] The Moroccan government banned the magazine, and those members who did not end up in jail or in hiding fled the country. A few former members attempted to republish in exile in France, but they did not have the same impact; eventually the journal sank into oblivion.[108] Serfaty continued to work for Ilā al-Amām from his safe houses, living clandestinely with the woman who would later become his wife, Christine Daure. In November 1974, the police caught up with him, and he was imprisoned for seventeen years, serving out a sentence for "plotting against the state's security."[109]

WHERE ARE YOU NOW, MARIO, MY BROTHER IN ARMS?

In 1976, inside his Spartan cell in the Kenitra prison, just north of Rabat, from behind "its irreversible door / the jeering jaw of Judas," Abdellatif Laâbi wrote in a letter to his friend Mario de Andrade.[110] The letter was affectionate and melancholic, a testament to the importance the men played in each other's lives. "Where are you now, Mario?" Laâbi lamented. "War, prison, made us lose touch."[111] He explained that prison did not prevent him from following with close attention the struggles in Mozambique, Angola, and Guinea and the fall of Portuguese prime minister Marcello Caetano. All of their victories "were bonfires that warmed me and my comrades."[112]

Laâbi thanked Andrade, without whom the Luso-African crusade against the colonial powers would never have "erupted into the Arab consciousness."[113] For it was Andrade who introduced Laâbi to so many brave fighters for FRELIMO, the MPLA, and the PAIGC, such as Marcelino dos Santos. It was Andrade with whom Laâbi worked in Rabat and Algiers for the decolonization of the mind and against what Laâbi called "the windup monkeys," the turncoat African dictators who extolled a humanism à la European.[114] It was Andrade who was always at the forefront of a socialism that was neither "black, nor white, nor Muslim, nor animist, but simply socialist."[115] "Mario, my brother in arms," wrote Laâbi, "my wish is to hold you against me a day in Luanda in peace, to see in your laughing and intelligent eyes the joy and gravity that the tasks of rebuilding and the pursuit of the revolution inspire."[116] In closing his letter, Laâbi hoped that one day he would have good news to give Andrade about Morocco—a country he knew Andrade loved deeply.

It is unclear whether Laâbi and Andrade ever met again. Laâbi was released from prison in 1980 and moved to Paris in 1985, where he still lives today. After working with the MPLA up to the eve of Angolan independence, Andrade left the group after disagreements with Agostinho Neto. When Portugal finally conceded defeat and the Angolan people achieved their independence, Neto proclaimed himself president, and Andrade settled in Guinea-Bissau. From there, Andrade continued to publish edited volumes of African poetry and preach a vision of Africa that transcended the rigid borders of the nation-state.[117] In 1985, Laâbi sent Andrade an invitation to the L'Harmattan publishing house for a reading of his recently published *La brûlure des interrogations* and *Discours sur la colline*. "Perhaps we will finally see each other again," wrote Laâbi, "my faithful friend."[118]

The relationship between Laâbi and Andrade testifies to the fact that Morocco served as a transnational locus of resistance to colonialism and neocolonialism, and as a space to envision what African unity should look like. Their collaboration reveals that the militant-artists of the Maghreb Generation were not content with political decolonization. They fought relentlessly for a utopian form of freedom—a freedom of expression, of the mind, and of movement. It is precisely interactions with people such as Mario de Andrade, Amílcar Cabral, and the other Luso-Africans present in Rabat in the 1950s and 1960s that drove Moroccan intellectuals such as Laâbi to a militancy based on political organizing as well as cultural criticism. Through poetry, movement building, and armed resistance, the Moroccans and Luso-Africans created a vision of African unity that far transcended the rigid national or racial solidarities that postcolonial governments enforced—a dissenting Pan-Africanism that centered the Maghreb.

THREE

POETRY ON ALL FRONTS

Jean Sénac's Fight for Algeria's Airwaves

In the hour of cultural revolution, poetry is a rifle for sowing.

JEAN SÉNAC, 1969

ON JULY 21, 1969, AS the world toasted Neil Armstrong and Buzz Aldrin's historic moon landing, five thousand people gathered in Algeria for the Pan-African Festival of Algiers (PANAF). Not only were representatives from forty African countries present but radicals from around the world flocked to the city to support the country's fight against imperialism. At symposiums, concert halls, and art galleries, the Black Panthers mingled with Tunisian musicians, Algerian activists, and Senegalese filmmakers. The Algerian government hired Franco-American filmmaker William Klein to capture the festivities for posterity, and for those ten days of July 1969, the Algerian national press, as well as that of many other African countries, reported in detail on the plays, exhibitions, dances, and concerts.[1] If American eyes were turned to the moon, African gazes were set on Algiers.

Many of the men and women present at the PANAF's symposium in the western suburbs of the city advertised their radicalness; the PANAF, they claimed, was *the* revolutionary festival.[2] In July 1969, not only Algeria but all of Africa, it seemed, was celebrating Algeria's spectacular revolution and the model the country was setting for decolonized states around the world. The French chargé d'affaires at the festival wrote to the French minister of foreign affairs, explaining that after this festival no one would dare denigrate the foreign policy of the Algerian government: Algeria had established itself as the Mecca of Revolutionaries.[3]

But not all in Algiers were enthusiastic supporters of the Algerian government's bid for Pan-African leadership. As Algerian writer and actor Hocine Tandjaoui recalled in a December 2017 interview, in the summer of 1969, while Africans gathered in downtown Algiers to listen to Black American Archie Shepp's saxophone, "[Many] young Algerians realized they were screaming into a void. All these pretty people were coming to illustrate, to commemorate an African Revolution that was counterfeit, . . . and we, we contemplated our extreme solitude."[4] Born in 1949 in Constantine in eastern Algeria, Tandjaoui published his first poems in *Souffles* and was the journal's correspondent in Algeria. In 1969, he was just nineteen years old and already had little hope for the future of political art in his country. To him the PANAF was not an epic celebration of independence but a masterfully conducted public relations move, smoke and mirrors that left only faint traces. Some fifty years later, in 2016, he still remembered the festival as a farce:

> In this late spring we resist the syrupy tune
> Of a progressivist Algeria organizing
> This razzle-dazzle circus they call the Pan-African Festival
> We are incredulous, dissidents, xerophiles.[5]

Algerian student Boussad Ouadi agreed that the festival could not possibly change anything about the situation of Algerian youth—youth who had been suffering an unmitigated ordeal since Houari Boumédiène's 1965 coup d'état. "All organizations were forbidden," Ouadi bemoaned; "the ciné-clubs were closed, we were muzzled. . . . We didn't really believe in this festival, considering the overwhelming repression under which we were living."[6]

Most of the scholarship on the PANAF focuses on the glitz and glamor of the festival. I look here to what I call the Off-PANAF: the events that took place outside the control of the Algerian state among members of the Maghreb Generation. The chief coordinator of the Off-PANAF was the Algerian poet Jean Sénac, who does not figure in any of the articles or official documentation published by the Algerian government concerning the PANAF. Despite his status as a major figure of the Algerian literary scene, he was not invited to participate in the festival's symposium by an Algerian government with which he was on increasingly bad terms. Yet his diary from those ten days in July 1969 contains scribbled notes of dinner dates, concerts, and parties with poets and artists from across the globe.[7] These encounters are much more difficult to reconstitute than the PANAF's main events, as they took place in the shadows, away from William Klein's video camera and the scrutiny of the press. Sénac organized parties at his house, recorded interviews for his radio show *Poésie sur tous les fronts* (Poetry on all fronts), and scheduled public poetry readings apart from the official program of events.[8]

ALGIERS AS THE MECCA OF REVOLUTIONARIES

"Picture this with me for a minute," described Algerian painter Denis Martinez in an interview in March 2018. "You see here there was this café where we met with Sénac, and then Mario [de Andrade] and his friends would be at this café, and there was also the Tahar Abderrahmane circle, the Brasserie, the Milk Bar, and the Cinémathèque, all along the street where we would circulate and sit outside in the terraces, and we would drink and smoke and talk."[9] Denis Martinez, born in 1941 in Oran in western Algeria, had been a professor at the Algiers Fine Art School since 1963. Much like the Moroccan artists of the Casablanca school, Martinez, together with some of his Algerian peers, created their own aesthetic, Aouchem—a modern art rooted in Algerian tradition blending geometric shapes and letters of the Tifinagh alphabet.[10] "Aouchem was born thousands of years ago, on the walls of a cave in the Tassili," Martinez and his friends wrote in their founding manifesto.[11]

For Martinez, reminiscing in his dusty and colorful apartment in Blida, the 1960s were a time of cultural and political ebullience. He and his friends would hitchhike the fifty kilometers to Algiers, borrow tapes from the Cinemathèque, have coffee with a couple of exiled revolutionaries, and then head back to Blida to show the movie in the main square. As one US journalist writing for the *New York Times* observed in 1965, "Young African exiles, some with beards or goatees, all with plenty of time for all-night talk, give cafés in downtown Algiers a look of the Left Bank in Paris."[12] Amílcar Cabral famously called Algiers the Mecca of Revolutionaries. When asked to elaborate he reportedly said: "Muslims make the pilgrimage to Mecca, Christians to the Vatican, and Revolutionaries to Algiers."[13]

As the mid-1950s turned into the late 1960s, whatever revolutionary clout Morocco had earned in the early years of the postcolonial era quickly faded away. Tensions with Algeria had been building since Morocco's independence, in great part because, in the lead-up to Moroccan independence, the French and Moroccan governments had failed to delineate the desert border between Algeria and Morocco. The French did not believe that such a stretch of arid and dusty land would ever be of value, but when oil companies discovered seas of petroleum under the desert sands, the land became priceless, and the two Maghrebi countries struggled over the exact location of the border.[14] Moroccans, Tunisians, and Algerians had collaborated in their struggles against the French colonial power, with the newly independent Moroccan and Tunisian governments even giving the Algerian Front de Libération Nationale (FLN) access to training camps along their Algerian borders. Despite these outward signs of collaboration, the messy aftermath of French colonialism and this question of desert borders rendered the three Maghrebi countries vulnerable in regard to their national sovereignties. Moreover, the three heads of state, Ahmed Ben Bella in Algeria, Mohammed V in Morocco, and Habib Bourguiba in Tunisia, were very different people, with very different visions for their respective countries, the Maghreb, and the Pan-African project. As early as 1956, behind the bars of his French prison cell, Ben Bella allegedly asserted that a "Sékou Touré [Guinean president] in Morocco and a Modibo Keita [Malian president] in Tunis, that would be perfect for us." Bourguiba and Mohammed V were not radical enough for Ben Bella, who believed they were in collusion with the West.[15]

The 1963 War of the Sands started with a series of desert skirmishes along the Algerian-Moroccan desert border. At first it seemed that this struggle would interfere with Algeria's emergence as a revolutionary powerhouse, because the war invariably turned the Algerian government's attention back to regional politics and away from the Third World. However, the Algerian government managed to use the war both to strengthen a sense of national unity and to blemish Morocco's already dwindling reputation as a revolutionary patron.[16] After the War of the Sands, King Hassan II turned his attention toward western Europe and toward Islamic trans-Saharan solidarities, forgoing the non-alignment of his father and the Casablanca group.[17]

For the Maghreb Generation, Algiers was the new place to be. The Algerian people had fought a drawn-out and bloody war against the French—a war that had made the front page of newspapers across the world through the slogan "Only one hero: the people."[18] As the Mecca of Revolutionaries, Algiers attracted militants such as the African National Congress (ANC) leader Nelson Mandela. "Algeria was his second home," remembered Mandela's grandson Chief Mandela in a hotel in Zeralda, near Algiers, in 2018:

> Algeria played a crucial role because this is where he came to get his military training but it was also a place where he came to connect to the entire continent, to the liberation movement, and to the revolutionaries of the time. While he was here, in and around leaders like Agostinho Neto, he was able to broaden his understanding of the plight of Africans and not just look at our own struggle in South Africa as an isolated problem; he came to view the struggle of Africans in its entirety."[19]

At the first OAU summit in Addis-Ababa in 1963, Ben Bella built on the overwhelming support for Algeria's struggle for independence and furthered the country's revolutionary rhetoric. "Pushing his notes aside, pounding the podium with both hands, very pale," one attending journalist recorded, "the Algerian leader made an impassioned appeal in a breathless voice for aid to the Angolan rebels. . . . I do not think that I had ever had such a profound sense of African unity as when I listened to Ben Bella, tears in his eyes, visibly moved, urge his listeners to rush to the assistance of the men dying south of the equator."[20] Indeed, Algeria turned to Africa first and foremost.[21] Emerging from a difficult and violent decolonization struggle, Algeria "had arms enough to supply the whole of the Africa continent," explained one US journalist.[22] And supply it did. No other African country was willing to support subversive transnational groups to the same extent—particularly in terms of military assistance; they were afraid of diplomatic reprisal or of undermining their own national sovereignties.[23]

On June 19, 1965, the inhabitants of Algiers woke up to find military tanks in the streets and armed soldiers at every important intersection. In the night, Colonel Houari Boumédiène and those loyal to him in the Algerian army (Armée de Libération National; ALN) had arrested Ahmed Ben Bella in his house. The coup was bloodless, and many Algerians believed the tanks were in place to film Gillo Pontecorvo's film *La bataille d'Alger* (*The Battle of Algiers*, 1966).[24] The coup installed the austere but charismatic military man Boumédiène, who vowed to continue the Pan-African policies of the predecessor he had ousted. But to many young Algerians, including Hocine Tandjaoui, Jean Sénac, and Denis Martinez, the coup was the beginning of their disenchantment with the revolution and postindependence Algeria.

"When I say that Algiers was the capital of the African liberation movements," clarified Denis Martinez, "I don't mean that it was the capital of African culture, except of course during the PANAF. . . . We yearned for Algiers to become a cultural capital, like Paris, . . . for artists to come from all over Africa."[25] In the summer of 1969, the young painter's dream came true. The PANAF was an ambitious project led by the Algerian government and partly funded by the OAU. The new Algerian president, Houari Boumédiène, whose legitimacy as a leader of the Third World was shaky at best following his 1965 coup, was attempting to grow the regime's base among the youth and to renew Algeria's reputation as a Pan-African power. As Black Panther Kathleen Cleaver remembered, "The stern, colorless colonel who replaced Ben Bella was virtually unknown outside of Algeria." According to Cleaver, "part of Boumédiène's strategy for asserting Algerian leadership on an international level; one plank in his comprehensive program to place Algeria in the political leadership of Africa, the Arab world, and nonaligned nations, was hosting the First Pan-African Cultural Festival."[26] The festival was also meant to showcase the steps that Algeria had taken toward financial independence after political independence and to encourage international investments.[27]

At the same time, the festival enabled the Algerian government to control the Pan-African cultural networks emerging in and around Algiers. By organizing the PANAF, Algerian officials could try to manipulate what was already happening in bars and cafés outside their direct supervision. The Algerian government threw this gigantic party in the streets of Algiers with the intent of producing and distributing a certain type of Pan-African culture that coincided with their political project. The PANAF was a political-aesthetic project. The culture that the Algerian government displayed and created at the festival contradicted everything that the European powers circulated about culture and the arts. "The occidental idea of culture . . . practically goes to say that culture and domination, culture and luxury, are intimately linked," reads one pamphlet published by the Algerian government for the festival.[28] The Algerian government put on display its rejection of such a concept of culture. In Africa, the authors of the pamphlet claim, culture had always had a functional and initiatory role: "Functional from the beginning and an auxiliary weapon later in our struggle for liberation, culture today in Africa is indissolubly linked to the development and to the social progress of our peoples."[29] The members of the Maghreb Generation who attended the festival, however, did not have faith in the Algerian government's effort to create a culture of and for the people.

Many members of the Maghreb Generation felt that the festival functioned as a façade, erected to conceal the decaying ideals that had once sustained the Algerian Revolution. In the handful of articles about the festival, scholars have tended to present the PANAF as a momentous occasion for the continent.[30] We have tended to serve up the same anecdotes, about the PANAF's iconic moments, such as Archie Shepp's concert, Nina Simone's first rendition of "Ne me quitte pas," the Black Panther Party press conference, Miriam Makeba singing in Arabic, and the dancing parade throughout the streets of Algiers. We have relied on the sources published by the Algerian government, in the form of pamphlets, government-sponsored newspapers, and interviews with government officials, and in so doing we have repeatedly concluded that the liveliest debate took place in the Palais des Nations between those who espoused *négritude* and those who abhorred it.[31] While there was a spirited debate at the symposium between these two positions, the protagonists of this chapter have time and time again dismissed this debate as passé—a hollow shell. Instead, they have emphasized the widening gap between the politicians and the militant-artists, between those who were bound to an institution and those who were free to think and criticize, between the Maghrebi state's vision of Pan-Africanism and their own dissenting Pan-Africanism. To them the festival represented the end of an era of true revolutionary change, one last big hurrah before the descent into censorship and the narrowing of cultural possibilities. This is not to say that they did not enjoy the opportunities the festival presented; but for the most part they shunned the official gatherings and stayed in the cafés and bars along the rue Didouche Mourad or at Jean Sénac's apartment, where they materialized a community of belonging that they had been creating for a decade on paper and through the airwaves.

JEAN SÉNAC: A CENTRAL FIGURE IN THE ALGERIAN LITERARY SCENE

Jean Sénac was born in the region of Oran to a poor woman of Catalan origin who had fled her hometown of Béni Saf after being raped. He grew up feeling excluded from the *pied-noir* population on account of his poverty and illegitimacy; he did not "feel of their race."[32] On the contrary, Sénac identified with the working people of Algeria, with Arabic, "this stony language," with a country where the "coffee was good . . . where the plates were oily and the food red."[33] Sénac was a poet, a socialist with an anarchist sense of humor, a lapsed Christian, a homosexual, and above all a prolific writer who penned words on any material he could find—bus tickets, toilet paper, and city walls included.[34]

While living in Algiers in the early 1950s, Sénac started two literary journals in quick succession: *Soleil* and its sequel *Terrasses*. Both journals included works by young Algerian writers who would later become important members of postcolonial Algeria's literary world, writers such as Mohammed Dib, Mouloud Mammeri, Kateb Yacine, and Mouloud Feraoun. Increasingly close to the Algerian nationalist movement, Sénac was tired of the cultural atrophy of Algiers, which he saw as a direct result of colonialism. On French writer Albert Camus's invitation, Sénac moved to Paris in the second half of the 1950s. His move did not put an end to his struggle for Algerian independence—quite the contrary. In Paris, Sénac joined the FLN, took part in clandestine operations, such as creating the underground newspaper *El-Moudjahid* (The holy warrior), and published the militant *Matinales de mon people* (The eve of my people) in 1961. His relationship with Camus became increasingly strained; Sénac could not understand why Camus would not side with the Algerian independentists. He organized multiple meetings between exiled FLN leaders and his intellectual mentor, to no avail. Eventually, Sénac chose to end the relationship.[35]

On the day of Algerian independence, Tuesday, July 3, 1962, Sénac marked his calendar with a brilliant sun.[36] Three months later, in October 1962, he returned to what he considered his rightful nation, ready to take up his responsibilities as a poet of the revolution. In his 1963 poem "Poème-programme," published in the paper *La République*, Sénac appraised the work that lay ahead, listing the spaces in which the revolution needed to persevere (the stadiums, factories, and movie theaters), and emphasizing the popular nature of all postcolonial projects.

Here
in Algeria
because we are writing for a people
of twelve million
here
we will break with the old selfish world
dust off our soles
dip our hearts in the fountain
and sing.
For an entire people
that will recognize
in the stadiums
at the factory
in the theaters
in the douars [villages]
. . . .
O brothers,
Algeria the democratic and popular
is waiting for its poets to speak.
They are here,
. . . .
at the front line of the people;
for them,
they will give the people's words
popular fervor.[37]

The new postcolonial Algeria celebrated Sénac as a revolutionary poet. He integrated Ben Bella's government as a consultant to the minister of national education and helped rebuild the Library of Algiers that the OAS (Organisation Armée Secrète) had burned down.[38] An enthusiastic supporter of the government, he wrote poems glorifying the revolution and exalted socialist self-management with this famous line: "Tu es belle comme un comité de gestion" (You are as beautiful as a management committee).[39] Sénac became the secretary of the Union of Algerian Writers in 1963, right after its creation. Through the union, Algerian writers hoped to participate fully in the construction of a socialist Algerian state and to become the voices of the Algerian masses.[40] One of the union's principal objectives was to "tighten the links with their brothers of the Maghreb, of the Arab world, of Africa and the Third World, in a revolutionary perspective."[41] But the union was immediately weakened by the conflicting views of its members, and Sénac quit shortly after Boumédiène's 1965 coup.

Sénac was rapidly becoming aware of the revolutionary rhetoric brandished by an Algerian government that was happy to have militant-poets writing on its behalf, but only when they did not demand full freedom of expression. Unlike some of his colleagues in the union who, according to Sénac, lolled in the comfort of writing for themselves, Sénac demanded that the union be awarded a budget from the Algerian state, in addition to full editorial independence, so that they might fulfill the mission of continuing the Algerian Revolution through their verses. [42] Even after quitting the union, Sénac continued to work to tighten links between Africa and the Arab world, and in doing so garnered a significant following. Young writers flocked to him for help, for advice, and for friendship. Sénac published the first anthology of young francophone Algerian poets in 1971, including many who went on to become renowned Algerian poets.

From 1969 to 1972, Sénac hosted two radio programs: *Poète dans la cité* (Poet in the city) and then *Poésie sur tous les fronts* (Poetry on all fronts), both of which were popular among young Algerians. An August 1971, an *El-Moudjahid* article lauded the wide reach of Sénac's show, the unnamed journalist in Algiers writing that on Monday, August 3, toward 9:10 p.m., he had heard *Poetry on All Front*'s opening credits wafting out of several apartments in the city's projects. "Only great radio shows can compete with the television screen," the journalist remarked.[43] Sénac received boxes of fan mail from young admirers, some only in middle school, asking him to review their poems and raving about how transformative and inspiring his show was. One young man, Mohamed Khodja, told Sénac that he came to life when he heard the poetry of his brothers "screaming their madness and their misery."[44] Djaffar Ait and Kaci Djerbit, two high schoolers from Tizi Ouzou, wrote to request paper copies of his shows, since their high school forbade the radio. *Poetry on All Fronts,* they explained, "allows us to understand the reality that surrounds us and in which we are immersed body and soul. Russian poetry, Black American poetry, national poetry, never leave us indifferent but penetrate us and bring us face-to-face with problems that we have no right to ignore."[45] Over the course of *Poetry on All Fronts'* five years on air, Sénac broadcast the voices of Algerian poets (writing in French, Arabic, or Tamazigh) and the voices of radical poets from around the world, from the anti-apartheid poets to Turkish poet Nâzim Hikmet and the American Beat poets.

Through his radio show, Sénac helped young Algerians understand that territorial independence was not enough, that they needed to labor on to achieve cultural and intellectual decolonization. As one young Frenchman living in Algiers noted, "All these young people to whom we kept on repeating your country is free, they realized upon hearing Sénac that there were many more chains to break, even in their own consciousness. His voice was a breath of fresh air for an entire generation that was being force-fed empty rhetoric."[46] Hocine Tandjaoui, another young Algerian who discovered Sénac through his radio show, was one of those who had made the "pilgrimage" to Sénac's basement apartment.[47] Tandjaoui remembered Sénac's being an inspiration for many young Algerians who were disillusioned with the Algerian Revolution and the absence of cultural and political possibilities in post-1965 Algeria. "Sénac was important for us," remembered Tandjaoui, "for he was a dissident voice from the beginning."[48] Sénac revealed to a generation of young Algerians that the FLN leadership was not working for the promised freedom and equality of the postcolonial world but instead consisted of a "bunch of puritan-bourgeois" working to line their own pockets.[49]

Houari Boumédiène's 1965 coup altered Sénac's relationship with the Algerian government and his vision of the revolution. Sénac did not hesitate to critique what he saw as a slippage into dictatorship, into corruption, as this June 1970 diatribe against the Algerian publishing world testifies: "The SNED [Société Nationale d'Édition et de Diffusion] more than ever is filth and a major crime against the spirit of the revolution, more than ever, dough and cops, censorship, cowardice, incompetence, disaster, and a bureaucracy of losers. . . . Crime! Crime! Crime!"[50] His friends and fellow writers Kateb Yacine and Malek Haddad turned against him, questioning his Algerianity—a sore point for Sénac, who constantly felt like an outsider, worried that people saw him as a *gaouri* (Algerian for an outsider, or foreigner, often French).[51]

Sénac, broke, moved out of his house at Pointe Pescade and into a basement apartment in downtown Algiers on rue Elysée Reclus—an apartment that he famously called his "cave-vigie" (basement-watchtower). His poetry became increasingly dark. The hope and determination inflecting earlier poems such as "Poème-programme" evaporated; he was left with an overwhelming sense of fear. In a 1971 poem titled "Cette ville" (This city), anxiety took over Sénac's voice. No longer did he speak for the people; he now wrote of feeling watched, spied upon, and lied to: "In this city / we no longer go out / rats snuff it under our hearts . . . the walls can decay / but these looks . . . build the future with what? On rage, dirt and vulgarity . . . miserly nationalism, religion, race. . . . In this city youth is a crime, intelligence is a crime, beauty is a crime," he lamented. "Mediocrity is the only law / poetry beat to the blood / In this city / we no longer talk / we lie to each other / . . . we are scared."[52]

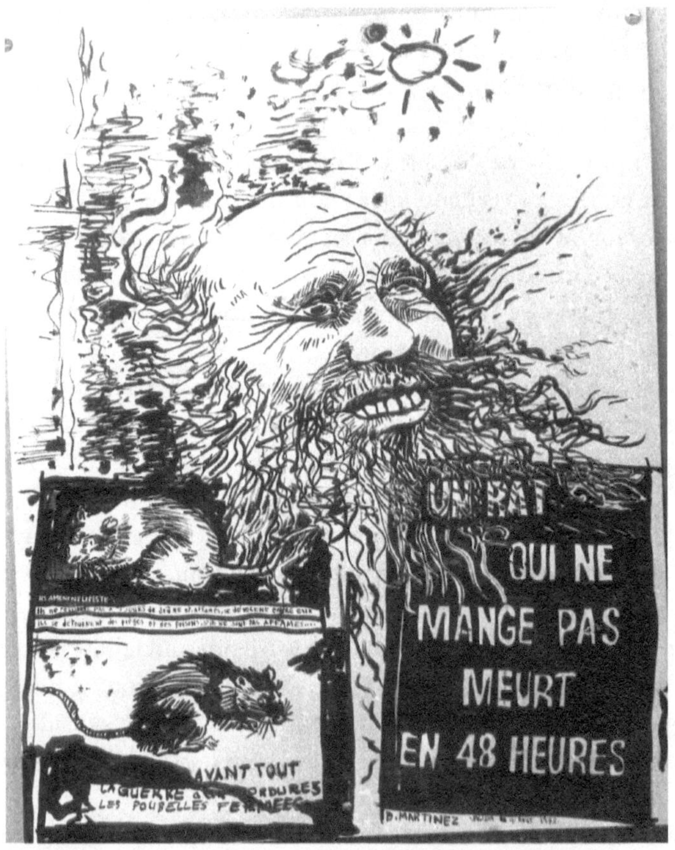

FIGURE 10. Painter Denis Martinez's portrait of Jean Sénac, created shortly before Sénac's murder in August 1973. "A rat that does not eat dies in 48 hours." Apparently Sénac never saw it; the rats indicate Sénac's squalid living conditions. Reprint courtesy of Denis Martinez.

And indeed, Sénac faced many threats. As early as 1968, some of his friends grew worried for his safety. Patrick MacAvoy pleaded with him to move to France, asking him to abandon this "realm of country bumpkins such as Kateb Yacine," and revealed to Sénac that their mutual friend, Jacques, had dreamed that Sénac was being lynched.[53] Yet Sénac never gave up hope, as this June 1970 letter to Jean Breton testifies: "Here the fight continues, at the radio, at the university, at the theater, in the street, each second, to save still a little of this revolution, a little poetry, a little beauty, while the gutters invade the beach. With the most generous, the most lucid of us, we try to wash away the pustules, to maintain a true sun."[54]

Young French diplomat Gilles Gauthier, who was living in Algiers at the time, commented on the decrepitude of Sénac's living conditions: "At the end of a sinister hallway, there were two small rooms, a kitchen with a sink and as the only source of light two windows that gave onto a light well. The floor was covered in books, which we were not allowed to touch." Nevertheless, Gauthier noted, Sénac continued to assemble his radio shows with passion, always in a hurry, navigating with ease between the piles of books in his apartment to find one passage or another. "When I asked him how he could do this that fast," Gauthier wrote, "he would quote this Picasso anecdote: an American was complaining about the price Picasso had set for a piece of tablecloth that he had scribbled on in only five minutes. Apparently, Picasso told the American man: yes, but it took me fifty years to learn how to do this in five minutes."[55] In June 1972, to Sénac's dismay, the Algerian government canceled his radio show *Poetry on All Fronts*.[56] In his show, his letters, and his conversations, Sénac had not hesitated to critique what he saw as the government's slow turn to dictatorship and corruption. This criticism no doubt had something to do with his show's cancellation. Incensed, Sénac quit the radio altogether.

In 1972, Sénac gathered young Algerian poets, many of whom had gotten to know him through *Poetry on All Fronts*, in Constantine to discuss the connection between the political and the artistic roles of the poet. The despair of the young Algerian poets is obvious in Sénac's notes on the meeting. Like Hocine Tandjaoui in 1969, the young poets in Constantine spoke of their solitude. They lamented the lack of infrastructure for publishing their poems, as well as the absence of critics and of an audience. They spoke of community censorship when it came to some of the themes they wanted to write about, such as sex and suicide. Algerian poetry was clearly in crisis.[57]

Jean Sénac was assassinated in his apartment in the night of August 30, 1973, and quickly buried and forgotten. Though Sénac had wanted to be interred in a Muslim cemetery, as he clearly stated in his last will and testament, the Algerian state refused, and he was buried instead in a Christian *pied-noir* cemetery in Algiers.[58] The Algerian press declined to announce the date of his funeral, and not a single Algerian official came to pay homage to a man who had fought for Algerian independence and been part of the government after the revolution. "Nobody wants to talk about Sénac in Algeria," wrote Tahar Ben Jelloun in September 1973.[59] The investigation into his murder led by the Algerian government produced no evidence other than a petty crime (linked to his homosexuality—a lover?), and the possible suspect was soon released.[60] *El-Moudjahid* only published a tiny paragraph announcing Sénac's death. Testifying to Sénac's stature in the Algerian literary scene, both francophone and arabophone, an Arabic-language magazine, *Al-Sh'b al-Thaqāfy*, published an in-depth and laudatory homage to Sénac, with testimonies from several admirers, calling him the poet of love and freedom, and the poet who shone the light upon the truth.[61] Rachid Boudjedra, one of Sénac's many pupils and friends, wrote: "Jean Sénac was the first victim of Algerian Islamic fundamentalism. He was stabbed to death in an atrocious way in September 1973 because he was a *pied-noir*, because of his French origins. A symbol of multiracial and multireligious Algeria . . . Jean Sénac, the *gaouri*, was assassinated by fundamentalists out of hatred for intelligence and the other."[62]

JEAN SÉNAC: THE CONVENER OF THE OFF-PANAF

Jean Sénac is nowhere to be found in state-sponsored documentation about the PANAF. He was not invited to participate in the festival's symposium, nor did he appear in the many pictures published by the state newspaper *El-Moudjahid*. He did not contribute articles to pamphlets published about the festival, nor did he feature in William Klein's documentary. And yet, to this day, many of the members of the Maghreb Generation who traveled to Algiers in the summer of 1969 remember meeting with Sénac. "Jean Sénac," René Depestre exclaimed in 2017, "oh, he was a solar man!" According to Depestre, it was thanks to Sénac that he met many of the poets and thinkers who were in Algiers in July 1969. To Depestre, Sénac was a Pan-African convener.

Indeed, if Sénac was a giant on the Algerian literary-political scene, he was equally important in the Pan-African literary world. Mario de Andrade, Amílcar Cabral, Marcelino dos Santos, René Depestre, Ted Joans, Sarah Maldoror, Archie Shepp, the members of *Souffles*—all knew and admired him. "When you meet Sénac, Madam, you respect him," insisted Guadeloupian film director Sarah Maldoror; "he's a fighter, you don't always fight with arms, he fought with his words."[63] Throughout his life, Sénac labored for the revolution—the one that would completely liberate his Algerian people together with all people from Africa. On his deathbed, he wrote that he wanted people to dance the twist, "dance breathlessly for Africa the liberated / . . . you will build a culture without races."[64]

In the summer of 1969, Sénac's biweekly show, *Poetry on All Fronts,* was an all-Africa affair: from Andrade and the members of *Souffles* to Depestre and the anti-apartheid poets.[65] Sénac was determined to give his many listeners a taste of what a dissenting Pan-African poetic community could look like, outside the walls of the PANAF's official symposium. He started each episode with these words: "Algerian brothers, here are your poets. Foreign friends, here are the poets of your people. Together we will live a moment of truth, a moment of trust. For poetry is truth, poetry is brotherly communication, poetry is light and trust, or it is nothing."[66] Just as the members of *Souffles* had worked hard to turn their journal into a Pan-African forum, one independent from state supervision and honoring the voice of the people, Sénac struggled to create a space for Pan-African poetry in an Algiers that was becoming increasingly repressive. This was the mission of *Poetry on All Fronts.*

"If I tell you that Africans are born poets, you are going to laugh, Ma'am, but it's true," explained Sarah Maldoror in an August 2018 interview.[67] To Maldoror, Jean Sénac and Mario de Andrade, her partner, were two such men. Maldoror and her daughters, Henda and Anouchka, remembered that they spent significant amounts of time with Sénac while living in Algiers. Anouchka, still a child at the time, recalled being impressed by the length of Sénac's beard and by the poet's assertion that "it was the longest in the world."[68] The Maldoror-Andrade family had been living in Algiers since their move from Rabat in 1966. The FLN had become an important ally of the MPLA, and the Algerian government provided the family with a white villa overlooking the sea in Bab El Oued. From there, Andrade organized the resistance to Portuguese colonialism and helped the Algerian government train guerilla fighters.

It is hard to know the nature and extent of Andrade's interactions with Sénac during this period. Certainly, my interviewees make it sound like the world of revolutionary poetry was a tight-knit community, but few traces are left of the exchanges between various members of these circles, as most of the conversations probably occurred in cafés or bars and most of the participants are now dead. I have found only two letters from Andrade to Sénac, in Sénac's archives, but both reveal a familiarity that comes from frequent encounters. In Andrade's archives, I found a careful cutout of the tiny paragraph in the journal *El-Moudjahid* published at the time of Sénac's death.[69] Sénac was assassinated just eight months after Andrade's dear friend and Anouchka's godfather Amílcar Cabral was also assassinated. "It was a very hard year for Mario," remembered Henda Ducados, Andrade's daughter.[70]

Sénac and Andrade first met in Paris, where they both contributed to the journal *Présence africaine*.[71] It was Andrade who relayed Sénac's message-poem to the 1956 First International Congress of Black Writers and Artists in Paris—a message signed by several other young Algerian writers who stood in solidarity with their African counterparts. This was the first of many times Sénac would position himself at the center of solidarity efforts between Algerian and Black writers. This was in September 1956, before Algeria was anywhere near gaining its independence and while other *pied-noir* writers were shying away from making any clear declarations of support for the Algerian struggle. Through this message-poem, Sénac was not only outing himself as a resister, an Algerian, a victim of colonialism, but he was also already working to create a united front with Black artists and poets.

Salute to the Black Writers and Artists
Us, African Writers,
Salute the First World Congress
Of Black Writers and Artists,
By the cry of our executed;
The pain of our women
And this crime:
The bitterness of our children.
We salute them by all the blood
Of our people on our words,
By all the black of our people
On our hands of mad frost,

....
O brothers! If our syntax itself
Is not a cog of liberty
If our books must still weigh
Upon the back of the docker,
If our voice is not the relay of stars
For the railroader and the shepherd,
If our poems are not also the weapons of justice
In the hands of our people
Let us be quiet!
Black brothers, the Algerian Writers
If they dare raise their voice while their brothers fall,
It is to transmit this message of Hope.[72]

The "Salute to the Black Writers and Artists" was a rallying cry for poets of the African continent. In the poem, Sénac united all people of Africa around a single experience of pain and positioned the poet not only as the spokesperson for the oppressed but also as the voice that could lead people out of their misery and suffering.[73] Sénac took on the color of blackness, "his black hands of mad frost," demonstrating his sense that he and his fellow African poets wrote as one hand—transcribing the message of their people. This was very different from Jean Paul Sartre's introduction to Frantz Fanon's *Wretched of the Earth*; through his "Salute to the Black Artists and Writers," Sénac positioned himself as an insider, as a Black artist himself, not as an approving European onlooker.[74]

Mario de Andrade read Sénac's message of support to the congress, and it was he and Frantz Fanon who pushed for a reference to the Algerian War in its final resolution.[75] Through his friendship with Fanon and Sénac, Andrade stood by the Algerian cause. This explains why, in his 1961 collection, *Matinales de mon peuple,* Sénac wrote a poem titled "Angola," which he dedicated to Andrade. "Mario de Andrade, my brother," he began, "I do not forget that at the darkest hour of Algeria's history, you were by our side against the same enemies."[76] In the manner of Aimé Césaire in *Cahier d'un retour au pays natal,* the poem describes the rotting faces of their common enemy. Sénac wrote of the decaying European civilization confronting, for one last night, the strength that is Africa, that is Angola, that is Hope and Brotherhood. Demonstrating his commitment to Angolan independence,

Sénac ended the poem with "Black brothers, I salute your rippling blood / The rogue and generous river of independent Angola."[77]

Unlike Jean Sénac, and because of his close ties to the Algerian government, Andrade was invited to participate in the PANAF's official symposium at the Club des Pins. At the symposium, Andrade delivered a speech on behalf of the MPLA, FRELIMO, and the PAIGC. In contrast to many of the other countries' spokespeople, who expounded vaguely on the role of culture in the current African political climate, Andrade was very clear: "The war of liberation that we are conducting in Angola, Guinea, and Mozambique, is the only way we can exist culturally." Like Sénac, Andrade believed that the writer's role was to communicate the world, the experiences, the "syntax" of the people. Andrade ended his speech with a call to African poets and filmmakers from the recently independent nations to come witness the struggles of their people in the Angolan *maquis* and the Mozambican jails. "Where are you?" he asked. "You must come, there is still time!"[78]

In the summer of 1969, Sénac dedicated at least three of his shows from *Poetry on All Fronts,* one in July and two in August 1969, to the poetry inspired by Mario de Andrade. Unfortunately, the recordings of the show were destroyed after Sénac resigned from the radio in 1972, and the paper traces are limited to a few discontinuous pages, haphazardly stored in a box in his Algerian archive. But from the bits and pieces of the show that I've been able to cobble together, Sénac shows a boundless admiration for the work of such poets as Mario de Andrade, Agostinho Neto, Marcelino dos Santos, and others. Acting as the relay of the Algerian people, in a continent still alive with the hope conveyed by the Algerian Revolution, Sénac explained that the battle-poetry of Angola, Mozambique, Guinea, and Cap Verde would break down the artificial boundaries of the African continent.[79] "Whether they exalt the heroic gestures of the war, or compose popular songs to the glory of national edification," claimed Sénac, "the poets in both cases are at the forefront of African unity. . . . As such, the situation of African poetry at the turn of the 1960s is characterized by a Pan-African thematic."[80]

Even though Sénac's position in the Algerian political world was becoming precarious, and even though he was not fooled by his government's revolutionary rhetoric, Sénac had not quite lost hope for the future of militant-poet dissent. Through his contacts with poets from across Africa and the Black Diaspora, Sénac tended to the movement of revolutionary poetics by connecting those in Algeria (his audience) that still valued the freedom to express resistance to those in Lusophone Africa who were fighting for the freedom to exist.

It was through Mario de Andrade and at the PANAF that Jean Sénac first encountered the Haitian poet René Depestre. In a December 2017 interview, Depestre said that he and Sénac were close friends and wrote each other until Sénac's death, though no traces of their correspondence remain in either of the poets' archives. Sénac knew of Depestre before they met—he had read the Haitian poet in *Souffles* and had received Depestre's *Anthology of Cuban Poetry* in 1967, through Andrade. "The relays of the revolution are numerous, and, on all fronts, poetry lights up a little more our dream,"[81] Sénac explained when presenting Depestre's anthology on the radio. In 2017, Depestre did not remember much about the PANAF, other than a rather risqué sexual adventure.[82] He did, however, recall that it was the PANAF that brought together the Black African and the Maghrebi writers, which, he claimed, took place in Jean Sénac's apartment.

While Depestre was close to such figures of the *négritude* movement as Aimé Césaire, Léon-Gontran Damas, Alioune Diop, and Léopold Sédar Senghor, he was not a follower of the *négritude* movement. His poetry certainly drew inspiration from *négritude* literature and developed some of its themes, but to Depestre, *négritude* had become synonymous with the dictatorial regime of Papa Doc Duvalier, from which he fled his homeland of Haiti. For Depestre, *négritude* had been an enlightening and nourishing cultural *marronage* that had helped the people from the Antilles gain a better sense of themselves.[83] But by 1969, *négritude* had become the "evil engine of pseudo-decolonization. *Négritude* [was] papadoc-ized to the bone."[84] While the previous generation of *négritude* poets, such as Senghor and Césaire, may have used poetry to recover human dignity, Depestre, along with the rest of the Maghreb Generation, stood firmly in the ranks of those who believed that poetry's primary purpose was to bring about the revolution.

As such, Depestre found solace in the struggles of his friends Jean Sénac and Mario de Andrade. He recognized that the struggle for freedom of speech and against censorship was ongoing in Algeria and stood on the side of those, like Sénac, who defied the government's move to stifle dissent. "Sénac was in the opposition," Depestre remembered, "and he was right; I was very well received, because of my friendship with Fanon, but I led my own investigation while in Algiers, and I saw that the leaders of the FLN were a real mixed bag."[85] Unlike Sénac, however, Depestre participated in the festival's official symposium, and his speech was referenced at length in a variety of official channels, such as *El-Moudjahid*. At the symposium, Depestre gave a moderating speech about the damages of colonialism and the use of ideologies such as *négritude* to regain a sense of humanhood. But after establishing these well-worn positions, Depestre moved on to evoke the dangers that awaited the postcolonial nation. Using Haiti as an illustration of the failure of revolution, he warned his audience against the "Indigenization" of colonial violence. Depestre offered Cuba as an example of a successful revolution—a revolution that filtered into all aspects of Cuban daily life and broke the "old animal reflexes that capitalism and racism had implanted in the people's unhappy minds."[86] He argued that there could be no real decolonization if it was not revolutionary, for only through a revolution could the people truly take hold of their history. Depestre thus stood firmly in line with the revolutionary trajectory of countries such as Cuba and Algeria. However, he also conveyed a sense of empathy that was lacking from much of the Algerian government's official rhetoric. For Depestre, a true revolution could only survive through tenderness for the masses, not through dogma or cold isolation from the people. For Sénac, as for Depestre, love and revolution were intimately intertwined.

Outside the official lineup of events and dinners, Depestre met with Sénac to record an interview and to prepare two broadcasts for *Poetry on All Fronts*. Little remains of these recordings save their titles and the list of poems Sénac and his collaborators read during the show. In the same way he had used Andrade to introduce his audience to the world of Lusophone poetry, Sénac used Depestre as a gateway into the poetry and realities of the Caribbean. On September 15, 1969, Sénac aired a show titled "We Make the Revolution, Thus We Exist: The Great Fraternal Voice of René Depestre," which included the first part of an interview he had recorded with Depestre on topics as varied as poetry, Haiti, Cuba, surrealism, voodoo, and revolution. On September 22, 1969, the second part of the Depestre interview aired in a show titled "Poet in Cuba."[87] In both of these shows, Sénac chose to include some of the most explicitly Third Worldist of Depestre's poems, such as "L'âge du Vietnam" (The era of Vietnam), an homage to the human victims of war and to the similarities of suffering among them. Much like Sénac in his "Salute to Black Writers and Artists," in "The Era of Vietnam"

Depestre united all of humankind around a single experience of life and a single heart: "Me the man I have these tides in me / I have my ugliness, my pettiness / my fake gods, my lies sometimes / but somewhere in me, maybe / in my very heart, there is the sea."[88]

In Sénac's correspondence, I found several references to Depestre's poetry. Clearly Sénac's showcasing of the Haitian's poems on *Poetry on All Fronts* had garnered some admiration. One such letter was from Hamid Nacer-Khodja: "I haven't been listening to *Poetry on All Fronts* for long, but I am already a fervent fan. Last week and yesterday I heard and admired René Depestre's beautiful poems. . . . The result, sir, is this: I would be overjoyed if you could send me the unpublished poems of René Depestre. I cannot get them; I do not have the means."[89] This letter marked the beginning of Hamid Nacer-Khodja's lifelong commitment to Sénac and to rehabilitating his memory after his assassination.

Before interviewing Depestre, Sénac had met him at a party on August 2, 1969, in his "basement-watchtower." If one is to believe Sénac's calendar for that week, the party was an all-night affair: the next day the only note in his calendar was "sleep."[90] There are practically no traces left of the conversations that occurred between the many militant-poets present that night; only a single record survives in Jean Sénac's archives: a poster of a poem by Depestre, "The Era of Vietnam," tagged with the signatures of those present that night. The poster, clearly a gift for Sénac, contains thank-yous for the encounters he had facilitated and is signed by Abdallah Stouky, René Depestre, Mohammed Akmoun, and others whose names are more difficult to read. Some of the tags are clearly inside jokes; others simply thank him for a marvelous evening spent with other revolutionary poets. One note in the margin ties Depestre's printed poem about Vietnam to the revolutions in Algeria and Cuba. Perhaps it is then that Sénac decided to include Depestre's "The Era of Vietnam" in his radio show.

According to Depestre, in any case, it was on that same night that he met the group from *Souffles* for the first time, though only Abdallah Stouky's name appears on the poster. At this point, Depestre had already contributed a couple of texts to the nascent journal—texts that he had written within the context of the Cultural Congress of Havana.[91] But these contributions had been relayed through Mario de Andrade and, according to Depestre, it wasn't until the PANAF that he and the *Souffles* group finally met; with the help of Jean Sénac, the Maghreb Generation came together.

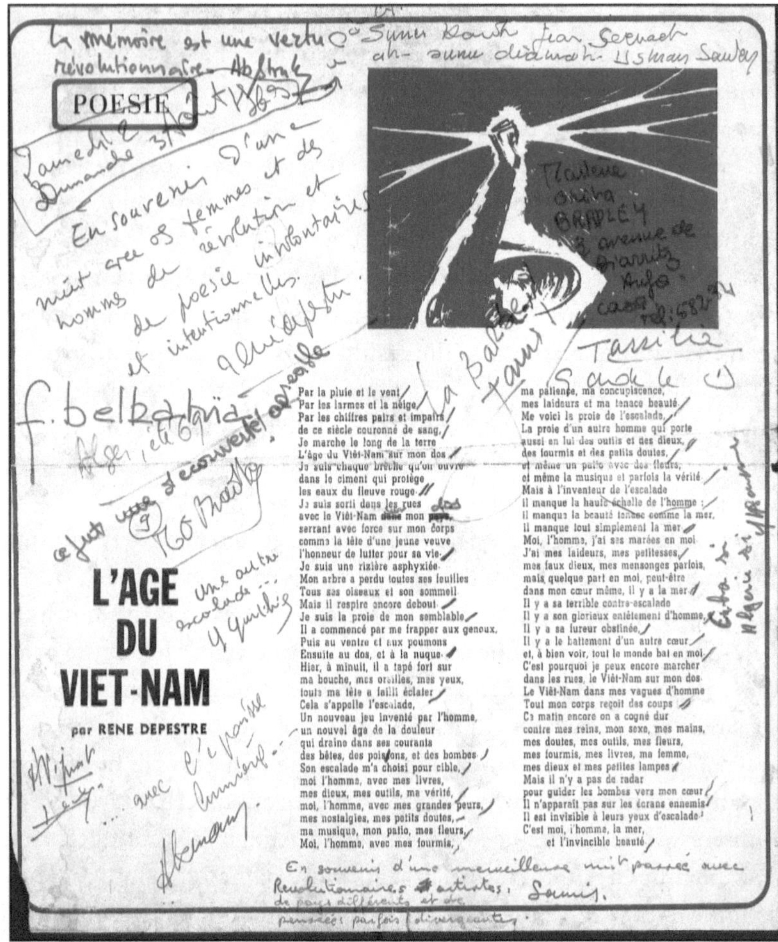

FIGURE 11. **"L'âge du Vietnam." Poster-poem by René Depestre signed by those present at the party held on August 2, 1969, in Algiers. Source: Jean Sénac Archives, Algerian National Library, Algiers.**

In July and August 1969, *Souffles* was still a small publication with a limited distribution; most of those in Algeria who had read issues of the journal had received it from friends such as Hocine Tandjaoui, *Souffles*' representative in Algeria. As many of the survivors of that generation reminisce wistfully, copies were shared or dittoed in accordance with the collective ethos that characterized the Maghreb Generation.[92] Sénac had been in contact with the *Souffles* group for a few years and had relayed their message in Algeria. Just a month before the inauguration of the PANAF, in June 1969, he had dedicated four consecutive broadcasts to the young Moroccan poets of *Souffles*. Under the general title "The Poets of the Journal *Souffles*," Sénac delineated the poetic and theoretical concepts of the literary journal. He insisted on the originality of this group, open to exchanging ideas—a group that questioned "the deepest foundations of their souls" and that of the Arab world.

In introducing *Souffles*, Sénac listed what he considered to be the journal's founding texts. For him, Mario de Andrade and René Depestre's contributions figured alongside Laâbi's prologue as the ideological cornerstones of the *Souffles* project. Sénac cast *Souffles* as the advent of a community, civilization, and way of thinking that he, along with Karl Marx and Frantz Fanon, had long yearned for. This was a community like the one he was building through *Poetry on All Fronts*—a community of militant-artists from across Africa that could not and would not settle for an authoritarian nation-state and the perpetuation of imperialism by Indigenous state officials. This was the Maghreb Generation.

Sénac worked hard not only to broadcast but also to physically bring together the members of the Maghreb Generation. Hence, when the editorial board of *Souffles* set off on the long desert road to Algiers in the summer of 1969, they moved toward a community of belonging already being formed on the radio waves, if not yet in the streets and cafés. Seven of *Souffles'* members traveled to Algiers in July 1969: Tahar Ben Jelloun, Abdellatif Laâbi, Jocelyne Laâbi, Toni Maraini, Mohamed Melehi, Abraham Serfaty, and Abdallah Stouky. In a January 2018 email, Toni Maraini recounted a long, tiring, but beautiful car journey to Algiers that culminated in a messy but euphoric arrival to the city. She, together with her husband, the painter Mohamed Melehi, and Abdellatif Laâbi had come mainly to meet with other artists of the Maghreb Generation (including Sénac and the painter Mohammed Khadda), to distribute a catalogue Melehi had made of young Moroccan painters and to meet with potential contributors to *Souffles*. They did attend a few events, however, such as the projection of Ousmane Sembène's movie *Le mandat*.[93] But the festival came with its load of controversies, Maraini noted, perhaps unavoidable in the founding of a true Pan-African community.

In January 1970, *Souffles* published an entire issue dedicated to the PANAF, with a split cover featuring a Black musician on one side and a military man fleeing from an explosion on the other. The cover played into the rhetoric of the festival—an event meant to aesthetically knit together resistance and culture, art and revolution, rather than actually incubating a culture of resistance and revolutionary art. Complete with excerpts from the symposium speeches, the Black Panthers' Ten-Points Program, an interview with Senegalese filmmaker Ousmane Sembène, and book reviews, the issue is one of the most thorough coverages the festival received outside of Algeria.[94] Following in Sénac's footsteps, the group from *Souffles* decided to focus on Andrade's and Depestre's contributions to the symposium, which they reproduced in full and accompanied with pictures of the two men.

Apart from Andrade's and Depestre's contributions, however, the editors of *Souffles* were not enthusiastic about the official events of the PANAF. By lauding the interventions of the Guineans, MPLA, Depestre, and the Black Panthers, they aligned themselves to the left of the Algerian government's official rhetoric and showed signs of hesitation and doubt about the true intentions of the African and Maghrebi regimes. Maraini's husband, Mohamed Melehi, preserved a bleak image of their time in Algiers: "We went to the festival; there were Algerian cops beating up Africans in front of the Hotel Aletti. I have only this memory, for the Africans were the honored

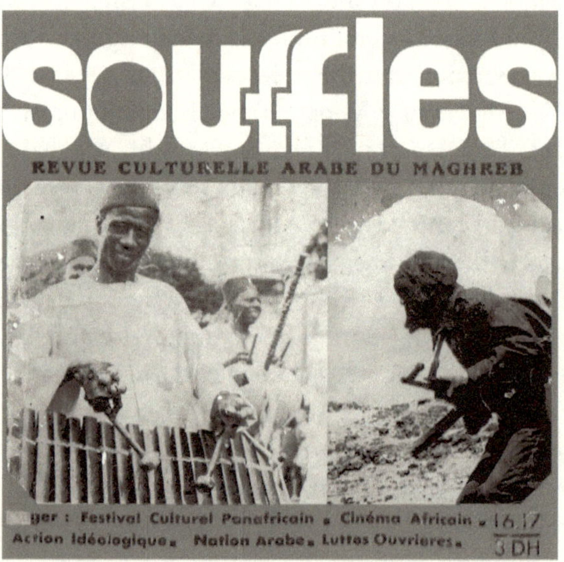

FIGURE 12. Cover of "Algiers: Panafrican Cultural Festival." *Souffles*, nos. 16–17 (1969). Reprint courtesy of Abdellatif Laâbi.

guests. . . . I was scandalized; this arrogance shocked me. I'm not sure Algiers was ready for this festival. It was only for show"[95]—a show that, according to Tahar Ben Jelloun, revealed the inability of the Algerian government to break down the imprint of colonialism. A few months later, the young Moroccan poet commented on the decoration of the city, describing the effort as one "of incredible mediocrity, Africa viewed by colonial Europe of the turn of the century."[96] In a 1970 letter to Hocine Tandjaoui, Abdellatif Laâbi also expressed his disappointment with the trip. He and the other members of *Souffles* hadn't come for the festival—it was the least of their reasons for being there—but to meet Algerian comrades who could help with the journal; but everyone was busy, and he had "had enough of pretty speeches and made-in-Africa beats."[97] The members of *Souffles* who attended the PANAF expressed doubts both publicly and privately about the revolutionary potential of such an event; in fact, many of their critiques resembled those that *Souffles* had articulated in 1966 about Léopold Sédar Senghor's First World Festival of Black Arts in Dakar. What the young poets and painters of the Maghreb Generation were interested in were the meetings with militant-artists from Africa, Asia, and Latin America that took place outside the official events; these were the encounters that allowed them to begin a dialogue, encounters such as those fostered by Jean Sénac.

Of all those present at the PANAF, it was the group of Black American poets and thinkers that most impressed the members of *Souffles*. Every night, Abraham Serfaty remembers, he would go to listen to the Black Panthers' poetry, discover "their struggles, their chants, their recaptured dignity."[98] To Serfaty, Black American culture was a model for humankind; indeed, he explained, Black Americans knew, unlike their white enslavers, that you could not separate art from life. Black Americans had "been submitted to the worst and longest of oppressions," and yet, he marveled, "they emerged as accusers and renovators, as combatants and constructors."[99] One of the most appealing aspects of the Black American struggle, Serfaty felt, was their pragmatism and their contact with the reality of the world. In his two-page article "Salute to the African-Americans," published in the sixteenth issue of *Souffles*, Serfaty denigrated those in Algiers who, "pretentious enough to invest themselves with the quality of specialists in revolutionary integrity," forgot Lenin's famous reference to Goethe in April 1917: "Grey is theory, my friend, and green the eternal tree of life."[100] The Black Americans, Serfaty explained, were smart enough to know that the only color that mattered was green, not gray, white, or black. They knew that resolving the issues of US society involved deep reflection on the historical processes of economic, social, and cultural stratification and not on a theoretical, mystical, or racial reality. To Serfaty, these men and women should become the African revolutionaries' tutors, for their experience of trauma had made them lucid. Enthralled, Serfaty raised his glass to Malcolm X, Don Lee (otherwise known as Haki R. Madhubuti), Bobby Seale, and Fred Hampton.

Sénac was also an admirer of Black American poets and revolutionaries. In July 1967, he had already conducted a two-part radio show on the Black American poets, titled "The Great Protest of the American Poets of African Descent." The first part, "Misery," presented the poetry of slavery and suffering. "You, listener friends, listen to the voice of those that come from Black America. They tell us of pains that you know for having lived them," Sénac began.[101] He drew a parallel between the second-class status of Algerians during French rule and that of Black Americans in the United States. Beginning with a letter-poem by Phillis Wheatley and ending with a long-form prose-poem by Margaret Abigail Walker, Sénac revealed the sufferings and longings of Black American poets, the pain and loneliness that life in the United States entailed. He chose poems that brought together Africa and the United States, the suffering of the past and of the present, such as Langston Hughes's "Afraid," where Hughes compared skyscrapers to palm trees:

> We cry among the skyscrapers
> As our ancestors
> Cried among the palms in Africa
> Because we are alone
> It is night,
> And we're afraid.

Sénac cited another poem that evoked Africa through references to palm trees—William Waring Cuney's poem "No Images," about a Black woman who does not know her own beauty:

> If she could dance
> naked
> under palm trees,

And see her image in the river
she would know

But there are no palm trees
on the street
And dishwater gives back
no images.

Through these excerpts Sénac attempted to guide his listeners through the central trauma of the Black American experience: not knowing who or where one was because of forcible removal from one's homeland. To Sénac, this experience was like that of the Algerians who had been intellectually and emotionally colonized by the French until they knew not who they were or where they were from—"for we do not come from the Gauls / our ancestors were eaten away at by the sun / and their pores were punctured by the winds of the desert."[102]

The second part of Sénac's show on American poets of African descent was titled "Revolt." In this part, Sénac cited Black American Pan-African activist Stokely Carmichael at length, who was in fact in Algeria at the time. A guest of the Algerian government, Carmichael was vocal in his disdain for US imperialism. His trip was avidly covered by *Révolution africaine* and *El Djeich*, and Carmichael himself remembered being treated like a *rais* (head chief).[103] Algeria was open to Carmichael's reading of power. "The former slave, the ever-marginalized citizen no longer responds to oppression through blues but through 'black power' and, in the same movement, joins the international struggle against imperialism and all manners of alienation," reads Sénac's translation of Carmichael.[104] For far too long, Western white society had imposed its own heroes on colonized peoples. Now, Sénac and Carmichael believed, Black people were engaged in a struggle to find new heroes, such as Malcolm X, W. E. B. Du Bois, and Fanon—the very Fanon who had led the Black American people to Algeria.

Through this cry to revolt and with figures like Stokely Carmichael and poets like Ted Joans, Sénac explained, the people of Harlem had finally joined the people of Algiers, Havana, Hanoi, and Conakry in the global fight against imperialism and in the Pan-African family. To Sénac, and to all those he admired in the Black Power movement, this fight was not a somber march toward victory but a dance, as Sénac's reading of Black American poet Ted Joans's poem testifies: "The moment has come for everyone to swing (life does not have meaning / if it has no swing) yes it is quite true."[105] Unlike the *Souffles* editors who felt some discomfort with the term *négritude* and more generally had a difficult time identifying with the concept of Blackness, Sénac showed no such resistance. For him, the Black Power movement was inspiring for its mix of guerilla warfare and cultural resistance—it was a movement to which he felt he belonged.

Less than a year later, in an April 8, 1968, show, four days after Martin Luther King Jr.'s assassination, Sénac once more reached out to Black Americans, comparing the assassinations of MLK and Malcolm X to those of Ali la Pointe and Mouloud Feraoun.[106] Opening with Senghor's homage to the Senegalese soldiers who died for France in World War II, Sénac not only mourned the deaths of all Black people along with that of the United States' great pacifist Black leader but reminded his audience that the only way forward was through violence, or else others would lie dead along the roads like "svelte poplars."[107] Like many Black Americans in April 1968, Sénac saw MLK's assassination as a call to violence. "To the question 'The voting slip or the gun?' the assassins of Malcolm X in 1965 and those of MLK have just given us an answer," cried Sénac. The world revolution and the power of the guerilla had entered the heart of the United States, Sénac continued, claiming that Che Guevara's portrait illuminated homes from Harlem to the US South. To Sénac, MLK's death represented a rallying cry for the Pan-African revolution—while people such as MLK, Mouloud Feraoun, and Senghor may have been a poetic and political inspiration, their message of peace and nonviolent activism rang false in 1968, with MLK's body still warm in the grave.

Thus, by July 1969 and the opening of the PANAF, Sénac was already well acquainted with the Black American poetic scene and with many Black American activists. He had probably met Stokely Carmichael and Miriam Makeba on one of their trips to Algeria. In fact, in November 1969, while embroiled in a bureaucratic mess with the Algerian government over obtaining his Algerian citizenship, Sénac complained that they had given it easily to such people as Makeba.[108] Sénac likely read the *Autobiography of Malcolm X*, published in French by Maspero in 1968, as it appears in his personal book collection at the Algerian National Archives. While he may have been well acquainted with the ideas of the Black Power movement, it is hard to tell whom exactly Sénac met in July 1969. Many Black American poets and activists were present, and the possibilities for encounter were as numerous as they were fleeting. Sénac probably attended Eldridge Cleaver's presentation, as his journal and the copies of the *Black Panther Journal* in his archives testify.

One Black American artist that it is certain Sénac befriended during the PANAF was the Free Jazz poet Ted Joans. Their friendship lasted until Sénac's death. Ted Joans wrote Sénac twice from Marrakech in January and February 1972, promising to visit Algeria soon and asking for news. In his second letter, he thanked Sénac for his *Anthology of New Algerian Poetry*, which he read with an English-to-French dictionary. He explained that he hoped to meet young poets such as Rachid Boudjedra, Lâadi Flici, and Hamid Skif—who was "really swinging sensual"—on his visit to Algiers in February.[109] He told Sénac that jazz was a weapon, that jazz was the same thing as Black Power, and that his poetry was based on that understanding. Finally, he signed with a short poem that he himself had translated into French: "If one day you should see a man / walking down a crowded street / talking to himself / don't run in the opposite direction / run towards him for he is a poet / Ted Joans and you have / nothing to fear from the poet / other than the Truth."[110]

These multiple encounters with Black American poets, in books and in real life, had a significant influence on Sénac's perception of the role of music and poetry in the fight against oppression. Like the members of *Souffles*, and Serfaty in particular, Sénac admired the generosity of the Black American artists toward the downtrodden. In the poets of the Black Power movement, Sénac found the tolerance and acceptance that he sometimes missed at home. "By placing the demands of homosexuals, women, and all the oppressed of the Third World on the same plane," Sénac marveled, "Huey Newton and the Black Panthers swept away in one fell swoop the obstacles and taboos that mutilate our societies."[111] The Black American poets embodied the diptych so central to Sénac's life: Love and Revolution, which is clear in Sénac's "Ode to Black America," written in Algiers in November 1970:

> Free Man smokes. He blows his smoke into my mouth . . .
>
> . . . .
>
> We are not black-white I am beautiful because I am black I
>   am beautiful because I am white. We are beautiful
> Blood is the color of Jericho roses, . . .

. . . .

Free man speaks. Between his hands a fabulous geography is born.

. . . .

Free man watches. . . .

. . . .

Watches the black, the woman, the homosexual, the druggy, the white, the green, the blue. Free Man
Fixes man's destiny in his iris,
Leads him to the crest of fire. Under
The cobblestones the beach. Thank you Comrades! Free man
Smokes. And Ho and Mao and Che and Palestine
And Crazy Horse
And November and May the zodiac
Of autogestion and $E = mc^2$ the
Goodness of Einstein and Char and Fanon
And Artaud and
Angela who holds the thread of the Minotaur
And Genet on all the chests and all the fleeces of all the freedoms
And Ginsberg and Voznesensky and Ted Joans and Retamar and Guillen and Hikmet and Patrick MacAvoy and
Sonia Sanchez and Depestre and Blas de Otero and
Darwich and Khaïr-Eddine and Adonis and Cernuda and
Whitman and
The electronic tam-tams the song the percussion all
The song of Reason and of Poetry and
The Folly of sweet lips of buttered bread on the hearts of the children of Archie Shepp
In the embers between his three fingers
Testifies . . .

. . . .

And the great raft of America in tears drifts in the fascinated oriental night
fuming rears and dislocates. Free Man
Sings. On his lyric thighs
The poem is no longer a sob.[112]

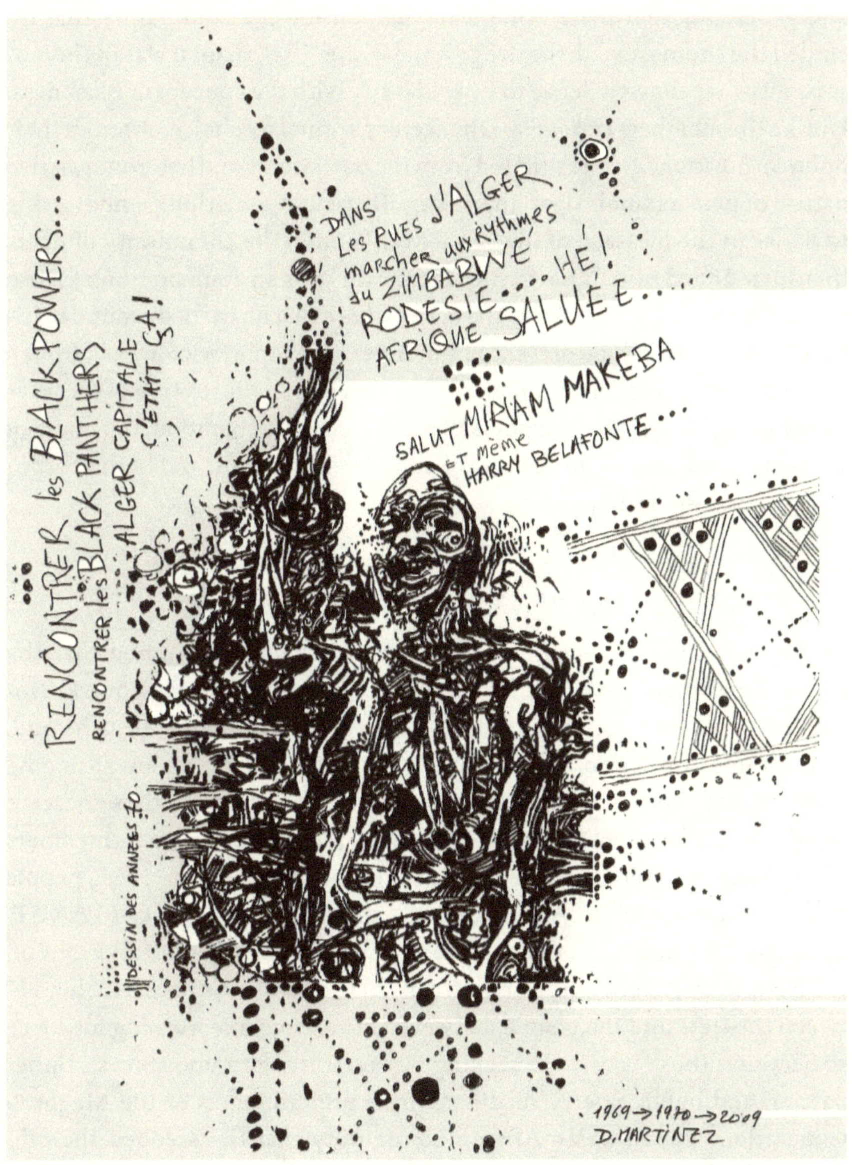

FIGURE 13. Denis Martinez's depiction of the 1969 festival and its most memorable moments. Reprint courtesy of Denis Martinez.

Once again, Sénac easily took on the mantle of Blackness, repeating with glee "I am black I am beautiful."[113] Sénac identified with the community and geography that Black Americans had built—the community that included the "homosexual, the druggy, the white."[114] Perhaps it was his homosexuality that allowed Sénac to fully identify with the concept of Blackness. Unlike the members of *Souffles* who were marginal by choice, through their political positions, Sénac suffered from the patriarchal and heteronormative nature of postcolonial Algerian society. There was something empowering to Sénac in the message of the "Free Man" and in the community of poets that surrounded him. "Ode to Black America" was an enumeration of those who influenced Sénac's poetic life, of the voices that he carried around in his head and with which he presented the Algerian people twice a week from 9 to 9:15 p.m. on *Poetry on All Fronts*. This poem was an illustration of the ways Sénac brought together the poets of the Maghreb Generation, in a mess of languages and sounds, in the cafés and in his apartment, and in the corporality of mouths and thighs.

THE END OF THE ERA OF REVOLUTIONARY POETICS

In his interview in December 2018, Hocine Tandjaoui claimed that the PANAF was organized "just for the pictures."[115] The Algerian government needed to reassert its revolutionary clout on the international scene and, at the same time, wanted to control the culture of militancy springing from its cafés and cinemas. It was impossible, however, for these nascent Maghrebi governments to control all the interactions between members of the Maghreb Generation. And so, alongside the official PANAF, people such as Sénac, Depestre, Andrade, Joans, and Laâbi met at the Off-PANAF. Through these meetings, these militant-poets asserted that the divisions on the African continent were not between "Black" and "White" Africa but between the state and the people, between those who were working for a free society and those who were seeking power. Through radio shows, dinner parties, and public poetry readings, these militant-poets of the Maghreb Generation created a Pan-African community that transcended the official channels of the PANAF as well as the artificial boundaries between nation-states.

The fate of these poets demonstrates the very real threat that they posed their nation-states. In the decade following the PANAF, Sénac and Cabral were murdered; Laâbi was imprisoned; Depestre was kicked out of Cuba for speaking out against Fidel Castro's authoritarianism; and Andrade was marginalized by the new Angolan state. Ultimately, of those that survived, many moved to Paris. After Rabat, Algiers too lost its status as the Mecca of Revolutionaries. The PANAF became the principal illustration of the apex of Algiers' Pan-African and Third World status. But what remains of the festival is mostly the Algerian state's narrative in the form of pamphlets, government-sponsored newspaper articles, and reports from the festival's symposium. The differing accounts in this chapter and the next uncover the many tensions at play in the underbelly of the Mecca of Revolutionaries. They also reveal that at the very moment when African states were busy reinforcing their national identities, artists and militants from the postcolonial world ignored their governments' call to protect the nation-state, creating instead a transnational network that undermined the very foundations of these new nations. These are important narratives, as they demonstrate that the hardening of national borders, the construction of the nation-state, and the expansion of capitalism that followed decolonization were not inevitable but that people such as Joans, Andrade, Laâbi, Sénac, and Depestre offered an alternative world every step of the way.

Through the creation of journals such as *Souffles* and radio shows such as *Poetry on All Fronts*, the Maghreb Generation built a worldwide movement that imbued poetry with revolutionary potential. Throughout the 1960s, the movement took strength from the many voices that joined it from across Africa, Europe, and the Americas. But in the decade following independence, this revolution of poetry increasingly ran up against powerful postcolonial forces that attempted to consolidate the new nations and perceived poetry as a threat to the nation-state, and so these poets were silenced.[116] But the Maghreb was not done being the home of militant-artists from across the globe. With Sénac buried and the *Souffles* members in prison, militant-artists turned to film, gathering every couple of years in Tunis for the JCC.[117]

FOUR

NOTHING TO FEAR FROM THE POET

Hooking Up at the Pan-African Festival of Algiers

There is nothing to fear from the poet
Other than the Truth

TED JOANS to Jean Sénac, 1972

IN THE SPRING OF 1969, Eldridge and Kathleen Cleaver, fleeing a US government intent on putting Eldridge in jail, absconded to Cuba and then to Algeria. They arrived in Algiers a couple of days before the start of the PANAF.[1] The Algerian government extended an invitation to the revolutionary couple, and as a result, Algiers became the headquarters of the international division of the Black Panther Party from 1969 to 1972. The Cleavers attracted a host of other Panther members, who moved to Algiers, toddlers in tow, and filled the Pointe Pescade house provided by the Algerian government.[2]

Though the Black Panthers were excited about the Algerian government's support and yearned to collaborate with the Algerian people, they had a hard time fitting in. The Panthers were highly visible and at times controversial guests in a socially conservative environment.[3] Speeding down rue Didouche Mourad in a shiny red convertible, accompanied by Algerian women, the Panthers did not always make a good impression.[4] According to the Panthers' guide and translator in Algiers, white American Elaine

Mokhtefi, women were the Panthers' only Algerian visitors at Pointe Pescade. Charlotte Hill, one of the Panther members who sojourned in Algeria in the early 1970s, recalled how smitten Algerian women were with the Panthers: "The Algerian women were very drawn to the brothers; many of them would come to the headquarters and try to catch [them]."[5] Algerian Boussad Ouadi, a twenty-year-old college student at the time of the PANAF, was shocked by the Black Panthers' behavior toward Algerian women: "They [the Panthers] were so American. They walked around the Casbah, half-naked, [and] behaved with the girls in ways that we found insufferable; that was their GI side."[6] Eventually, this drew the ire of the Algerians, and when the Panthers vacated Algiers in 1972, they left sensing they would never belong. "We saw that we would never be able to be really comfortable there, raising our children there," remembered Hill.[7]

The documents the Algerian government produced for the PANAF tell a story of revolutionary glamour, one that does not acknowledge the disenchantment and despair of many young Algerians. To chronicle the Off-PANAF, I conducted interviews and mined the Maghreb Generation's personal papers. During these interviews, I always asked my respondents if they had experienced or witnessed instances of racism, xenophobia, or other forms of discrimination during the PANAF. Most of the time their response was a categorical no. When I asked my male interlocutors if they had noticed any sexism at the PANAF, their answer was swifter still: no. Often accompanied by a statement such as "The 1970s were so different, Algeria was so advanced, if you looked at pictures in front of high schools there were girls all over in miniskirts, no veils, nothing. . . . Now the women are in their sad hijabs."[8] For the women who attended the PANAF, however, the mere ability to wear a miniskirt might not have been a cause for celebration, nor did their relative ability to choose their clothing give them access to the conversations about African unity occurring throughout the PANAF.

In 2017 and 2018 (when I conducted most of the interviews for this book), the Maghreb Generation cultivated rosy memories of their encounters with militant-artists from across the world.[9] When remembering the PANAF, nostalgia crept into their voices, and they were reluctant to acknowledge the existence of any obstacles to the creation of a dissident Pan-African community. The tensions were with the state, they insisted, not with other militant-artists. Only in conversations about sex—a topic that my male interlocutors brought up unprompted—did racist tropes surface. While many of the male members of the Maghreb Generation denied the presence of bigotry at the PANAF, when it came to assessing and accessing women's bodies, racial worries and fetishes surfaced. While the bodies of real women, such as Kathleen Cleaver, were the unwilling loci of racial tensions, in many of these men's minds the bodies of imagined women came to represent the project of Pan-African unity. In the end, the men of the Maghreb Generation created a community premised on revolutionary masculinity, casting women as ahistorical and apolitical symbols of Africa to conquer and collect through sex.[10]

OF PAN-AFRICAN UNITY AND MINISKIRTS

The government-backed press coverage of the 1969 PANAF showcased Algeria not only as a member of the Pan-African community but as its leader. Government newspapers such as *Algérie actualité* and *El-Moudjahid* sported headlines such as "Algiers: Crossroads of African Culture," "We Discovered Africa," "Africa Celebrates Its Reunion," and "The Festival Is an Enthusiastic and Lucid Assertion of Our Culture."[11] An op-ed in *El-Moudjahid* mentioned the "intensely African nature" of Algiers, while an interview conducted by an *El-Moudjahid* reporter detailed the supposed delight of the various African delegations at their living conditions in Algiers.[12] The head of the Cameroonian delegation reportedly told *El-Moudjahid* that "before this festival, most of our countrymen, who are peasants, would not have thought that a Black person could be the brother of a White person. This festival will have showcased this fraternity for all to see."[13] According to paper, the festival even exceeded the Algerian government's hope of unity, as illustrated by a man from the Ivory Coast talking to an Algerian taxi driver in Arabic.[14] The French chargé d'affaires in Algiers also noted, with some condescension, that while at first the Algerian people were "unused to the Africa of masks and sorcerers," little by little they relaxed, and by the last night the city was a scene of jubilation, with "the Blacks participating happily."[15] As emissaries of the Algerian government, newspapers and journals such as *El-Moudjahid* and *Algérie actualité* wanted to make one thing clear to their readers: Algeria's reunion with "Black Africa" was going forward unobstructed.[16]

"The PANAF was the only time that the word 'fraternity' was palpable," reminisced Algerian writer Salah Guemriche in June 2018 in his sunlit apartment in Angers, France. Guemriche, who was just twenty-three at the time of the PANAF, remembered being surprised by the lack of tensions at the festival. "We were expecting, well . . . there's always anti-Black racism among the Arabs . . . but there was none of all that. People were dazzled by Black Africa, by the dances, by the costumes."[17] In interviews, Algerian participants and officials acknowledged that Algerians may have been prejudiced toward "Black Africans" before the PANAF—a bias they claimed to have inherited from the French-colonial partition of Africa—but that the PANAF had changed Algeria's perception of "Black Africa."[18] Algerian student Boussad Ouadi first met members of the MPLA and FRELIMO liberation movements in the early 1960s when they were training together at the Algiers Technology Academy. In a 2014 interview, Ouadi recalled that his Algerian peers at the technical school would jeer when the liberation group members showed pictures of their children back home. "Oh, look [the baby is] all naked," Ouadi's peers would snicker; "they walk around all naked in their countries, see, that's what Africa is like."[19] Ouadi's own mother had feared Black people before 1969, Ouadi acknowledged, claiming it was due to trauma from the Algerian War of Independence and to the presence, in Algiers, of Black men who were conscripted into the French army. "These guys did terrible things, they would come in, break everything, terrorize women and children, just by their appearance even," remembered Ouadi.[20] But with the festival, Ouadi explained, everyone realized that these were not men to be afraid of but that they were brothers. "It was absolutely amazing, explosive," recollected Algerian artist Houari Niati in 2012. "People were embracing each other, there was a total acceptance of what they were seeing. It was very pure, very untouched: raw Africa."[21] If the official Algerian accounts of the festival in *El-Moudjahid* and the charming memories of Algerian spectators such as Ouadi, Niati, and Guemriche, are to be believed, the PANAF motivated Algerians to transcend their prejudices.

While the Maghrebi spectators I interviewed were reluctant to bring up race, racial tropes emerged nonetheless, particularly when my interviewees started talking about the women they encountered, and ogled, at the PANAF. Indeed, even as Ouadi described the festival as a moment of bonding with Africa, he could not help but comment with a condescending amusement and titillation on the African women's clothing. For him, one of the most exciting moments of the festival was when the young Black women started dancing in the streets:

> You should have seen these African troops, these natural and fresh troops, the girls were dancing, someone had put clothing on them, poor girls, and visibly they were not used to being dressed, so they would blow off the bras, and they would dance on the main square in front of the Grande Poste, and all the young people were there, and they had never seen that in their lives, young girls dancing like that bare-chested on the square.[22]

Time and time again the Algerian men brought up, with a mix of excitement and condescension, these "poor girls" who had been forced to wear clothing.[23] Denis Martinez also remembered the parade of shirtless Black women: "There was no taboo," he smiled; everybody was applauding and mesmerized.[24] Black women only appeared in these arousing recollections as tantalizing bodies to watch dance or walk past. None of the interviewees remembered actually talking or interacting with Black American or African women.[25]

The political spaces the Maghreb Generation labored so hard to create were, for the most part, closed to women. *Souffles*, the PANAF, and *Poetry on All Fronts* were men's worlds in which women were, at best, background characters. [26] Women performed the editorial tasks, typing and revising articles, like Jocelyne Laâbi and Toni Maraini, who, although they both attended the PANAF, are named nowhere in *Souffles'* special edition on the PANAF. Women traveled alongside their husbands, moving children halfway across the world, making new homes for their families in unfamiliar lands. Women gave birth in extreme conditions, like Kathleen Cleaver, who during the PANAF had to be driven to a hospital in the outskirts of Algiers in the middle of the night accompanied by men she barely knew. Despite their presence at the PANAF's main events as coordinators, babysitters, typists, and translators, women appear in neither the official nor the Off-PANAF archives.[27]

When I asked my male interviewees about the role of women militant-artists at events such as the PANAF, the men professed their own dedication to the struggle for women's liberation. But they almost exclusively framed this struggle in terms of sexual liberation, concerned with liberating women's bodies from the oppression of colonial chastity. It was as if the emotional and intellectual decolonization that these men so ardently sought for themselves could not apply to women. For many of these men, sexual liberation was the pinnacle of female liberation. They did not mention the fight for women's economic, political, or educational liberation. They did not make space in *Souffles* or *Poetry on All Fronts* for women's voices. Even in the spaces that Maghreb Generation men had worked hard to carve out for themselves, women had no footing.

When she first arrived in Algiers in 1969, Black Panther Kathleen Cleaver was pregnant, and her husband, Eldridge, was still in Cuba. She did not speak French or Arabic but hoped that Algeria would offer some peace or a sense of homecoming after months as an exile. In a 2015 interview, she remembered:

> When I got there, I thought I was in Africa. I thought this was North Africa, Africa, and I remember saying something to a storekeeper, in some kind of broken French—I'm sure he thought I was crazy—about how we are in Africa, and you are African, and I'm African American, and he said "Africa's over there." Africa's on the other side of the Sahara, in their mind. It was very interesting. I didn't understand that idea: they felt Mediterranean, all the people I was meeting were Berber. They did not think they were African. They thought Africans were Black people. They hadn't figured out how we could be White and African.[28]

Kathleen Cleaver had expected to feel welcome in Algeria. Instead, because of her light skin and American style of dress, she was treated as a white woman. A few weeks later, once Eldridge had joined her, the Cleavers would walk around the streets of Algiers, and men would congratulate Eldridge on securing a white woman. Bewildered by the mistranslation of her racial identity, Cleaver did not feel at home in Algiers. Black Panther Charlotte Hill also remembers sticking out in the streets of Algiers. "Here we were wearing miniskirts, where the Muslim sisters there they might have miniskirts under their hijabs, but they were draped down, we would be walking through the streets and men would be harassing us," she recalled, reasoning that "I think most of us thought it was just racism, but in hindsight it was the way we were looking in miniskirts, you know, in a society where the women were supposed to be very modest."[29]

Despite spending significant time in the city as exiles, Kathleen Cleaver and Charlotte Hill never overcame the sense of isolation they felt in Algiers. For Cleaver, Algeria and the Maghreb as a whole was no place of poetic inspiration; instead, it was a place of banishment from which to continue the fight in the United States. On top of the frequent racial or racist remarks

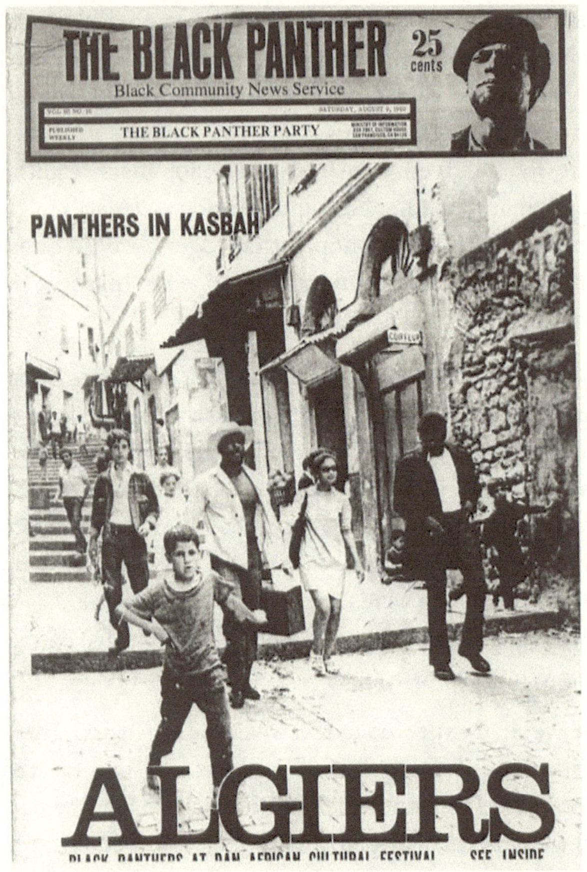

THE BLACK PANTHER
25 cents
Black Community News Service
THE BLACK PANTHER PARTY
PANTHERS IN KASBAH
ALGIERS

FIGURE 14. The Black Panthers in the Algiers casbah. Cover of *Black Panther Journal* 3, no. 16 (August 9, 1969).

regarding her supposed whiteness and Eldridge's Blackness that Kathleen endured when walking around Algiers, the Cleavers also faced numerous problems. They were unable to make friends; their Algerian neighbors refused to speak to them, as the Black Americans were under police surveillance. They couldn't read the newpapers or understand what was happening on television. Everything, from daily life to political organizing, was an ordeal:

> We didn't know anything about how you negotiate with Third World governments. Which is not a direct way; you essentially work things out bit

> by bit, and it depends on who you know and what they say. And Algeria in particular was a very, very opaque society. So, you really never know who is who, or what anybody knows; you just operate with a very limited amount of information—everybody, not just us, it's about the whole culture, but particularly for people from America who aren't particularly French or Arabic and had never been in Algeria and weren't planning on going to Algeria.[30]

Unlike many of the men I interviewed, Kathleen Cleaver did not remember her time at the PANAF fondly because, as a woman, she was excluded from much of the fun of Algiers during the PANAF. Despite the cultural and linguistic isolation of Algerian society for both Eldridge and Kathleen, Eldridge had significantly more freedom of movement. In fact, the Algerian government invited Eldridge to speak at a panel at the PANAF about the situation of Black Americans in the United States. During Eldridge's speech, the crowd was loud and enthusiastic. Kathleen was not invited to voice her opinion in the debates. The panel did not include any Panther women, though Julia Wright did serve as an interpreter. "I did not really have a role in this festival; I was just there," remembered Kathleen.[31]

In Algiers, Kathleen Cleaver was sidelined by the unfamiliar culture and the denial of her racial and political identity. As she noted, the culture of secrecy in Algeria suited Eldridge: he was a secretive man; moreover, secrets were usually shared with him. But for Kathleen, this meant that most of the time she had no idea what was going on.[32] And while she was unable to make any Algerian friends—men or women—many of the men who came to the PANAF fondly remember meeting Algerian women.

OF BLACK MEN AND PAN-AFRICAN QUEENS

When, in a 2018 interview, I asked Elaine Mokhtefi, the Cleavers' guide and translator in Algiers, if she thought the Black Panthers and the other Black Americans who were in Algiers for the festival had experienced any racism, she responded: "I don't think they ever felt discriminated against; it's not like today. [Algerians] saw Black people all the time. . . . Everyone was aware of the problem of racism, but I think they handled it well."[33] But Mokhtefi, a white American, was not best suited to speak on the lived experience of anti-Black racism in North Africa. While many white Algerian spectators believed there was no racism at the PANAF, a few people exhibited a keener sense of observation. One French bystander, who by July 1969 had been living in Algiers for some time, remembers that the children in the street would scream "Nègre, nègre, nègre!" when they saw a Black person walk by. For the Black men who attended the festival, reactions were mixed. Some, such as American poet Ted Joans, chose to ignore racism and the apparent whiteness of Algeria in their search for communion with the Algerian people.[34] Others, such as Ivoirian playwright Bitty Moro, could not. Indeed, Black American artists in their search for a Pan-African community seemed eager to find solidarity and solace in Maghrebi culture and politics, while some Africans considered the possibility of African cultural unity much more tentatively.[35]

On the night of July 28, 1969, in front of the Grande Poste in Algiers, Ted Joans stood up and recited: "We are still black, and we have come back. *Nous sommes revenus.* We have come back and brought back to our land, Africa, the music of Africa. Jazz is a Black Power!"[36] He made no distinction between North Africa and the rest of the continent; to him it was all Black Africa. An outspoken poet and prose writer, Joans was never reluctant to talk about race, yet in North Africa he often willfully ignored racial differences and tensions, convinced that in the free countries of Africa, racism was already history.[37]

Ted Joans was born in 1928, in Cairo, Illinois, to a riverboat entertainer killed during the 1943 race riot in Detroit, Michigan.[38] In 1961, Joans fled the violent racism of the United States and chose exile. He did not, however, opt to leave the United States for Europe, as did his mentors and friends such as Black American writers Chester Himes, Richard Wright, and James Baldwin. Joans merely passed through Paris on his way to Africa. He developed a love/hate relationship with the French capital. In Paris, he met the surrealist poet André Breton, one of the major sources of inspiration for his work, as well as *négritude* poets Léopold Sédar Senghor and Aimé Césaire. Like Mario de Andrade, Marcelino dos Santos, and others before him, meeting Africans in Paris convinced Joans that it was time to get out of Europe and start exploring the African continent. And so he traveled to Morocco, where the images of the "motherland" he had nursed for years came face-to-face with the reality of the African continent.

Prior to traveling to Africa in the 1960s, Joans wrote about the continent with an idealized and stereotypical imagery. In a poem from in the mid-

1950s titled "Going Home," he described the African continent as a place where antelopes frolicked in jungles, perhaps unaware that antelopes prefer the abundant grass of the savannahs to the density of jungles.[39] In one of his first poems from Africa, in 1960, he wrote, "Africa is the land where Rhinos roam."[40] Joans even created a stamp that featured his name and the outline of a rhinoceros with which he stamped many of his poems.

But beneath that veneer of wild reverie, the reality of traveling was not always pleasant for Joans. In 1961, as he was fleeing American racism and sailing to France aboard the ship *Lyautey,* he scrawled a small note, a sort of diary entry, featuring racist tropes about his fellow travelers. Joans complained about the number of Muslims on the ship, "more than a thousand," and of the "filth" that they brought to the cabins; "they spit and pee everywhere."[41] When the captain agreed to change his living quarters, Joans wrote, "It is good to be away from those Moslems. They are not clean people."[42] Some of those "Moslems" that Joans met on board the *Lyautey,* a French ship, were most certainly North Africans. Indeed, Joans seemed unaware that such a large portion of the African continent was Muslim. The continent that he had dreamed about from afar for so long was now taking a bewildering shape in front of his eyes. His awareness of racial tropes did not extend abroad, and not to Muslims, at least not at first. Like so many Black Americans who came to Algiers for the PANAF, he was baffled by the hard reality of life in Africa, by the smells, the poverty, and the difficult traveling conditions. Joans, on board the *Lyautey,* was above all a man of the First World.

Despite his initial aversion to Muslims, Joans settled between Tangiers and Timbuktu, crossing the desert regularly, writing and painting, even exhibiting his work at the Librairie des Colonnes in Tangier.[43] As the landscape of his life transformed, the linguistic topography in Joans's poetry also changed: little by little, jungles were replaced by deserts, antelopes by camels, and references to Berbers and Tuaregs became frequent. He fell in love with Morocco and with the Maghreb in general, a region that eventually came to represent the entire African continent in his mind. He signed his name in long lines reminiscent of Arabic script and started to integrate words of Arabic into his writing. His archives contain several press clippings in Arabic and collages that integrate Arabic text into the piece.[44] Joans could not read Arabic; he was no doubt using the Arabic text for a purely visual effect, creating pieces that combined nude women with press clippings on military espionage in the Maghreb.[45] Poems such as his unpublished March 1965 "Twin Sounds" offered a window into the multilingual and multicultural milieu he inhabited. In a smoky, surrealist reverie, he wrote of sex and race, weaving together French, English, and Arabic.[46] After visiting the exhibit of contemporary art at the PANAF—which featured Mohamed Melehi and where Joans met Tahar Ben Jelloun—he was enthralled by the Moroccan visual artists. "These honest, non-commercial artists of Maroc who paint like saints in love breathing whiffs of kif and incense through their pores," Joans scrawled on his PANAF program.[47]

It was in North Africa that Joans felt the most at home. He seemed wholly unaware of the racial tensions between Arab and Black or Arab and Amazigh within the Maghreb and between the Maghreb and the rest of the continent. "There is no racism in the independent countries of Africa, so leave your racist bag at home," he wrote in the introduction to his unpublished *Black Man's Guide to Africa*.[48] He credited the absence of racism in Africa to Islam,[49] explaining that the Arabs had brought Islam, the great unifier, to Africa, as well as "fine arts and handicrafts, the Arabic language (which unified the people), and a new way of life."[50]

Shortly after leaving Algiers in 1970, Joans published a collection of poems titled *Afrodisia*. The book is divided in two: half of the poems are dedicated to Africa, the other half to Eros, the Greek god of love. As the title suggests, both themes intertwine.[51] For this collection, Joans wrote several of the poems during the PANAF; many more referenced the PANAF or alluded to encounters he had in Algiers. *Afrodisia* contains a poem titled "The Pieds Noirs," in reference to the French Algerians who left Algeria after the country's independence. The poem demonstrates Joans's identification with Algerians. "They are gone," he applauded, referring to the *pieds-noirs*; "they have sunk into / the earth or gone back / to their European cemeteries / they are gone long gone / we are glad that they are gone."[52] Using "we" to encompass both himself and the Algerians, Joans demonstrated his identification with the Algerian people, through their communal resistance to colonialism. Other poems refer to the idea of return, such as "Home," in which he celebrates being "back with my tribe again / I have returned / back home again / glad to be back / with my tribe black."[53] Another PANAF poem describes the visit Joans and the Black American poet Don Lee paid to the National Museum of Fine Arts of Algiers, a visit to see "where the black in us begin[s]."[54] To Joans, it seems, Algeria was undeniably, unproblematically Black and African. "Algeria is really an 'A' for Africa country," he wrote in his *Black Man's Guide to Africa*.[55] This was because its people had fought and won their independence from France; Algeria was Black because it had struggled against colonialism. Like many of the members of the Maghreb Generation, including Jean Sénac, Joans had come to associate Blackness with resistance. Discursively racializing resistance, he welcomed a range of militants (white, Brown, and Black) into his Pan-African family.

Nowhere in his writings on North Africa does Joans note discomfort with being a Black man in a multiracial African world. When his skin color attracted attention in the Maghreb, he seems to have enjoyed it. On his first visit to Algeria, shortly after the country's revolution, a young man in Sétif called Joans "someone of the jazz music tribe," a comment Joans relished.[56] He attracted attention in Algeria, but it did not seem to bother him. If anything, what bothered him more was being a man of the First World living in the Third World. No matter how open-minded he claimed to be, or wanted to be, living in North Africa was difficult at times; he wrote of the smells and sounds of the medina with a certain touch of repugnance, expressing a sensory overload that ranged from immense pleasure to visceral disgust. He was troubled by the hunger and begging he saw in the streets.[57] During the PANAF, as they rode together in a slow, crowded bus, Don Lee remarked to Joans, "I never knew how spoiled the Man had made us, until I ran into this natural scene, right here that I'm in, it's really tough and rough on the mind. Damn, just think, I was brought up in the Chi slums too, but this is really something!"[58] What most baffled Black Americans like Joans and Lee was not that Algerians were not the Black Africans they had imagined but that Africa was poor. It was the material rather than the racial reality of coming to a festival in a recently decolonized area that made them feel that they didn't quite belong.

When Joans, Lee, and the editor Hoyt Fuller explored Algiers during the PANAF, Joans noted that "the people were very friendly to us because we were Black Americans and NOT imperialist negro Americans."[59] Perhaps they were also friendly to him because they were Black Americans and not Black Africans or Black Maghrebis. While Joans's economic status and geographic origins made adapting to the material conditions of the Maghreb difficult, they also protected him from some of the anti-Black racism Algerians reserved for those who were darker-skinned and native to the continent, such as the Ivoirian Bitty Moro. Furthermore, protected by his masculinity,

Joans was given room to express his Africanness in political—rather than racial—terms.

Indeed, not all Black men who traveled to Algiers for the PANAF had as pleasant an experience as Joans. The Senegalese delegates—120 people strong including Alioune Diop representing the literary magazine *Présence africaine* and filmmaker Ousmane Sembène—were unhappy with their time in Algiers. In a document published by the Senegalese administration and destined for UNESCO (United Nations Educational, Scientific, and Cultural Organization), they expressed their "sharp discontent." "Apart from the very bad technical organization," they continued, "the behavior of the Algerians vis-à-vis the Senegalese was less than courteous and often fringed on odious. The Senegalese were hurt by the Algerians' lack of hospitality."[60] Theater director Bitty Moro, who traveled to Algiers from the Ivory Coast, also had mostly negative recollections of the festival. First, he explained in a May 2014 interview, everyone treated the artists from the Ivory Coast as neocolonialists, as capitalists.[61] The Ivory Coast, under Félix Houphouët-Boigny's rule, was no friend of the Algerians, and the theater troupe fell victim to the considerable political differences between the two regimes.[62] Second, Moro explained, in Algiers he and his theater troupe were "just *nègres,* in the pejorative sense of the word, that's who we are to them."[63] West African men were not baffled by the material conditions of the Maghreb, but they did have a clearer sense of racial divisions that still plagued the African continent, and they were more suspicious of Algeria's intent in organizing this festival.[64]

Moro's stories of racism were always intertwined with issues of sex. In the restaurant where he and his theater troupe went for lunch, Moro recounted, the server kept his daughters away from them. "So, I told him," he related, "we come to your restaurant to eat, and you have these beautiful daughters. Why do you lock them up? They must come to talk with us to know our bit of the world."[65] Moro interpreted this incident as a racial slight, bristling at the idea that Algerian men might be hiding their daughters away from him because he was a Black man, but of course the server might very well have hidden his daughters away from any man who entered the establishment. Another anecdote Moro reported took place in Tunis around the time of the festival. He had been walking in the streets of Tunis with Algerian writer Kateb Yacine's wife, Zobaida Sharghi, when a group of young Tunisians came up to tell him that it was forbidden for a Black man to go out with a white woman. Backed up against a wall, Moro called out to the police to extricate himself from this quagmire. The Maghrebi men in Moro's anecdotes expressed deep anxieties about sex and the reproduction of racial categories. The idea of a Black man sleeping with one of their Maghrebi daughters, or more generally one of "their women," challenged their continued identification as white Africans and their notions of racialized power; it threatened their racial understanding of themselves and their country.[66]

It was not only individual Algerian men who hid the women in their family, recalled Moro. "You know, when I got to Algiers, they had locked up all the prostitutes of the city," he mocked. "I don't know where they put them, but no *nègre* could go visit a prostitute in Algiers, ah, because there were too many *nègres* in the city. . . . Ha! How can we cooperate with that?"[67] It is difficult to verify Moro's claim of such a decision on the part of the Algerian government without access to government archives, but many of the people interviewed for this project noted that the Algerian government had "cleaned up" the city for the PANAF, which could be an allusion to the removal of sex workers from the streets of Algiers, certainly a common practice for many cities ahead of large international events.[68] On the other hand, this anecdote suggests that Morro anticipated that the Algerian people and the Algerian state would consider him a racial and sexual threat, even to those at the bottom of the social ladder: sex workers.[69] Denied access to the bodies of Algerian women, Bitty Moro felt excluded from the Pan-African project.

Bitty Moro and Ted Joans had two very different experiences of the PANAF. Much of this difference was due to their place of origin. Joans first traveled to the Maghreb with a limited understanding of Africa. Over the course of the many years that he lived between the Maghreb and Timbuktu, crisscrossing the continent, he did acquire a finer understanding of Africa, one that he shared with his Black American audience through his *Black Man's Guide to Africa*. But his guidebook also demonstrated a determination to find a sense of home, of kinship, with the continent, and in particular with North Africa. Moro, of course, was born and raised on the African continent; he was not in search of belonging in Algiers. Furthermore, Joans, as a Black American, was either less aware of or spared a portion of the bigotry that Black men from the continent suffered in Algeria.

If Moro felt ostracized at the PANAF by the Algerians' unwillingness to share their women, Ted Joans and Haitian poet René Depestre felt enthusiastically Pan-African precisely because of their sexual encounters with Algerian women. In their poetry, both Joans and Depestre celebrated the availability of women in the Maghreb. Through sex with the bodies of Algerian women, they were able to actualize the Pan-African community they so yearned for. "I don't remember much of those couple of weeks in Algiers," confessed Depestre in December 2017. Giggling with a boyish timbre for a man of ninety years, he recounted what little he did recall: a sexual adventure involving two sisters in his Algerian hotel room. "It was the most unusual experience of my life," he continued, bringing the anecdote up multiple times over the course of our two-hour-long interview.[70] Depestre had been living in Fidel Castro's Cuba for several years, in exile from Haitian dictator Papa Doc Duvalier's reign of terror. In 1969, he traveled to the PANAF in hopes of meeting other young artists equally dedicated to the project of intellectual decolonization and Pan-Africanism. However, the only memory Depestre retained from the PANAF was that of gaining access to Algerian women's bodies; it was this experience that came to symbolize Pan-African unity in Depestre's mind.

In his post-PANAF poetry collection, *Afrodisia*, Joans included a poem called "My Trip." Mingling erotic language with that of political liberation, he conflated his discovery of Africa with his sexual feats, alluding to the many women he encountered during his trek across Africa. Through these women, Joans claimed to have become Moroccan, Algerian, and Tunisian. "I have been to the desert I have lived with the blue men, the Tuaregs," he wrote, "That / was my trip / I have drunk mint tea while sitting on my Harlemese / haunches after Saharan hospitality lunches. I have hitchhiked with my / fly wide open and spurted hot sperm into wide pelvic Berber women. . . . That is my trip I have Moroccod / Algeried / Tunised."[71] This is one of several poems Joans wrote in the 1960s that described his sexual encounters with a Berber woman.[72] In the text, his Berber companion has no name, personality, or memorable characteristic other than her Berber-ness and wide pelvis; it is unclear whether each encounter is even with the same woman. The Berber woman is a vessel, both physically and figuratively: physically, the woman is a vessel for Joans's sperm, a way for him to plant a little of himself in Africa; figuratively, she adds a bit of Berber-ness to his poetry, not as an active participant but as a conquered body. Despite Joans's revolutionary ideals, the North African woman in his poetry is no more than an object to be conquered, a bit of Africa to reclaim from white male colonizers. Joans and Depestre, far from being colonizers, were radical anticolonial visionaries, yet their political project remained patriarchal, analogous to colonial fantasies about African land, as they relegated the women they encountered to a realm beyond history and erased their individuality, thereby depoliticizing them.[73]

Both men were titillated by their time in Algeria, enthralled by the cultural of modesty, mesmerized by the veils.[74] "Moroccan girls / are often covered / in kaftans / shawls / djellabahs / some wear small hankie veils / Moroccan girls / utilize flirty eyes / a welcome and / a double dare stare," wrote Joans.[75] "The Arab woman is very sensual because, you see, Islam is a very erotic religion," Depestre explained to me in December 2017, "despite its macho attitude . . . and, you see, the Arab woman makes love like a fairy."[76] Like many European men, Depestre disapproved of what he perceived as chauvinism in Muslim culture and thought that Arab woman should be liberated from the oppression of chastity. And for that project, he was offering his help.

Much like many of the men who came to the PANAF, including some of the Black Panthers, Depestre and Joans related to the Algerian nation through its women, or rather through sexual fantasies about imagined Algerian women. In the process of telling me about their time at the PANAF or other Pan-African cultural events, my male interviewees repeatedly and unprompted told me of the women they had sexual encounters with. My first response was often discomfort—I was, after all, often meeting these men for the first time, alone in their homes. I then wondered if these largely elderly men were endeavoring to establish their virility. Eventually I realized that many of these encounters with women had come to embody their entire experience at the PANAF; it had morphed into a mythical event, personified by a woman.

Shortly after the PANAF, Joans wrote a poem titled "As Don Took Off at Dawn." The poem combined descriptions of traveling back from Algiers to Morocco with impressions from the festival: "Miriam the queen is crowned queen / . . . Archie elephant steps the Joy / black Africa black at last / black African back to black / black power free at last / drums roar from mudhut centers / diplomats' naked chests shine black / protocol: a smile, a couch, a pow-pow / Pan-African frying white whales / pole puke rocketed to the moon."[77] In rich, confusing, and at times disturbing surrealist language, Joans divulged his vision of Pan-Africanism. He dreamed of Pan-Africa as a woman: "Inchallah today or this morn / a pair of arms await her torso / she will be here to hear it / she will be here to taste it / she will be here to see it / she will be here to dance it / she will be here to smell it / the smell is stench of passion / stink of paradise on my shirt."[78]

Instead of admitting women to the debates over African unity during the PANAF, the male members of the Pan-African community came to see the bodies of women as conduits for creating a tighter Pan-African network. For these men who found themselves in an unknown land and culture, sex with Algerian women was a way to link themselves to Algeria.[79] As Depestre explained to me, "Through my sexual relations in Algiers and Morocco I discovered Arab poetry, Arab culture, the great sociologists of the past. . . . Making love was an act of civilization."[80] Depestre intellectualized his sexual desire, transforming it into a tool of community creation, of network building.[81]

In his poem "Eros and Revolution," Depestre mandated:

> Your gun in one hand
> Your right to orgasm in the other
> Run naked toward the sun
> Raise your barricades
> Make your revolution.[82]

In the Pan-African network of the 1960s and 1970s, masculinity was a staging ground of anti-imperial political subjectivity.[83] The unabashed and unapologetic hypersexualization that Joans, Depestre, and their peers deployed was central to their ideology—an ideology of revolutionary masculinity.[84] They were on a quest for male independence, freed from the puritanical chains of Western domination. Their sexual desires were not limited to white women; the diversity of geographies to which the women in Joans's and Depestre's stories are connected indicate a desire to transcend the Black/White, colonized/colonizer binary. Perhaps this is why they thought their conquests were revolutionary. Through their sexual adventures, they defied white and Maghrebi fears of miscegenation and created a world that they believed to be more equal.

Joans's and Depestre's sexual accounts are suffused with the language of public service. They fashioned themselves as selfless agents of African freedom—through their erotic poetry they hoped to free the "Cuntinent," a term that Joans joyously coined, from what he called "the weak men with turtlenecked sweaters."[85] But in the "selfless" act of liberating, they conquered too. Joans ends his poem "Cuntinent" with "body cuntinent I have claimed you / body cuntinent I have conquered you all / body cuntinent you are mine." Relegated to the realm of body and landmass, women had little room to articulate a different vision of the postcolonial world; freedom was still premised on gendered notions of power, conquest, and the ability to claim a little bit of Africa through sex. Depestre and Joans thus joined the hundreds of Black intellectuals who, as Black feminist scholar bell hooks explained, believed that the battle against white supremacy and imperialism could be waged not merely as "decolonized free subjects in struggle but as 'men.'"[86] Depestre and Joans were asserting their freedom in the postcolonial world by demonstrating their revolutionary manhood—their power to conquer and to control women.[87]

ON SEX, GENDER, AND PAN-AFRICANISM

Much of the literature on Pan-African and Third-Worldist politics focuses on the extraordinary alliances forged across oceans and continents, between people who did not speak the same language but who, through their desire to build something other than an imperialist world, managed to connect. The scholarship on the PANAF, which has largely relied on sources published by the Algerian government in the form of pamphlets, government-sponsored newspapers, and reports from the festival's official symposium, is no exception. The Algerian government has worked hard to portray the PANAF as the culminating event of Algiers's era as the Mecca of Revolutionaries. In 2009, the Algerian government organized with great pomp the Second Pan-African Cultural Festival of Algiers, which was widely considered a flop by those who had been to the 1969 iteration.

Looking beyond the state-produced documents, however, one finds a very different account of the first PANAF. Some militant-artists from the Maghreb Generation, despite their cynicism about the Algerian government's intentions in organizing the festival, were able to forge a community at the PANAF, although this community was often premised on notions of revolutionary masculinity. Men such as Ted Joans and René Depestre challenged the colonial division of Africa and the power of white hegemonic masculinity by lusting after the bodies of Algerian women. Through the language of lust and love, they took Africa out of the hands of Western sexual imperialism and made it their own, yet at the same time, they reproduced European colonial tropes of luscious, highly sexual Africa and gendered power, undermining their anticolonial liberatory projects of racial and cultural solidarity. Conflating oppression with repression, structural liberation with sexual liberation, political liberation with personal liberation, these men sought to free African women, and in particular Algerian women, by means of sex.

The world of the Maghreb Generation was not free from cultural tension and miscommunication, as evidenced by the experiences of the Cleavers, Moro, Depestre, and Joans. The variety of cultures, the disparity in incomes and ability to travel, the rift between racial perceptions, and the barriers of gender and sex were but a few of the barriers between members of the Maghreb Generation. The men who traveled to Algeria in the summer of 1969 had to navigate through layers of myth about Africa and Algeria's place on the continent and in the world. Men such as Joans and Depestre believed that they had managed to surmount these hurdles, that they had "Arabized" or "Algerianized"; they failed to realize how their sexual conquests, both imagined and real, created hierarchical power dynamics between them and the Algerians—especially the Algerian women, bound to a static Algeria, doomed to remain mere embodiments of the erotic Arab woman. Algerian participants and the Algerian government fell victim to a similar, overly simplified imaginary, arguing that if only for that month in the summer of 1969, they had transcended the long shadow that trans-Saharan slavery cast over the African continent. But the Black men and women who attended the PANAF felt similarly pigeon-holed by Algerian stereotypes. Unfortunately, and perhaps predictably, the fantasies that surrounded Black bodies, Arab bodies, and female bodies of all racial backgrounds, which had developed over centuries of the slave trade and colonialism, were too deeply embedded to evaporate in the heat of a July in Algiers.

FIVE

THE RED IN RED-CARPET

The Journées Cinématographiques de Carthage

Europe is a periphery of Africa. See, they stayed at my place for over a hundred years, and they don't speak the language, I speak their language. . . . If you take the map of Africa and you put Europe and America in it, you still have room. This tropism . . . why would you want me to be the sunflower turning toward the sun? I am the sun!

OUSMANE SEMBÈNE, 1983

THE STORY GOES SOMETHING LIKE this: Tunisian film critic Tahar Cheriaa traveled to the Cannes Film Festival in May 1966. There, for the first time, like many of the other attendees, he discovered African cinema through Senegalese director Ousmane Sembène's first feature film, *La noire de . . .* (Black girl), a film about the dehumanizing effects of racism on a young Senegalese woman.[1] The young woman works for a French couple who treat her so horribly that she considers suicide as the only option for regaining her liberty.[2] Upon seeing Sembène's film, it dawned on Cheriaa that cinema was a powerful tool that could illustrate the African experience for the masses. He invited Sembène to participate in the inaugural Journées Cinématographiques de Carthage (JCC) in October 1966. Sembène received the festival's first prize, the Tanit d'Or, that October, and inspired scores of young African filmmakers to create their own films. So goes the tale of the first encounter between Tahar Cheriaa and Ousmane Sembène and the subsequent creation of the JCC. In the decades since, both men have been lionized in films and documentaries such as Mohamed Challouf's film *Tahar Cheriaa: À l'ombre du baobab* (*Tahar Cheriaa: In the Shade of the Baobab*) and Samba Gadjigo's *Sembène!*[3] The story of Cheriaa and Sembène's friendship is a central component of African film's founding myth. Not only did the poster for the JCC's twenty-sixth session feature both men's contented faces, proudly puffing away at their pipes, but many of my interviewees refer to this creation story to illustrate Tunisia's particular claim to Pan-African leadership.[4] As Tunisian director Férid Boughedir claimed in a 2018 interview, "Tunisia remains the most Pan-African of the Maghrebi countries, when it comes to film, and to culture in general."[5] Boughedir, whose 1983 documentary *Caméra d'Afrique* chronicles the first twenty years of African cinema, is perhaps Tunisia's best-known film director and one who, in our 2018 interview, still expressed his commitment to the JCC's Pan-African origins.

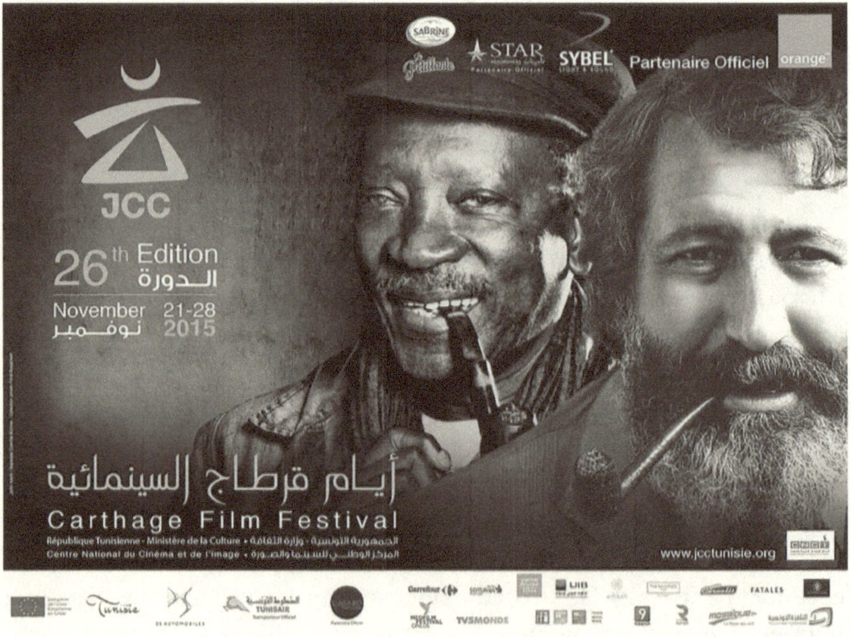

FIGURE 15. Poster for the twenty-sixth edition of the JCC, November 21–28, 2015, featuring Tahar Cheriaa (right) and Ousmane Sembène (left). Available online.

In 1966, the Tunisian Ministry of Culture created the JCC to compete with Algeria and Morocco on the African cultural scene. The JCC's beginnings were geared toward European approval. Under the joint leadership of Tahar Cheriaa and Ousmane Sembène, however, the biennale gradually emerged as a Pan-African forum for debates on the role of the postcolonial state and the relationship between artists and their people. Through interviews with JCC participants and administrators, JCC pamphlets, press coverage, and personal correspondence, this last chapter reveals the little-known story of the JCC as the final home of the Maghreb Generation in the mid-1970s.

TUNISIA'S FORGOTTEN PAN-AFRICANISM

To an even greater extent than Morocco, Tunisia's role in hosting liberation movements in the 1960s and 1970s, particularly those invested in revolutionary culture, is virtually unknown. Historical scholarship on the Maghreb has mostly focused on Algeria—and even then, mostly on the Algerian War of Independence—and has left Tunisia understudied.[6] When scholars do refer to Tunisia, it is often to use it as a counterexample to the antidemocratic tendencies of other Arab or African countries. Until the 2011 Tunisian Revolution that ignited the Arab Spring, the scant scholarship painted the country as a "little Europe of the Enlightenment," as somewhat insignificant, especially compared to its rowdy next-door neighbors.[7]

Scholars have portrayed Tunisia as a country turned northward, toward the Mediterranean, and not as a country that sought to develop Pan-African solidarities.[8] European scholars and journalists have characterized independent Tunisia's first president, Habib Bourguiba, as a modernist, a man who cared about the subaltern and about women in particular—in short, as a man who followed in Europe's footsteps. This is not to say that Europeans created this image out of thin air.[9] Bourguiba's government played an important role in exporting the image of a country on the cusp of modernity. Bourguiba's state doctrine, *bourguibisme*, rested on the values of liberalism, state-controlled Islam, and autonomy from the Arab world. Central to his doctrine was the idea of "politique des étapes," a step-by-step process toward political achievement; he was not one to throw his country into some kind of rash pursuit. "I am a realist," he explained. "To be a realist is to prefer a modest reform to an impossible miracle."[10]

Europeans and Americans were enthusiastic about Bourguiba's doctrine of *bourguibisme*. A June 1972 article published in the French daily *Le Monde* during Bourguiba's visit to France, highlighted the French perspective on his state doctrine: "[French] public opinion has recognized the command with which Bourguiba has directed the evolution of his country, the wisdom of his positions in the great conflicts that divide the world. The capacity to ally patience and good timing with audaciousness and decision-making, is the essence of 'Bourguibisme.'"[11] The European press turned a blind eye to the repression endured by Tunisians who dissented from Bourguiba's vision. A 1964 article in *Le Monde* spoke of Bourguiba as a strong man with a clear idea of Tunisia's future, who, while he did not tolerate criticism very well, was "not made of the same wood as real dictators."[12] Throughout his tenure, Bourguiba drew heavily on the language of Tunisian exceptionalism and on Europe's idealization of Tunisia to cast a leaden shroud over all forms of opposition in the country.

Despite what the European zeitgeist wanted to believe; the Tunisian government did not entirely disavow Pan-African ties. In the context of the Cold War, Tunisia, as a recently independent country, had to show nominal signs of nonalignment. And so, in search for moderate nonalignment partners, Bourguiba first turned east, and when that failed, turned south to the African continent.

In the first few years of Tunisian independence, Bourguiba did not seem to show much interest in Africa or in highlighting Tunisia's Africanity. In 1963, at the first OAU summit in Addis Ababa—the very same summit where Ben Bella had made a passionate plea for support of the Angolan independence struggle—Bourguiba showed some reticence at the idea of rushing into African unity. "We barely know each other," explained Bourguiba, "and we haven't had the time to figure out what brings us together and what divides us. We must erase all the walls built by the colonial period. We must not forget that Africa was for a long time a continent open to the world but closed to itself."[13] He felt more connected to the Middle East than to Africa, a position that he made clear at the second conference of the OAU when he insisted that there could be no Pan-African solidarity if African leaders did not stand with the Palestinian people.[14]

Bourguiba traveled to the Middle East in 1965, where he delivered an infamous speech in Jericho on March 3. The address hinted at the fact that Arab countries needed to work with Israel toward a peaceful solution to the Palestinian problem. His appeal provoked an uproar across the Arab world, spurring demonstrations and forcing Bourguiba to cancel a trip to Iraq. As a result, he was vilified by several Arab leaders and their people. [15] Disappointed by this reaction, Bourguiba turned his attention south and decided to deploy *bourguibisme* and Tunisian soft power upon the African continent instead.

On November 15, 1965, just six months after his Jericho debacle, the Tunisian president set off on a month-long trip across West Africa, which took him to Mauritania, Liberia, Senegal, Mali, the Ivory Coast, the Central African Republic, Cameroon, and Niger.[16] Throughout this trip he promoted *bourguibisme* as the only way to unite the countries of Africa. Positioning himself as the reasonable Tunisian patriarch, he deliberately differentiated himself from Algeria's revolutionary rhetoric. In a speech delivered to the Senegalese parliament, he called for a "commonwealth à la française."[17] This was Bourguiba's kind of Pan-Africanism, a rhetorical union premised on developing cultural exchange that posed little to no political threat to his regime.[18]

When, in 1966, Tunisian film critic Tahar Cheriaa and Tunisian minister of culture Chedli Klibi came to Bourguiba and asked to create the Journées Cinématographiques de Carthage under the umbrella of the Tunisian Ministry of Culture, Bourguiba gave the project his blessing. To the Tunisian president, the JCC probably resembled other trans-Saharan cultural exchanges that he had set up while in West Africa, such as the Tunisian Art Institute in Dakar; there was thus nothing to worry about. By subsidizing such festivals as the JCC, Bourguiba assumed, Tunisia could compete with Algeria's Pan-African draw, all the while attracting artists over militants and filmmakers over rabble-rousers. Little did he know what the festival would become.

In the late 1960s and early 1970s, African filmmakers benefited from some state support, especially in Tunisia, Algeria, and Morocco. However, according to Tunisian director Abdellatif Ben Amar, politicians did not necessarily promote cinema for cultural reasons but because they saw it as a way of "restoring the image of independence leaders, of the war of independence, of showcasing the courage of our leaders who had participated in the liberation struggles."[19] And so, in the hopes of creating blockbusters glorifying the Tunisian, Moroccan, and Algerian independence struggles, Maghrebi politicians began to invest in building movie theaters, circulating cinema minibuses, funding festivals, and nationalizing the Maghrebi screens. Of course, explained Ben Amar, Maghrebi filmmakers were not interested in lingering on the past, on the events of independence: "It's as if French filmmakers had only made films about de Gaulle on June 18th. The African filmmaker lived in the present; he was interested in the question of women, in denouncing the abuse of power, and so this did not make the state happy."[20]

What Maghrebi filmmakers did have in common with the Maghrebi states was their interest in Pan-Africanism, which came naturally to Maghrebi filmmakers, as both Ben Amar and Tahar Cheriaa agreed. Maghrebi films were very similar to other francophone African films in both content and form because, wrote Cheriaa, "the influence of French culture, academic and cinephile, is often quite dominant."[21] Just as the writers of *Souffles* had argued in the mid-1960s, the Tunisian filmmakers felt they shared much more with their African counterparts than with those of the Levant: the experience of colonialism directed their subject matter and their artistic priorities, and this drove them to make much more political and sober films.

While intellectual networks that transcended the nation-state posed a threat to the new African states, many of the themes dear to Pan-Africanism converged with the preoccupations and ideologies of the Maghrebi nation-states and therefore did not seem threatening at first. For Bourguiba, the JCC and its Pan-African ideology would respect the popular and Manichaean divide between Africans, on the one hand, and Europeans, on the other. As Tunisian producer Hassan Daldoul explained, "Pan-Africanism is not nationalism, it's just culture. There is no ethnicity in Pan-Africanism, unlike Pan-Arabism."[22] Thus, while Pan-Arabism may have seemed hazardous to Bourguiba's regime and risked unsettling Tunisian nationalism, Pan-Africanism, an ideology that hinged primarily on culture, did not seem to rest on strong-enough foundations to pose much of a threat. To many Maghrebi directors, however, pursuing Pan-African networks became a relatively safe way of expressing resistance and evading the nation-state.

THE MAGHREB GENERATION'S TURN TO FILM

If the 1960s was the decade of liberation, the 1970s was the decade of disillusion, a decade during which newly independent countries failed to provide for their inhabitants and sank into dictatorship.[23] The domain of the political was slowly closing to all but a few men. But not everyone in Africa gave up on political projects; much as they had in the previous decade, the realm of culture—the cinemas and cultural clubs, literary reviews, and cultural festivals—served as a space in which to dream and construct a different vision of society. Since the assassination of Jean Sénac in 1973, however, and the imprisonment of the *Souffles* writers and editors, the viability of literary culture as a revolutionary weapon was swiftly fading in North Africa.

The Maghreb Generation's cultural revolt against imperialism and neocolonialism was revitalized when militant-artists turned to film as the newest weapon in their arsenal, exchanging cameras and cameramen and carrying reels halfway across the continent to show in cinematheques and town squares. Filming in grainy black and white with borrowed cameras, filmmakers managed to create a cinematic culture in countries with no film industry. In some cases, filmmakers received support from national leaders eager to restore their image or glorify their independence struggle. More often than not, however, despite the lack of money and infrastructure, young African filmmakers made do with what they had at hand, in the process creating cult classics. Poet and *Souffles* contributor André Laude, who collaborated with Mauritanian director Med Hondo, recalled that he and Hondo would buy film by the foot. "Friends would steal film from the companies they worked at. We had an old, busted camera . . . wobbly. . . . We would find old excerpts of documentaries and just glue them onto the film."[24]

In the early 1960s, when Senegalese writer Ousmane Sembène returned to Africa after ten years spent as a dock worker in Marseille, he started to think of film as a more effective tool for reaching his people, since so many were illiterate. Sembène was born in Zinguinchor in 1923, served as a Tirailleur Sénégalais during World War II, joined the French Communist Party in going on strike against the war in Vietnam, and published the now famous novels *Black Docker* (1956) and *God's Bits of Wood* (1960).[25] Sembène, who was an ardent supporter of leftist economic movements such as the Senegalese railroad workers' strike (1945–46), traveled to Moscow in 1961 to study film at the Moscow Film Society and train as a filmmaker of the people.[26] When he returned, he made his first short film, *Borom Sarett* (The wagoner), which follows a cart driver around Dakar for eighteen minutes, showcasing the difficulty of life in the city, where independence did not solve all the problems of the Senegalese people. Critics hailed the film as a landmark in the history of African cinema, some scholars even arguing that African film was born in Senegal in 1962 with *Borom Sarett*.[27] Many African artists soon followed in Sembène's footsteps and turned to film. Angolan militant-poet Mario de Andrade started to collaborate with his companion, Sarah Maldoror, in producing movies about the struggle against Portuguese colonialism. Mauritanian actor Med Hondo turned away from theater in 1968 because, he claimed, theater was too ephemeral, whereas film "was an art that left its traces"—an art that had larger political implications and potential audiences.[28]

Like their poet peers, African filmmakers realized that Western encroachment was ongoing despite territorial decolonization. Perhaps more than any other artists, filmmakers felt the weight of American and European cultural imperialism. Filming a full-length motion picture necessitated more expensive technology, more people, and generally more infrastructure than producing a radio show or poetry magazine. What little money African filmmakers had access to was distributed sparingly by European agencies such as the French Centre National de la Cinématographie (CNC)—a system that allowed these agencies to control the themes and messages of the films emerging from the African continent.[29] Furthermore, European and American distribution agencies retained significant control over what African cinemas projected on their screens. This, claimed Mauritanian director Med Hondo, was an effective way of penetrating the minds of African people, "influencing their everyday social behavior, directing them, and diverting them from their historic national responsibilities."[30] Hondo argued that, through such films as Hollywood westerns, European and American governments were insidiously imposing alien models and references on Africans, ultimately damaging African cultural development. Not only that, Hondo continued:

> [This blocked] true communication between Africans and Arabs, brothers and friends who have been historically united for thousands of years. This alienation disseminated through the image is all the more dangerous

> for being insidious, uncontroversial, "accepted," seemingly inoffensive and neutral. It needs no armed forces and no permanent program of education by those seeking to maintain the division of the African and Arab peoples—their weakness, submission, servitude, their ignorance of each other and of their own industry. They forget their positive heritage, united through their foremothers with all humanity.[31]

Hondo and his peers of the Maghreb Generation held that Africans needed to claim their own cinemas. If they could gain control of the screen, they could project a positive image of Africa, rooted in African concerns and made for an African audience. Hondo and Sembène were weary of performing for a European audience, of being forced to take a back seat (*strapontin*) or of serving as a hint of exotic flavor in European film festivals.[32] To be an African filmmaker, Hondo and Sembène believed, was to be a revolutionary, to cease filming postcard documentaries for European tourists, to revolt against the idea of "art for art's sake," and to break out of the confinement of "technical cooperation" with Europe, which the two men considered to be just a thinly veiled, polite form of neocolonialism.[33] Like the poets and writer of the Maghreb Generation, the filmmakers of that generation rejected the Western interlocutor and viewed art and revolutionary politics as inseparable.

Sembène was careful to pinpoint the difference between a European rebel—the discontented youth who knew not what to do with their time—and the African revolutionary—a youth who was working toward a very specific goal: that of serving the African masses.[34] Hondo and Sembène were deeply influenced by the Third Cinema movement coming out of Latin America; like their peers in Latin America, they struggled to forge a new path between the commercial films of Hollywood and the auteur cinema of Europe. They argued that cinema should not be commercial or represent the view of a single individual; instead, it should give voice to the struggles of the people and inspire them to revolutionary action.[35] As Tunisian director Nouri Bouzid remembered, in the 1960s he and his peers waged war on Hollywood and on Egyptian cinema, which had shaped the Arab cinema market with its melodramas. They also waged war on aesthetics: "We sometimes went so far as to reject plot and anecdote, considering that it was too easy to tell a story."[36] Like the writers of *Souffles*, the Luso-Africans, Jean Sénac, Ted Joans, and René Depestre, the filmmakers of the Maghreb Generation rejected art for art's sake, arguing that beauty should be searched for in the heat of battle and the cries of the people.

TRACING THE JCC'S HISTORICAL EVOLUTION

Tahar Cheriaa, born in 1927 in Sayada, Tunisia, has been called the "father of Tunisian and African cinema" and was dedicated to the Pan-African cause.[37] A functionary of the state, an intellectual, a communist, a cinephile, a womanizer, and a "Nietzschean with no mercy," Cheriaa had many faces, but seemingly all of them were Pan-African.[38] In 1962, Bourguiba appointed him cinema director in the Ministry of Culture and Information. Cheriaa, whose love of film began when he joined the Sfax ciné-club in 1954, spent years studying the economy of film and writing reports for the Tunisian government and UNESCO, eventually concluding that whoever controlled the distribution networks controlled cinema.[39] In 1964, despairing over the lack of Tunisian films being screened in Tunisian cinemas and the overwhelming presence of Hollywood, he attempted to pass a decree forcing theaters to show at least one Tunisian short film per trimester. According to Tunisian director Férid Boughedir, "Tunisia was immediately placed on a blacklist. For an entire year the whole country was deprived of any new films. The American ambassador even personally asked Bourguiba who this Cheriaa, this Bolshevik, was, he who attempted to hinder the free circulation of American films."[40] It was in the aftermath of this experience that Cheriaa decided to create the Journées Cinématographiques de Carthage, under the auspices of the Tunisian government.

The Tunisian film directors and JCC participants I interviewed seemed to think of Cheriaa as either a radical who knew how to use government money to benefit his own projects or a compliant bureaucrat of the Tunisian state. In 1956, in an article titled "Potential Futures for Cinema in Tunisia," Cheriaa wrote that cinema was the ideal instrument of "interior and exterior propaganda," concluding that cinema was thus "an essential element of the cultural and spiritual patrimony of the nation."[41] Perhaps he was trying to convince the Tunisian government to invest in cinema production, arguing that this would be an ideal way to spread the message of *bourguibisme* and the hopes for Tunisian nationalism, or perhaps he was indeed a proponent of Bourguiba's regime. Historian Kmar Bendana, who knew him, claimed that Cheriaa was just a professor like others, that there were "fifty possible Cheriaas; he was simply a functionary of the state."[42]

To directors Mohammed Challouf and Férid Boughedir, however, Cheriaa was a revolutionary, a communist—albeit not a card-carrying member—someone who was looking for a revolutionary transformation of society.[43] In Boughedir's view, Cheriaa had fulfilled Frantz Fanon's dream of uniting the revolutionary Third World, by bringing together people such as Ousmane Sembène and Egyptian director Tawfiq Saleh; he was therefore an essential link in the Maghreb Generation network. Cheriaa was no doubt conscious of the double personality he conveyed. At a UNESCO colloquium in the summer of 1970, on the theme of the artist-creator's responsibilities in a violent society, Cheriaa wondered ironically if having him deliver a speech about artistic freedom was "a purposeful punishment given to this monster of contradiction, friend of the arts, defender of artists, supporter of freedom of expression, but nevertheless meticulous censor with the evil scissors, whose uncomfortable reputation I've acquired."[44]

In JCC lore, Sembène and Cheriaa are often portrayed side by side. In interviews, Challouf and Kaiser Cheriaa (Tahar Cheriaa's eldest son) stressed the enduring love the two men bore each other. Kaiser Cheriaa recounted meeting Sembène's son a few years after Sembène's and Cheriaa's respective deaths. "When I talked to him, it was crazy, I found the same behavior," he recalled. "Sembène had the same relationship with his children—it was like Jean-Jacques Rousseau, you know, who talked of social contract but then put his kids in an orphanage. It was the same thing: they were adored, they were gods, but they were not fathers."[45] Though Kaiser had no fond memories of Cheriaa as a father, he remembered with admiration his dad's devotion to young filmmakers, whether they were Tunisian or from anywhere else on the African continent, and his enduring friendship with Sembène.

But the two men did not agree about everything. If Cheriaa was a functionary of the Tunisian government, Sembène was in an all-out battle with the Senegalese state: his films were often censored, and he openly spoke out against Senegalese president Léopold Sédar Senghor's regime. Already in 1967, after Sembène claimed that African states were not ready to listen to African filmmakers and their problems and that the struggle for freedom of speech was a top priority, Cheriaa tempered Sembène's rhetoric, claiming that freedom of speech was only secondary to reclaiming the means of production.[46]

No matter where Cheriaa's heart lay, with the help of the new minister of culture, Chedli Klibi, Cheriaa was able to create the first independent film festival on the African continent. In October 1966, the festival exhibited only one African film, *La noire de . . .* by Sembène, a film which, according to one Lebanese newspaper, *Al-Nahār,* "opened wide the doors of the cinema to the African continent."[47] The other films were primarily from countries bordering the Mediterranean; most had already been screened in Europe, and many festival participants felt that this first test run did not distinguish itself sufficiently from other, European festivals.[48] Some Tunisian papers, however, were pleased with the Mediterranean inclinations of the JCC's first session, like the Arabic-language newspaper *Al-'Amal,* which lauded the JCC's efforts at returning Carthage to its "rich past as the center of the Mediterranean."[49] Many international observers and journalists also seemed content with the festival, writing reviews that commended Bourguiba for his forward thinking—further evidence of Europeans' tendency to view Tunisia through rose-colored glasses.

One francophone Lebanese journalist, Mary Azoury, noted that she felt the "Tunisians had faith in the future. We've had the time to talk with many people; all trust their government; they know these politicians work for the general good. Many African countries wonder how to catch up. Tunisians do not ask such questions. Their country is sailing on the wind of miracles, and the magician's name is Bourguiba."[50] French producer Christine Gouze-Rénal saw "extraordinary passion" among young Tunisian directors. "But," she warned, "though your country is marvelous, and has so much drive, you must leave behind your own problems. . . . You must enlarge your ideas, maybe talk about other people's problems."[51] Gouze-Rénal's condescending tone aside, her comment reveals that she, like many of the festival's audience, had not understood the point of the festival to be Pan-Africanism; instead, she read this as one more attempt on the part of Africans to show that they were worthy men and women of culture. She was not wrong. In its first incarnation, the JCC's goal was "to show the West, where the film market is fiercely guarded against all foreign input, that talented filmmakers also exist in other places."[52] In other words, the JCC was still very much geared toward the West.

This did not last long. Sembène, one of the founders of JCC and a fierce opponent of ideologies such as *négritude,* was busy lobbying for African filmmakers "to repudiate the West and to deal only with local problems. . . . The filmmaker must always take the side of the oppressed: decolonization is not over."[53] Indeed, though the Tunisian regime, the Tunisian minister of culture, and the foreign press may not have understood the JCC as a Pan-

African or militant space, at the post-screening debates and symposiums African film enthusiasts were coming together and comparing the problems they faced. "There were filmmakers from all over, from Senegal, Sudan, Somalia," remembered Tunisian director Hassan Daldoul. "That's when we started to realize, to debate, to think, and to build a Pan-African consciousness."[54] According to many of the people I interviewed, the movies themselves mattered less than the debates and discussions that occurred in the hallways, between movies, in the cafés, and around kitchen tables. It was in those spaces, outside the control of the Tunisian state, that the Maghreb Generation filmmakers met and started building the Pan-African culture of dissent that would flourish at the JCC in the 1970s.

As Tunisian producer Néjib Ayed explained, although the JCC was created with the blessing of the Tunisian government, the Tunisian government didn't have the expertise to put in place a festival of this scope. The Ministry of Culture thus placed the festival in the hands of the Fédération Tunisienne des Ciné-Clubs (FTCC), one of the few spaces where resistance to Bourguiba's regime thrived.[55] The FTCC, created in 1950, was one of the largest nongovernmental organizations in Tunisia: it had over 100,000 members from across Tunisia and directed the cultural activities of ciné-clubs throughout the country. In some towns the ciné-clubs were one of very few places of socialization and entertainment for the generation coming of age after independence. Organizing projections of films, debates, and other cultural events in locations across Tunisia, including in very remote areas, the leaders of the FTCC had their finger on the political pulse of the country. While the Tunisian government may have directed the cinema sector in theory, in practice it was the FTCC that controlled what happened on the ground. Similarly, while the JCC was funded by the Tunisian state, the actual planning, including the choice of films, the organization of the debates, and the allotment of prizes, was under the FTCC's supervision.[56]

Between the first and the second sessions of the JCC, the FTCC changed the film festival's regulations. Many Tunisian and African observers and participants had put pressure on the festival's organizers to move away from emphasis on the Mediterranean and Europe. Starting in 1968, the new regulations stated that only African and Arab films could be showcased in the official competition.[57] This decision likely stemmed from the changing environment in Tunisia. Tunisian students and film buffs were tiring of Bourguiba's single-party regime. They began to fight against this monopoly on the streets, in seminars, in ciné-clubs, and in the JCC.

The 1960s were marked by a strong student resistance to the Bourguiba regime. As early as 1963, two student groups were formed: one was close to the Tunisian government and a member of the UGET (Union Générale des Étudiants de Tunisie); the other, the Perspectives group, was more left wing and socialist, and spoke out against Bourguiba's authoritarianism. Beginning in 1965, students started calling for strikes and demonstrations, which were violently put down by the police. The members of Perspectives used similar rhetoric to groups such as *Souffles* and those who participated in the Off-PANAF; they were not fooled by the pseudo anti-imperialism of their governments and denounced them for being full of turncoats. One 1967 Perspectives pamphlet reads: "Because the Tunisian leaders are part of this species, thankfully increasingly rare, of those who betray the oppressed and are in fact vassals of imperialism, we dedicate to them our utmost contempt."[58] In January 1968, when the US vice president Hubert Humphrey visited Tunis, Tunisian students flooded the streets to denounce US foreign policy—primarily the collusion between American imperialism and Zionism and the US war in Vietnam. On March 15, the students declared a general strike, which the Tunisian police crushed, imprisoning more than a hundred militants.[59]

In the world of Tunisian film, 1968 represented a changing of the guard.[60] It is no coincidence that many of the students who participated in the March 1968 protests were members of Tunisia's ciné-clubs: the ciné-clubs were spaces of politicization. In contrast to the early 1960s, when the network of ciné-clubs across Tunisia was mainly dominated by suited European or Euro-educated members, by the late 1960s a younger generation was showing interest in film—a generation that had come of age after independence and was less concerned with the colonial past than with the societies they currently inhabited. High school and college students, laborers, and others began to use the ciné-clubs as a space of socialization, as one of the few arenas in which they could express themselves free from parental and state supervision. This new generation was also strongly influenced by the Third Cinema movement and was thus much less concerned with art for art's sake or for commercial gain, instead hoping to mobilize the masses through film.[61] They began taking control of the ciné-clubs, every year gaining more elected seats on the ciné-clubs' boards.[62]

If these students were unafraid to show their political colors at the ciné-clubs, they were equally dauntless about exhibiting them at JCC events, under the very noses of Tunisian state officials. The French ambassador to Tunisia, who attended the 1968 JCC and reported back to the French Ministry of Foreign Affairs, noted that the festival was a mix of "Bensalism, Marxism, and Leftism," to the delight of Tahar Cheriaa and the Tunis University students.[63] In fact, the JCC opened with a documentary on Ben Salah, Bourguiba's primary opponent, one that was applauded by the students in attendance.[64] "The student audience, hostile to the festival in principle (which they consider an anachronistic and bourgeois event) showed their hostility several times," wrote the French ambassador, by "applauding when M. Ben Salah appeared on the screen, by violently criticizing the filmmakers and organizers around the morning debates, and by refusing the selection criteria of the films presented, instead wanting to see *Soleil Ô* [by radical Mauritanian director Med Hondo]."[65] Clearly, the Tunisian youth were not interested in Bourguiba's vision of soft Pan-Africanism. Instead, they sided with the militancy of films such as Hondo's *Soleil Ô*, a film that vividly denounced neocolonialism in its opening animated skit.

To compete with the ciné-clubs' radicalizing influence, Bourguiba's party, the Neo-Destour, created their own network of ciné-clubs.[66] This did not help de-radicalize the students, who continued to protest. "We wanted the liberty to think, to create, to critique, to talk about women's rights, injustices, abuses of power," explained Tunisian director Abdellatif Ben Amar, "but the state did not want us to question, it did not want us to help the masses understand that you couldn't just listen, couldn't just be the perfect pupils of the nation, that a leader could not think for us."[67] And so, the state started closing ciné-clubs operated by the FTCC and banning post-screening debates. In 1970, the film service at the Ministry of Cultural Affairs, under orders from the central government, expanded visa requirements for films to be shown in ciné-clubs. Even when the films had already been granted a visa, the ministry argued that these visas only covered a public screening, not a public debate.[68] "The scope of the repression grew," explained Tahar Cheriaa, "and any notion of debate became suspect and was repressed."[69]

The struggle between the members of the Ministry of Cultural Affairs and the central government was constant throughout the 1970s. The ministry was one of the few spaces in which resistance to Bourguiba's regime thrived, but it was under intense surveillance from the regime, which did not hesitate to arrest FTCC members and film directors when they took too much liberty. "We were surrounded by snitches," explained Hassan Daldoul. "All they [the snitches] needed to say was that you were preparing the revolution, and then direct to the *zalzal* [dungeon], where you were tortured. You can't imagine what they did to them."[70]

Tahar Cheriaa himself was imprisoned by the Tunisian government. The story of his imprisonment varies greatly depending on who tells it. According to Férid Boughedir, longtime admirer and friend of Cheriaa, it was Cheriaa's desire to liberate Tunisian screens from American and European control that resulted in his six-month-long imprisonment. Vexed by Cheriaa's efforts to gain control of Tunisian screens, the same companies that had boycotted Tunisia in 1964 created a damning file against Cheriaa. "They claimed that he stole money from cinemas, that he slept with his secretary, and all sorts of other calumnies," explained Boughedir.[71]

> They sent this to Bourguiba. Now usually, Bourguiba tore up this sort of thing, but this time there was this Algerian poet, Moufti Zakaria, who owned a movie theater in Tunis, who brought Bourguiba some poems, and among them was this file against Tahar Cheriaa, claiming that a communist had infiltrated Bourguiba's administration, and let's be clear, Bourguiba did not like communists or the Kremlin. And there was proof, since in 1964, when Cheriaa was trying to reclaim Tunisian screens, that he had traveled to Paris to visit Sov Export Films, and had asked them if, in case of an American boycott, they would be willing to provide films to Tunisian cinemas. This alone was proof to Bourguiba of Cheriaa's communist sympathies. So Bourguiba sent him to jail, because Bourguiba was very hotheaded, so without a trial or anything he sent him to jail. We went to visit him, he was our president, our director, we brought him oranges.[72]

According to Mohamed Challouf, Cheriaa was imprisoned for eight months and was only liberated with the help of his African colleagues, just in time to join the 1969 PANAF. Challouf explained that it was Ababacar Samb-Makharam, the Senegalese filmmaker, who circulated a petition at the PANAF film symposium demanding Cheriaa's release—a petition that filmmakers from across Africa signed and sent to Bourguiba.[73] Yet another version of the story of Cheriaa's imprisonment comes from Algerian film critic and administrator Ahmed Bedjaoui, who claimed that Cheriaa had been imprisoned by Bourguiba when the PANAF opened in Algiers. Filmmakers from across Africa, all present in Algiers, signed a petition that they delivered to Boumédiène, asking him to put pressure on Bourguiba to release Cheriaa. When Bourguiba did, Boumédiène chartered a plane to pick up Cheriaa from Tunis and deliver him straight to the PANAF.[74] All of these stories contributed to Cheriaa's lionization as the father of African cinema, as a Pan-African hero who used the medium of film and the film industry to defy the state.

If the ciné-clubs attracted and molded young activists who challenged the Tunisian government domestically, the JCC helped to inscribe this dissidence into a global network denouncing neocolonialism and authoritarianism across Africa. Beginning in 1968, what had started as a Tunisian project, a project conceived by Tunisian functionaries and subsidized by the Tunisian state, began to escape the Tunisian state's control and started broadcasting the Maghreb Generation's ideology of dissenting Pan-Africanism—an ideology far from Bourguiba's ideal foreign policy. Throughout the 1970s, the debates and screenings at the JCC were suffused with the language of revolution and militancy, often forgoing any aesthetic consideration and privileging films that felt radical or challenged the established power paradigms. To Sembène, the JCC was "Africa's vengeance;"[75] to Algerian Mahmoud Ben Salama, the JCC was a strategic nexus that worked fervently for an accelerated decolonization of subjugated cinemas.[76] But to European observers, this trend was threatening: Victor Bachy, from the Belgian daily newspaper *La Libre Belgique,* wrote that "the JCC has demonstrated the victory of militant movies. . . . It preaches, implicitly or not, violence, hate, and vengeance. It is a never-ending chain, alas."[77]

These changes in the JCC's rhetoric were largely spurred by the African filmmakers who had become staples of the Carthage festival, including Ousmane Sembène, Guadeloupean director Sarah Maldoror, and Mauritanian Med Hondo.[78] As Sembène noted in an interview with Tahar Cheriaa, "it [was] not Tunisia that made Carthage, it [was] the Africans."[79] Maldoror explained that Carthage was the city where African filmmakers learned to look at themselves: "We were watching our movies, our dances, our histories, our loves, and our dreams. There, by exchanging gazes, we understood our differences. We were watching others, no longer being watched."[80]

African liberation groups were a permanent fixture in Carthage until the end of the 1970s, explained festival director and producer Néjib Ayed.

Groups such as FRELIMO, the MPLA, the ANC, and others were at the center of all the discussions. "We would always remind everyone that they were there, why they were there, what the struggle was, and we would debate furiously about apartheid, colonialism, southern Rhodesia."[81] In constant contact with members of these liberation groups, the young Tunisians who attended the JCC nurtured the political consciousness that had been sowed in the ciné-clubs. "All of the African films were political, were in opposition to authoritarian states," remembered Hassan Daldoul. When these filmmakers came to Carthage, the young Tunisians peppered them with questions, begging for advice. "You can't imagine what kind of points of view they helped us develop, how they liberated our ideas," marveled Daldoul. "They were making oppositional films, critiquing religion, male domination, sexual repression . . ."[82]

The African directors also showed solidarity with Tunisia's disenchanted youth, urging them to continue to fight for freedom of speech in a country sinking deeper into authoritarianism. In her memoirs, *Instants de vie,* Tunisian writer and activist Jelila Hafsia recalls that in October 1968, during a JCC debate, the Greco-Ethiopan director Nikos Papatakis stood up in front of a crowded room and read a letter of protest. "The letter concerned the imprisoned students and the hunger strike that had started the previous day. Most of the people in the room, many of them festivalgoers, joined him in signing the letter of support."[83] Hafsia noted that "for all these countries, the problems are the same, and cinema is a weapon."[84]

THE FILMS AND DIRECTORS OF THE JCC

The JCC's most militant films were presented by African directors: direct critiques of the corruption and abuse of public funds such as Malian director Souleymane Cissé's *Baara.* But it was Sembène, above all, who dictated the rhetoric of the JCC. In heralding Sembène as the "father of American cinema," scholars have conveyed the impression that African film's dominant aesthetic was his own politically motivated social realism.[85] Sembène did not tell stories about the elite; instead, he filmed the working class, the farmers, to draw attention to the difficult conditions of their lives. Sembène embodied the image of a politically motivated director: during interviews he did not shy away from sharp accusations against the former colonial powers and the neocolonial states that replaced them.[86] The fact that he had trained in Moscow added to the image he projected of a director primarily interested in portraying the hardships of the working class. Like other members of the Maghreb Generation, Sembène was influenced by Amílcar Cabral and Frantz Fanon, and he rejected all forms of spiritual and cultural mystification. Instead, Sembène advocated direct action: "The gods never prevented colonialism from establishing itself," he argued in 1976; "when the enemy is right there, he has to be fought with weapons."[87] Though not all African directors necessarily followed in Sembène's social-realist footsteps, the call from Carthage was for ideologically motivated films and not for films that engaged in art for art's sake or personal pursuits.

Sarah Maldoror was one of the few female directors who won acclaim at the JCC in the 1970s. The JCC, like the PANAF, *Souffles,* and other Maghrebi cultural projects led by the Maghreb Generation was primarily the domain of men. Most of the men I interviewed commented on Maldoror's strength: she was a fighter, I heard again and again. Maldoror, whose father was Guadeloupean, was born in the South of France in 1929; like Sembène, she studied film at the Moscow Film Academy. While she and Mario de Andrade were living in Algiers with their two daughters, she assisted director Gillo Pontecorvo in filming *The Battle of Algiers.*

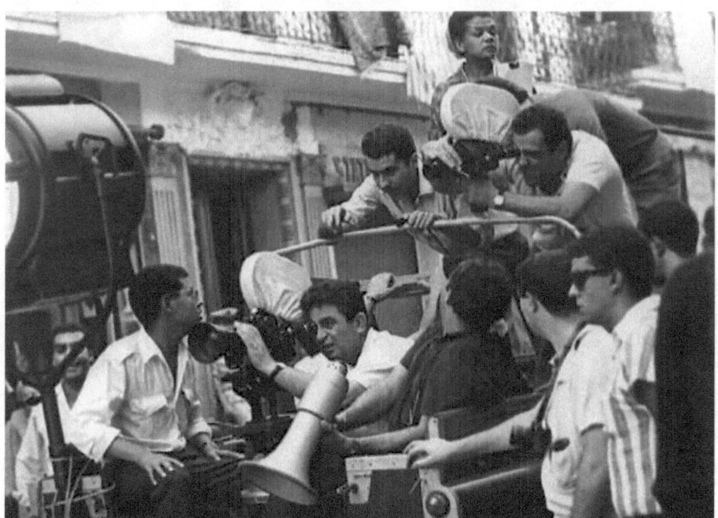

FIGURE 16. Sarah Maldoror surveying the scene during the filming of *The Battle of Algiers* (Gillo Pontecorvo, 1966). Reprint courtesy of Annouchka de Andrade and Henda Ducados.

In 1968, while living in Algiers, Maldoror made her first short film, *Monangambee,* based on a short story by the Angolan militant-writer José Luandino Vieira, funded by the Algerian government and including a large cast of Algerian actors playing Portuguese soldiers. "Monogambee" means "white death," an exclamation Angolans would apparently use as a warning cry when Portuguese soldiers approached.[88] The movie, only seventeen minutes long, tells the story of a woman who visits her husband, wrongfully imprisoned under suspicion of dissidence, in a jail cell in Luanda, Angola. The film centers around a linguistic misunderstanding between the woman and the Portuguese guards: the "completo," which the Angolans interpret as a three-course meal and the Portuguese guards as a three-piece suit. The film won the prize for best director at the JCC in 1970.

Maldoror's third film, *Sambizanga,* also won big at the JCC, garner-

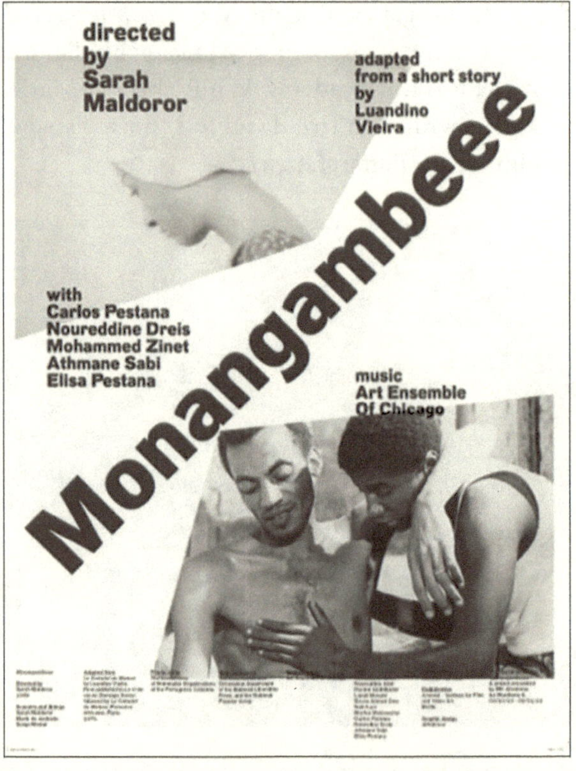

FIGURE 17. Poster for Sarah Maldoror's 1968 film *Monangambee.* Reprint courtesy of Annouchka de Andrade and Henda Ducados.

ing the prestigious Tanit d'or in 1972. The film tells the story of Maria and Domingos, who are blissfully enjoying life with their newborn baby until Domingos is arrested by the Portuguese authorities on charges of political activism. Maldoror's film follows Maria as she searches for her husband, is turned away by officials, and periodically cries "Domingos!"[89] The film features a gendered class analysis rather than a racial one—unlike, for instance, Sembène's film *La noire de . . .*, which is centered on racial violence. The emphasis is on the oppression of the poor by the rich, on a system that favors a minority over the majority. At one point, when Maria is escorted out of a police station by a Black police officer, she screams at him: "Get off me you shitty turncoat, you are with the Whites, you make us suffer!"[90] Maldoror was not interested in race or nationality. "What does it in fact mean to be French, Swedish, Senegalese, or Guadeloupian?" she asked in a 1974 interview. "Nationalities and borders between countries have to disappear. Besides this, the color of a person's skin is of no interest to me. What's important is what the person is doing."[91] Through films such as *Monogambee* and *Sambizanga,* Maldoror demonstrated that women were agents of change and mobilization in Angola and in Africa more generally, defying the pervasive perception of anticolonial liberation as the sole domain of male combatants.

Though Maldoror's style resembles Sembène's in its realistic depiction of poverty, injustice, and suffering, Maldoror was committed not only to a cinema for the people but to a cinema for women. "I'm only interested in women who struggle," she explained in the 1974 interview. By means of her films she hoped to inspire and support women who wanted to work in film, so that they would help grow the number of women in the film industry, since, she claimed, "Men aren't likely to help women do that. Both in Africa and in Europe woman remains the slave of man. That's why she must liberate herself."[92] Maldoror's commitment to telling women's stories came at a cost. In 1970, the Algerian government commissioned her to make a feature-length film about the PAIGC's struggle for independence in Guinea-Bissau. Maldoror centered *Des fusils pour Banta* on Awa, a young woman. When an Algerian official, unhappy with her choice of protagonist, confronted her, Maldoror retorted that he was just "a shit captain." The Algerian government swiftly confiscated her reels and expelled her from the country; the film has since disappeared.[93] Maldoror took her struggle for women's liberation to the JCC. Though she was practically the only woman

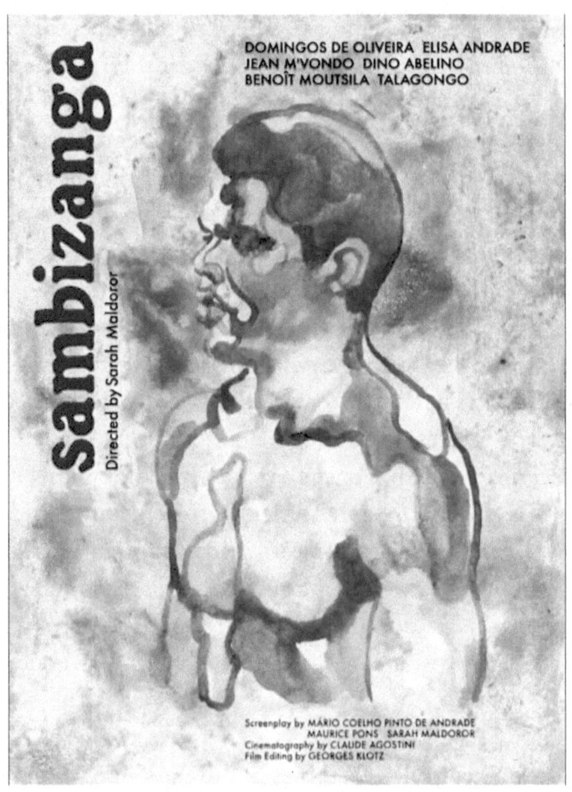

FIGURE 18. Poster for Sarah Maldoror's 1972 film *Sambizanga*. Reprint courtesy of Annouchka de Andrade and Henda Ducados.

to receive any acclaim in the 1970s, she wasn't one to accept a marginal position; she was there to fight for Africa and for women. She considered "film to be the best way of liberating women," remembered Tunisian Jelila Hafsia, who met Maldoror in Carthage.[94] Hassan Daldoul remembered her intensity: "Discussion about males and females, for that I adored her. She was violent, in-your-face. She defended Muslim women. Of course, I teased her, but she knew that I didn't mean it."[95] Daldoul went on to discuss how free Black women, as opposed to Arab women, were with their bodies.

Issues of race and sex were intimately intertwined during Pan-African reunions such as the JCC and the PANAF. Hassan Daldoul's supposed "teasing" of Maldoror and his comments on the "liberty" of Black women's bodies reveal the layers of harassment and stigma that women faced at the

JCC. In interviews conducted by the Tunisian press in the 1970s, Maldoror refused to discuss her private life and her companionship with Andrade, perhaps exasperated at being always associated with a man, or perhaps because, as a Black woman in the Maghreb, she needed to build walls around her personal life.[96]

Though Maldoror may have felt uncomfortable at the JCC, many Tunisian and African participants lauded Tunisia's treatment of women. Indeed, Bourguiba's government had worked hard to portray Tunisia as an exceptional place to be a woman in Africa and the Middle East. In January 1957, Bourguiba enacted the Code of Personal Status, a series of laws that granted women the right to choose their own husband, to demand monogamy, to divorce, and to adopt children without being married. A series of reforms introduced over the course of Bourguiba's first twenty years of rule authorized women to work, create bank accounts, start businesses, access abortions, and use contraception, all of this without the authorization of their husbands.[97]

In 2014, Charlotte Naccache, wife of Tunisian painter Edgar Naccache, talked of the political revolution that Bourguiba had orchestrated in order to liberate Tunisian woman, something hitherto unseen in the Arab world, she claimed, and perhaps even in the entire world. "Tunisian women should give their wedding bands, or even all of their gold jewelry, and melt it into a gigantic gold statue of Bourguiba to be placed right in the middle of Tunis," she said, her voice faltering with emotion. "The Tunisian woman owes everything to him!"[98] One JCC participant, Ynousse N'Diaye, star of Ousmane Sembène's film *Le mandat*, also remarked on how wonderful Tunisia was for women. "I admire Habib Bourguiba so much," she said in a 1968 interview. "We love him in Senegal. He is the only president who cares about the evolution of women."[99]

Another African filmmaker guiding the conversation at the JCC was Mauritanian director Med Hondo. Hondo's racial identity bridged the gap between North Africa and the rest of the continent. Born of a Mauritanian mother and Senegalese father, Hondo, like many other members of the Maghreb Generation, was multilingual: he spoke Wolof, French, and Arabic. Like Maldoror, Hondo was a darling of the JCC, where he won the 1974 Tanit d'or for his film *Les bicots-nègres vos voisins*, which denounced the living conditions of Black and Maghrebi immigrants in France. JCC spectators, including many of the Tunisian youth, loved Hondo's 1970 film *Soleil*

Ô, which began with an animated skit showing an African pawn of Western imperialism being catapulted to power, only to have that power taken away from him by that same imperialism.[100] Having lived in Paris for most of his life, in voluntary exile, Hondo turned to film, he explained, to find his place in the world and to make images of Africa for an African audience.[101] Much like Sembène, Hondo was a committed revolutionary; as his friend and *Souffles* contributor, poet André Laude, described him, Hondo "endured the tragedy of Africa and the Third World as if it was a cosmic event. He carried all the wounds of his brothers, of the marginalized, with him."[102] Hondo's films decried the living conditions of Black and Arab immigrants in France, but also the greed and corruption of African politicians. According to Laude, Hondo had a film project titled "Et sonnera l'heure des brasiers" (an homage to Argentine Fernando Solanas's 1968 film *La hora de los hornos*), which would portray the anti-neocolonial struggles in Africa and the "white-negroes who sold out their countries to the imperial power and blush with importance because, coming out of European universities and having become VIPs, they get to shake de Gaulle's hand, or that of humanity's butcher: Richard Nixon."[103] Hondo never made the film, but many of his films denounced what he called these "white-negroes," the turncoat dictators, the same people Jean Sénac called "monkeys" and Abdellatif Laâbi "windup monkeys."[104]

Hondo was convinced that Africa was not yet decolonized, that the relationships between the African continent and the rest of the world were still predicated on the whims of the imperial powers. Be it for "peanuts, tomatoes, fish, . . . or film, . . . there are people who produce, and people who consume," explained Hondo, "and be careful, because this could lead to a recolonization, and a much more subtle one. Before it was the big cannon that went boom, but now the cannon hurts a lot more and is invisible; it is much more subtle and much more pernicious and dangerous."[105]

Though Hondo's and Maldoror's cinematic styles differed considerably from Sembène's, they aligned with him on the matter of cinema's revolutionary purpose.[106] The general message of the JCC was that films that did not engage their audience politically were not welcome. The JCC thus became a bastion for the type of militant culture that thrived in Rabat in the early 1960s and in the margins of the PANAF in the late 1960s. This culture was one of revolutionary militancy, one that lauded military action, celebrated guns, and appealed primarily to male participants and spectators.

The JCC, however, seems to have had a bit more room for female participation than *Souffles* and the Off-PANAF. Perhaps this was thanks to Maldoror's constant struggle to portray, collaborate with, and train women, or because Bourguiba had indeed made Tunisia a more welcoming country for all women—at least, more so than Morocco and Algeria. The women around *Souffles* mainly took on secretarial roles, and those who appeared in the accounts of the PANAF were largely sexual representations of their race and nationality. At the JCC, however, not only were there some women participants, but many of the male filmmakers I interviewed discussed their desire to film movies about the social condition of women. Tunisian directors Abdellatif Ben Amar and Hassan Daldoul explained that they did not want to make movies glorifying Bourguiba's struggle for Tunisian independence; instead, they wanted to make movies defending women's causes. Both men expressed the same sort of nostalgia I had encountered when interviewing PANAF spectators, likewise noting the change in women's clothing and yearning for a time when women could walk around Tunis in miniskirts. Perhaps these men thought that this was the type of information a young French female researcher would want to hear—in any case, when talking about women's causes and women's rights, the male JCC participants only brought up a woman's right to dress as she pleased. This was not an issue at the top of Sarah Maldoror's agenda, however, who fought instead for women to find a place in the filmmaking world.

THE PAN-AFRICAN FEDERATION OF FILMMAKERS

Perhaps one of the largest and most enduring projects the JCC inspired was the creation of the Fédération Panafricaine des Cinéastes (Pan-African Federation of Filmmakers; FEPACI). Though many Algerian artists and filmmakers claim that the FEPACI was founded at the Pan-African festival of Algiers in 1969, Tunisian director Férid Boughedir insisted that though the idea was introduced in Algeria, it was at the 1970 JCC that the federation was born.[107] The real accomplishment of the FEPACI, according to Boughedir, was to unite filmmakers from different linguistic zones. This union worked because they were fighting a common enemy, he said: "the big Western film distribution companies that used African theaters to make their own films profitable and used all sorts of insidious methods to extinguish the budding cinema that is African cinema."[108] The members of FEPACI viewed companies such as the French Compagnie Africaine Cinématographique Industrielle et Commerciale (COMACICO) and the Society d'Exploitation Cinématographique Africaine (SECMA) as their primary enemies and endeavored to nationalize their cinemas, create their own distribution networks, and affiliate with African institutions such as the OAU. FEPACI members pressured their governments directly to nationalize the African distribution and exhibition sectors, which would break foreign monopolies and give African films a chance to appear on African screens. The FEPACI had some success: both Upper Volta and Mali nationalized their cinematographic industries in 1970; Senegal and Benin created their own distribution houses in 1974; and Madagascar nationalized its screens in 1975. Western distribution companies were enraged by these actions and launched a series of attacks on independent African cinematic industries, eventually managing to force many countries to reprivatize their screens or close their cinemas altogether.

Because most of the filmmakers and producers who created the FEPACI were leftists and Pan-Africanist members of the Maghreb Generation, the FEPACI's primary mission was to unite the continent and to use film to mobilize the African masses against neocolonialism and authoritarianism, which is why the FEPACI initially sought to be affiliated with the OAU.[109] "It was strange to see a professional federation of filmmakers have that much power," Boughedir noted. "The FEPACI was everywhere, . . . it had the status of observing member at the OAU, it had open access to all African governments, . . . it drafted bills, it was active, powerful."[110]

In January 1975, the filmmakers of the FEPACI met for a second congress in Algiers to clarify the federation's vision for the role of African filmmakers vis-à-vis their people. African filmmakers must refuse the stereotypical image of the solitary and marginal creator, resolved the Algiers Charter on African Cinema. "The African filmmakers must, on the contrary, consider themselves a creative artisan at the service of their people."[111] Thus, according to the charter, African filmmakers needed to be in solidarity with filmmakers from across the Third World who struggled against imperialism. Money should never be a gauge of success, warned the federation; instead, a successful African film should express the needs and aspirations of the African people. It appears that at the congress several filmmakers denounced movies such as *Pousse pousse* (1975) by Daniel Kamwa and *Le bracelet de bronze* (1974) by Tidiane Aw for being too sensationalist and not committed to the revolution against neocolonialism. On the other hand, the filmmakers present at the conference praised the films of Ousmane Sembène and Med Hondo because they prioritized the instructional use of cinema over its commercial and dramatic value.[112]

The manifesto ended by cautioning African governments to free African filmmakers from the shackles of censorship, for the "freedom of expression for film-makers is in fact one of the prerequisite conditions of their ability to contribute to the development of a critical understanding among the masses and the blossoming of their potentialities."[113] Indeed, one of the other main enemies of the FEPACI, which Boughedir did not mention in our interview, were African states themselves. The FEPACI stood firmly against any type of censorship that could "impoverish the creativity of the filmmaker and the democratic and responsible practice of his or her job."[114] While filmmakers struggled for the nationalization of distribution and exhibition, most resisted nationalizing the production sector. Filmmakers did not want to produce newsreels glorifying their own governments; they wanted—they needed—the freedom to express themselves in a way that did not always please their governments.[115]

In the 1960s and early 1970s, Tahar Cheriaa explained, thanks to a process of collective reflection made possible by the JCC and the FEPACI congresses, African filmmakers were able to make a realistic assessment of the cinematic situation in their own states. They were under the impression, however, that all they needed to do was pair their own desire to make film with that of the state, which they believed was also intent on creating national and Pan-African cinematic industries. "Feeling themselves so rich with things to say and imagining themselves to be free to say them," wrote Cheriaa, "they believed the states to be similarly disposed and never doubted their freedom of action."[116] They had no idea what the reality was, he bemoaned: while the goal of the FEPACI was to help African states nationalize their screens, all the while respecting the filmmakers' creative liberty, it rapidly became clear that many African governments were not working with the same objectives in mind.

The FEPACI was invested in producing Pan-African and revolutionary films, but the governments were generally more interested in nationalistic propaganda films. The Senegalese government, for instance, exported films that Sembène had financed independently, claiming that they were sponsored by the Senegalese government, all the while refusing to show the films on screens within Senegal. Sembène's harsh depictions of life in rural Senegal threatened the image of Senegal that Senghor wanted to circulate domestically. Yet Senghor took pride in having filmmakers of talent to export and showcase abroad; the Senegalese state capitalized on the aesthetic of the Maghreb Generation, the art of revolution, without suffering the consequences of what exhibiting that art domestically would mean for the regime's sovereignty.

Even within the halls of the FEPACI and among friends, accusations of collaboration flew. The shadows of Western distribution companies and controlling African governments lurked everywhere, and many filmmakers were charged with complacency, selling out, or worse, collaboration. Sarah Maldoror, one of the FEPACI's only women filmmakers, never one to mince words, exclaimed in 1972: "The struggle of the colonized peoples of Africa is continuing in solitude. Angolans, Mozambicans, and others are abandoned in a desert of fraternity, and maggoty solidarity. Everybody sympathizes, morally participates in our drama, but, each 'brother' country takes care of their own affairs, so for the safari pictures you can come back later!"[117]

THE JCC AS RED-CARPET REGALIA

In March 1982, the FEPACI met again in Niamey, Niger, to reassess the relationship between states and filmmakers. Members were disappointed in the fact that many African states had only financed films glorifying the government and the nation-state. While at the FEPACI's creation in 1970, as well as the second congress in Algiers in 1975, private companies had been portrayed as the agents of Western imperialism, in 1982 they were described as "economic operators" and portrayed as indispensable to the growth of African film.[118] The rhetoric of the FEPACI had changed. In order to move away from African governments considered too controlling, its leaders fell back into the arms of European cinema companies. Many of the people that I interviewed in 2018 deplored the current state of cinema production in Africa: "All we make now are movies about jihadists and immigrants," bemoaned Daldoul, "what the French are interested in."[119] In the end, wrote Tahar Cheriaa in 1978, "we underestimated the inexhaustible adaptability of the monopolies involved."[120]

Most of the filmmakers, producers, and film aficionados that I interviewed agreed that by the end of the 1970s the JCC had sold out. Explanations as to why differed. To some, such as Abdellatif Ben Amar, it was the creation of the Festival Panafricain du Cinéma et de la Télévision de Ouagadougou (FESPACO), the JCC's twin in Burkina Faso, that brought down Carthage. The FESPACO was founded as an alternative to the JCC, Ben Amar explained, because Carthage was gaining too much traction, so the French helped create the FESPACO—a festival that would promote a less threatening, exclusively Black identity and would no longer bring together the Maghreb Generation. In scholarship on African cinema, the FESPACO now largely dwarfs the JCC, which only appears in the footnotes of African cinema's founding texts.[121]

To others, like Néjib Ayed, it was the Tunisian state that betrayed the JCC by turning it into a stage for Egyptian stars to parade. Toward the end of the 1980s, Tunisian filmmaker Rachid Fachiouk inherited the direction of the festival. Fachiouk had many contacts in the Middle East. Under his supervision, explained Ayed, "we would invite all the Egyptian stars; the Egyptian delegation would come with fifty or sixty people, which was huge. At that point African film became marginal; that's when the big break happened."[122] The JCC's changing message was visible in the festival's program. The programs for the 1966, 1968, 1972, and 1974 festivals, all published by the Tunisian government, did not include any publicity. Starting in 1978, however, the programs, still published by the Tunisian government, contained many advertisements—in fact, the first nine pages of the 1978 program consisted solely of advertisements for hotels, beer, banks, Egyptair, and more. Clearly the years of revolutionary sympathy with the downtrodden were over.

The JCC, like many of the projects that *Maghreb Noir* explores, began as a state-sponsored cultural endeavor, one designed to propagate a certain conception of Pan-Africanism, in line with that of the Tunisian government and with Bourguiba's vision more specifically. But, as this book has illustrated through case studies from across the Maghreb, it was impossible for these young Maghrebi states to control interactions between members of the Maghreb Generation. In the end, the JCC went well beyond the initial desires of the Tunisian state, becoming a space for members of the Maghreb Generation to politicize themselves and others through film and in so doing create a dissident Pan-Africanism. Like their militant-poet peers, they argued that their mission was to use art to push African people to action, to drive them to reclaim power from the postcolonial states. It is true that by the 1980s the JCC had forsaken its original mission and espoused all the glitz and glamour of film festivals around the world. But the story of the JCC in the late 1960s and 1970s demonstrates that for a moment postcolonial culture did not belong only to the postcolonial states. Thanks to members of the Maghreb Generation such as Maldoror, Hondo, and their peers, postcolonial culture also thrived in the margins of state-sponsored events, taking advantage of the capital that the state invested while finding alternative sites to express outrage at the state's growing authoritarianism and searching for ways to combat it.

CONCLUSION

In the roar of weapons that are ripping apart the colonial night, young poets fight in the heart of the *maquis*. They know the necessary synthesis of political engagement and the inevitable need to say the truth, the just, the beautiful.

MARIO DE ANDRADE, 1966

BETWEEN 1976 AND 2003, Ted Joans traveled the world with something unusual in his luggage: an exquisite corpse. Creating an exquisite corpse is a game in which each participant takes turns drawing (or writing) on a piece of paper, folding it to conceal their contribution, and then passing it on to the next player. Surrealists first popularized the game, which has taken many different forms throughout the world today. Ted Joans's exquisite corpse, titled *Long-Distance,* was an oddity even for the genre. For nearly thirty years, Ted Joans transported *Long-Distance* from Marrakesh to Mexico City asking militant-artists from across the world to add to the drawing. *Long-Distance* includes 132 contributions from the myriad militant-artists Joans met throughout his travels, including *Souffles* writer André Laude, Mozambican painter Malangatana Ngwenya, and Moroccan painter Ahmed Yacoubi, as well as some names that may be more familiar to an American audience, such as white American writer and cartoonist Shel Silverstein and white American poet Allen Ginsberg. The result is a dizzying, thirty-foot-long ribbon of black ink on perforated computer printer paper.

I was fortunate to be able to view *Long-Distance* at an exhibit at the Metropolitan Museum of Fine Arts in New York City titled *Surrealism beyond Borders*. Walking along the 20-or-so-foot glass case in which *Long-Distance* was exhibited, one could appreciate the network that Joans captured with the piece. The drawing styles and subjects were radically different, ranging from the absurd and pornographic to the abstract and poetic. What is most striking, perhaps, about the piece is that it decenters Europe in the surrealist network. Joans gave each participant the same amount of space and the same instructions, letting artists from Morocco and Mozambique have an equal say in the project. This was also the goal of the organizers of *Surrealism beyond Borders*, to move away from a "Paris-centered viewpoint, to shed light on Surrealism's significance around the world from the 1920s until the late 1950s."[1] Surrealism was a shared means of revolt against the status quo, the exhibition's organizers argued, and could not fit into a simple linear trajectory of influence. The organizers of *Surrealism beyond Borders* acknowledged the importance of centers such as Paris and thinkers such as André Breton for the surrealist movement, but the exhibition untethered surrealism from both the city and the man, and in the process highlighted connections, geographies, and relationships that were yet underexplored.

Maghreb Noir does something similar. The militant-artists of the Maghreb Generation were influenced by the works of André Breton, the Beat poets, and the French existentialists. They traveled to Paris, London, and New York, read the international news, and listened to foreign radio stations. But what they yearned for, above all, was to connect with their peers. Again, in the words of Ousmane Sembène: "Let's not talk about the West. Let's talk about us."[2] The Maghreb Generation turned away from the Western interlocutor, pivoting inward to talk among themselves. But their refusal to comply with the terms of the former colonial powers did not mean that they were duped by their postcolonial states' call for national unity. As the new Maghrebi governments attempted to leverage power on the continent by organizing Pan-African cultural projects such as the PANAF, the members of the Maghreb Generation forged a dissenting Pan-African ideology that wove together poetry, film, anti-neocolonial writing, and direct political action against state authoritarianism. *Maghreb Noir* moves away from interrogating the persistence of the colonial discourse and North-South relationships and focuses instead on conversations occurring on the ground between members of the Maghreb Generation concerning the future of the postcolonial world.[3]

These men and women, many of whom have never been the subject of historical inquiry, spent their lives—and sometimes lost them—fighting for a postcolonial order in which they had agency, freedom, and beauty, regardless of manmade borders. Because many of them were poets and filmmakers, their demands may seem lyrical, nebulous, or even quixotic to historians who favor the authority of state archives. Perhaps this is why such figures as Jean Sénac, René Depestre, Sarah Maldoror, Med Hondo, Mario de Andrade, and Ted Joans have been restricted to the realm of literary critique or to art exhibitions, having yet to garner a prime spot in the historiography. It is my hope that this monograph has firmly placed them in scholarly conversations about Pan-Africanism. *Maghreb Noir* reveals that art is not antithetical, or a mere handmaiden, to politics. Along with their careers as militant poets and filmmakers, these men and women engaged in direct political action. In Rabat, Algiers, and Tunis, they participated in protests, shipped armaments, conducted military training, organized secret meetings, and disseminated banned literature—in short, they performed the work of revolution. By separating artistic production from political engagement, scholars have neglected the militant-artists who straddled the two worlds.

Another reason for the Maghreb Generation's anonymity has been scholars' marginalization of North Africa in Middle Eastern, Black Atlantic, and African history. That invisibility is what motivated me to start this project over eight years ago. At the time, there seemed to be a push to start including the Maghreb in histories of Africa. However, the Maghreb is still absent from many African history courses, while many academic positions are still advertised as professorships in sub-Saharan African history.[4] And yet the Maghreb is now, and has always been, a hub for people from Africa. Writing the history of the Maghreb's Africanity is essential to understanding the contemporary Maghreb and the present-day political demands of Black North Africans together with the thousands of Black migrants in Algiers, Tangier, and Tunis today.

Bridging the Saharan divide, the work of the Maghreb Generation demonstrates that scholars of the postcolonial period would do well to transcend linguistic, national, and racial divisions in the study of Africa and instead explore the ways in which individuals have always evaded the too easy appeal of restrictive categories. While the members of the Maghreb Generation sometimes envisioned themselves as part of a national community, they were just as likely to imagine themselves as part of a Pan-African community. Like many of us today, they conceived of their identities as intersectional. They spoke Arabic, Portuguese, English, French, Wolof, Kimbundu, and more, mixing these languages in their poetry and films. In many ways, they were the embodiment of the type of Creole community philosopher Édouard Glissant yearned for in *Poetics of Relation*—a community that refused to reduce itself to a single nature or single origin.[5] The Maghreb Generation annihilated all false universality, did away with the desire or need for a European audience, and celebrated its creolity (*creolité*) through the creation of art pieces like Joans's dizzying exquisite corpse.

My goal in this book, much like that of the organizers of *Surrealism beyond Borders*, is not to write a definitive history of postcolonial Pan-Africanism in the Maghreb, but rather to explore relationships, unearth archives, and highlight characters who have too often fallen through the cracks of our understanding of postcolonial Africa. I hope this will be just the beginning. The Maghreb Generation was a fluctuating group of individuals, of whom this book only highlights a fraction, who fought for a Pan-African future in the Maghreb; I hope others will add to this history.

ARCHIVING THE MAGHREB NOIR

The dreams of a transnational Pan-African project that motivated the men and women who are the subject of this book have collapsed. Rabat, Algiers, and Tunis have all lost their status as havens for the Maghreb Generation. As the 1970s turned into the 1980s, freedom of political and artistic expression was gradually crushed under the iron fist of the new postcolonial states of Hassan II, Houari Boumédiène, and Habib Bourguiba. The Soviets and Americans waged proxy wars in Angola, Mozambique, and elsewhere across the African continent, taking advantage of divisions between various factions all vying for power in the newly liberated states. These conflicts put an end to most hopes for Pan-African unity.[6] With the end of the Cold War, capitalism won the battle of ideologies, and both Morocco and Tunisia became playgrounds for wealthy European tourists and retirees, while Algeria sank into a decade-long civil war that has left Algerians reeling to this day and its artists looking for opportunities outside the country.[7]

The threat that the members of the Maghreb Generation posed to the Maghrebi governments has all but died out. In fact, in the past couple of decades, many Pan-African revolutionaries from the 1960s have been retrieved from collective amnesia by the very governments that imprisoned, tortured, and murdered them. In Morocco, *Souffles/Anfas* is no longer taboo; until the late 1990s, it was almost impossible to find copies of the journal, but between 1997 and 2004 two American professors, Thomas C. Spear and Anne George, digitized *Souffles/Anfas*, and the Moroccan Royal Library uploaded it to their website in 2010. The journal has now entered the pantheon of Moroccan national culture and is being reclaimed by the heir—King Mohammed VI—to the Moroccan government that imprisoned and tortured the journal's members. When I traveled to Tunis in November 2018 for the twenty-ninth edition of theJCC, the opening speeches and remarks all underscored the deep friendship between the Tunisian state and liberation movements from across Africa. Posters of *Soleil Ô* and *Sambizanga* were framed for all to see in the new, gigantic, and somewhat empty Cité de la Culture in downtown Tunis. Revolutionaries are now sexy.

The Maghrebi governments' renewed interest in their postcolonial Pan-Africanism has helped retrieve valuable archival documents. When, in 2009, the Algerian government organized a second Pan-African festival, pamphlets from the 1969 iteration were dug up and reprinted and William Klein's 1969 documentary on the PANAF, once very difficult to find, was restored with the help of the European TV channel ARTE.[8] The lack of historical research on the lives and work of the militant-artists of the Maghreb Generation has left a vacuum that the Maghrebi governments have moved happily to fill.

When I was in Rabat in February 2018, the Moroccan Royal Library hosted a conference on Morocco's assistance to the former Portuguese colonies in southern Africa, under the patronage of King Mohammed VI. El Mostafa El Ktiri, the Moroccan high commissioner to the former members of the resistance and the liberation army, opened the conference with a speech on the importance of shared memory. "We must not miss a chance to say and to repeat a certain number of truths about our collective memory and about Morocco's efforts for the liberation of these African countries [under Portuguese colonialism]," stressed El Ktiri.[9] He also expressed the Moroccan government's interest in projecting a uniform conception of the past that could serve a political point. To El Ktiri, historical research was important insofar as it allowed the Moroccan government to mine the past for evidence of Morocco's positive influence on other African countries—in other words, the Moroccan government's goal in resuscitating this "shared memory" should not be curiosity or the desire to question certain aspects of Moroccan history, but rather to serve the Moroccan government's political needs in the present.[10] Never did El Ktiri mention tensions between the Luso-African militants in Rabat and the Moroccan government; on the contrary, he lauded Moroccan king Hassan II for his total acceptance of all the Luso-Africans, never once indicating the reasons why the militant-artists eventually deserted Morocco.

The problem with leaving the Pan-African archives of the postcolonial Maghreb in the hands of government officials is that it will undoubtedly obscure the story of dissent against the postcolonial states' co-optation of the movement. As this book has demonstrated, while militant-artists of the Maghreb Generation used the states' Pan-African celebrations as points of convergence to meet and talk, they did not espouse the authoritarian tendencies of these states. In the margins of state-sponsored events such as the PANAF and the JCC, they created their own Pan-Africanism of dissent.

The archives of the Maghreb Generation are difficult to find; after all, the Maghrebi states had no interest in conserving these traces of dissent. Letters, poems, and drawings have disappeared, and the Maghrebi governments have confiscated and destroyed reels of film, zines, and manifestos. Many of the militant-artists of the 1960s, 1970s, and 1980s are aging, losing their memories, or now dead: Marcelino dos Santos died on February 10, 2020; Néjib Ayed, whom I was lucky to interview in June 2018, passed away in the fall of 2019, just before the thirtieth edition of the JCC; Sarah Maldoror, whom I interviewed in the summer of 2018, died of COVID-19 in March 2020. These men and women leave behind records that their spouses, children, or grandchildren are unsure how to process or share. Many of the descendants are aware of the historical significance of these items but do not have the infrastructure, money, or technical knowledge to sort and archive them. I fear that we may lose more valuable documentation if scholars and institutions do not help with this colossal enterprise.

In January 2022, I visited an exhibition at the Palais de Tokyo in Paris dedicated to Sarah Maldoror, titled *Sarah Maldoror: Cinema tricontinental*.[11] The exhibition included clips from Maldoror's films, letters, photographs, and art inspired by her work. According to the curators, one of the goals of the exhibition was to help the visitor understand that Maldoror's life was not linear but an archipelago of stories, people, and places. Much like the conservators of *Surrealism beyond Borders*, the *Sarah Maldoror* curators meant to bring visitors into the archive so that they might witness its richness, colorfulness, and messiness. My hope in ending this book on the question of archives is once again to highlight that *Maghreb Noir* is not intended as a definitive history of Pan-Africanism in the postcolonial Maghreb but that many more archives exist in people's attics, basements, and in their minds. It is our responsibility to find them.

ACKNOWLEDGMENTS

THE BACKBONE OF THIS BOOK are the people whom I interviewed and those who helped me on the ground to identify sources. The thirty-three people I interviewed volunteered their time and expertise, often inviting me into their homes and offering tea and sweets. I am grateful for their trust. I also want to thank those who do not appear in the list of interviewees but who took the time to have long conversations with me over coffee or tea, in Casablanca, Algiers, Tunis, and Paris. In particular, I would like to thank Kmar Bendana, Sayda Bourguiba, Morgan Corriou, Olivier Hadouchi, Claire Marynower, Maati Monjib, Kenza Sefraoui, and Ikbal Zalila for their assistance. A special thank-you to Insaf Machta and Pierre and Geneviève Masson, who provided housing and sustenance during my research sojourns. Thank you to the staff at the Glycines in Algiers—it was such a wonderful place to work. Thank you to Anouchka de Andrade and Henda Ducados for rereading my work, checking for factual inaccuracies, and allowing me to reprint their parents' documents. Thank you to Denis Martinez for allowing me to reproduce his beautiful artwork here. Thank you to Abdellatif Laâbi for allowing me to reproduce the covers and art of *Souffles.*

I could have not completed this project without the generous funding of multiple institutions. Thanks to the Foreign Language and Area Studies Fellowships and the American Institute of Maghreb Studies for subsidizing my research. Thank you to the staff of the countless libraries and archives that I visited during this research. Without their expertise and their willingness to forgo some of the bureaucracy, I would never have been able to gather all the information that I present in this book.

I have shared parts of this project at conferences across Europe, North Africa, and the United States. Thank you to those who organized those panels, who offered tips and critiques, and who helped publish the proceedings from those conferences. In that respect, I extend my sincere thanks to Samuel Anderson, Aomar Boum, Jeffrey James Byrne, Laryssa Chomiak, Muriam Haleh Davis, Yoav Di-Capua, Frank Gerits, Matteo Grilli, Chouki El Hamel, Kai Krienke, Afifa Ltifi, Nadia Marzouki, Pascal Menoret, and Cyrus Schayegh. Thank you to Hisham Aïdi, Nimrod Ben-Zeev, Caitlin Collis, Morgan Corriou, Lacy Feigh, Khaled Lyamlahy, and Marlen Rosas for carefully reading and commenting on several chapters of this book, or in Caitlin and Hisham's case, every single chapter. A heartfelt thank you to Brahim El Guabli, who has edited my work, written recommendation letters, and included me in every exciting new project he starts. Thank you to the *Arab Studies Journal* and the editors of *Visions of African Unity* for permitting to reprint here portions of articles I contributed.

I would like to thank the many teachers and mentors who have guided my work and channeled my enthusiasm into scholarly work. Naghmeh Sohrabi and Jocelyne Dakhlia were rigorous and generous mentors to me in my first years as a budding historian. Thank you to my Arabic teachers in Syria, Lebanon, and more recently to Atika Mekki for teaching me Algerian Darijah. The bulk of the research for this book was done at the University of Pennsylvania, under the mentorship of Cheikh Babou, whose intellect and rigor have been an inspiration for me throughout my career. Thank you to Eve Troutt Powell for her caring support and for training me as a cultural historian. And thank you to Roquinaldo Ferreira for his careful edits and comments on chapters and book proposals, and for his unfailingly enthusiastic support. Lee Cassanelli was always a generous and caring mentor, happy to provide me with sustenance in the form of breakfasts and lunches. My time at the University of Pennsylvania has been marked by many members of the current (and former) UPenn faculty and staff. I'm especially grateful to Ali Al-Dinar, Octavia Carr, John Ghazvinian, Peter Holquist, Lydie Moudileno, Benjamin Nathans, and Joan Plonski. UPenn would never have been as much fun or as intellectually stimulating without the friendships of everyone I met there, in particular Beeta Baghoolizadeh, Nimrod Ben-Zeev, Ezgi Çakmak, Caitlin Collis, Lacy Feigh, Ali Karjoo-Ravary, Rasul Miller, and Marlen Rosas. Thank you to the students that I taught at UPenn and Suffolk, who helped guide my thinking, asked probing questions, and reminded me what fun it is to teach.

Thank you to my editor at Stanford University Press, Kate Wahl, who believed in this project from the beginning and guided me through the entire process with generosity and expertise. I am grateful to the anonymous readers of the press for their plentiful and insightful comments on the manuscript. And to all the staff of SUP, including Gigi Mark, Christine Gever, and Marie-Catherine Pavel, thank you for making this a tangible book and not just a word document in the volatile Cloud.

Countless friends have supported me through the completion of this book. To all my old friends in France, in particular Marion Muscat and Eva Douaisi, who have fed me and housed me in Paris, taken me on vacations, and made me laugh for twenty years. Friends in the United States have made this country a new home for me; thank you to my Philadelphia, Los Angeles, and Boston communities (you know who you are). A special thank-you to Rivka Maizlish, who has always been one of my go-to editors for her amusing comments and love of writing. Thank you to my friends in Lebanon, in particular Adnan Akkad, who helped me work through some particularly difficult Arabic sources. And to my new friends and colleagues at Suffolk, including Bob Allison, Robert Hannigan, Michal Ben-Joseph Hirsch, Katy Lasdow, Michèle Plott, and Pat Reeve, for being so supportive as I finished this book.

Thank you to my parents, John Tolan and Michelle Szkilnik, who read the entire book, let me stay at their house during parts of my research, took me to the Algerian desert, always sent me articles they felt were relevant, taught me how to have fun and do work at the same time, and generally were great examples of how to be a scholar one would actually want to hang out with. Thank you to my sister, Marie Tolan, for helping me overcome almost all the anxieties brought on by academia. Thank you to my in-laws, Gloria Ramirez and Hailey Suárez, for always being supportive. And thank you to all the members of the Tolan and Szkilnik clans, and in particular to my goddaughter Maria Bardou, who was visiting as I completed this book.

And finally, to my wife, Camille Suárez. She read and line-edited this entire manuscript, visited me in Morocco and France, cooked for me, brought me flowers, and let me borrow her clothing, all the while writing her own book, getting jobs, and inspiring students from Los Angeles to Boston.

NOTES

All translations are mine, unless otherwise noted. For the Arabic transliteration I have adopted the guidelines put forth by the International Journal of Middle East Studies (IJMES) for the names of articles and books but have kept the most common spelling for people's names and for the names of organizations. Thank you to Brahim El Guabli for his help with the transliterations. All mistakes or inconsistencies in translation or transliteration are mine and mine alone.

Introduction

1. Ben Jelloun, "Entretien avec Ousmane Sembène," *Souffles*, nos. 16–17 (1970), 50. All citations to *Souffles* and *Anfas* may be found on the Royal Library of Morocco website, at http://bnm.bnrm.ma:86/ListeVol.aspx?IDC=3 and http://bnm.bnrm.ma:86/ListeVol.aspx?IDC=4.

2. Ibid.

3. Pamphlet published by the Algerian government for the PANAF, in Ted Joans, "Black Man's Guide to Africa," p. 64, BANC MSS 99/244, box 5, Bancroft Library, University of California, Berkeley (hereafter "Bancroft Library").

4. Hourari Boumédiène, in 1st Festival Culturel Panafricain Algiers 1969 / *La culture africaine: Le symposium d'Alger, 21 juillet–1er aout 1969* (Algiers: SNED, 1969), 15.

5. The FLN was an Algerian nationalist organization that fought against French colonial power, assisted by its military branch, the ALN. Upon independence the FLN crushed all other Algerian nationalist organizations, such as the Union Démocratique du Manifeste Algérien (UDMA) led by Ferhat Abbas and the Mouvement National Algérien (MNA) led by Messali Hadj, taking full control of the Algerian government and ruling over the country through a single-party system until 1989. See Malika Rahal's excellent article "Comment faire l'histoire de l'Al-

gérie indépendante." For a different history of independence in Algeria, see Rahal's recent book *Algérie 1962: Une histoire populaire,* as well as her history of the UDMA, *L'UDMA et les Udmistes.*

6. Yoav Di-Capua, *No Exit,* 14–16.

7. In his excellent 2016 monograph, *Mecca of Revolution,* historian Jeffrey James Byrne contends that the idealistic phase of decolonization in Algeria, in which a diversity of political ideals mingled and coexisted, ended as early as 1965. In the Third World order, Byrne claims, sovereignty and national authority were valued above all; "the state had become not only the sole legitimate manifestation of national liberation or 'freedom' but also the irreplaceable instrument of humanity's aspirations, for the wretched of the earth at least" (291). While Byrne limits his analysis to state actors, historian Yoav Di-Capua, tells the stories of a generation of Arab existentialists who did not hesitate to confront the "ubiquity of patriarchal norms, sexual repression, political impasse, state authoritarianism, violence and an overall absence of freedom and possibilities for self-liberation" (*No Exit,* 128). Indeed, intellectuals and artists repeatedly challenged nation-states' authoritarianism, careful not to confuse the construction of the postcolonial identity with a brand of nationalism that condoned exclusion and repression. Sovereignty and national liberation appealed to militant-artists only insofar as they did not interfere with their right to speak, create, and recite. Much like the Czech dissidents that historian Jonathan Bolton introduces in his *Worlds of Dissent,* these militant-artists "uncomfortably straddled two spaces—the space of a universal public, open to all interested parties, and that of a bounded public, theoretically open to all but also defined by particular customs, value, and goals" (16). For a discussion of the process of intellectual decolonization as autonomous from the state, see Wilder, *Freedom Time*; and Kumar, *Radical Equality.*

8. I use the term "Pan-Africanism" to refer to the desire to create an African cultural, political, and economic union. While presenting versions of this book at conferences, I have been asked why I choose to use the term "Pan-Africanism" rather than "Third-Worldism." My interlocutors point to the presence of peoples from Vietnam, ties with Cuba, and other signs that the Maghreb Generation network was not limited to the African continent. While I understand their argument, I prefer "Pan-Africanism" because that is the term used by my sources, even as they include militant-artists from Asia and Latin America in their networks. Their use of "Pan-Africanism" reflects the centrality of the African continent in the struggle for the postcolonial future. In the intellectual and artistic struggle against colonialism and neocolonialism, Africa was at the forefront.

9. In this book, I use the transliteration "Maghreb" for the Arabic term *Al-Maghrib.* Although "Maghrib" would be a more accurate transliteration, "Maghreb" is most commonly used in English-language scholarship.

10. See Sadai, "Racisme anti-Noirs au Maghreb: Dévoilement(s) d'un tabou," *Hérodote* 180, no. 1 (2021): 131–148; and Salah Trabelsi, "Racisme anti-Noir: 'Comment le Maghreb en est-il venu à rejeter son africanité?,'" *Le Monde*, February 24, 2019, https://www.lemonde.fr/afrique/article/2019/02/24/racisme-anti-noir-comment-le-maghreb-en-est-il-venu-a-rejeter-son-africanite_5427702_3212.html/.

11. Mrad Dali, "Les mobilisations des 'noirs tunisiens'"; Pouessel, "Les marges renaissantes." See also the BBC documentary by Nareeman Dosa, "Black and Arab: The Hidden Reality of Racism in Tunisia," BBC News, August 10, 2022, https://www.bbc.co.uk/programmes/pocs4kg8.

12. Some titles focusing on trans-Saharan trade include Ahmida, *Bridges across the Sahara*; Austen, *Trans-Saharan Africa in World History*; Cheikh, "La caravane et la caravelle"; Lydon, *On Trans-Saharan Trails*; and McDougall and Scheele, *Saharan Frontiers*. Other scholars have examined the construction and fluctuation of racial categories in the Sahara and the Sahel—that is, in the spaces of intersection between Black, White, Arab, Amazigh, and more. Some titles include but are not limited to Hall, *A History of Race in Muslim West Africa*; El Hamel, *Black Morocco*; Hunwick and Troutt Powell, *Same but Different*; Lewis, *Race and Slavery in the Middle East*; and Troutt-Powell, *A Different Shade of Colonialism*. There are many historians and anthropologists who study the history of Black Maghrebis, often placing their demands in the context of the Maghrebi regimes' attempts at making the nations more homogenous in the postcolonial period. See the works of Chouki El Hamel, Afifa Ltfi, M'hamed Oualdi, Stephanie Pouessel, and Marta Scaglioni, among others.

The postcolonial history of the Maghreb remains largely the history of the construction of the Algerian, Moroccan, and Tunisian nation-states. However, as established by scholars such as Malika Rahal ("Local Approach to the UDMA"), who reveals the diversity of political ideals within the Algerian resistance itself, it is important to historicize the diversity of the Maghreb and to show that if the Maghreb states have propagated an image of a homogenous North African nation, many North Africans had other visions for the postcolonial Maghreb. It is time to write the history of the postcolonial Maghreb with multiple identities, including African. See Aseraf's *Sur les traces de Messaoud Djebari* and El Guabli's dossier "Tankraa Tamazight" in the online journal *Jadaliyya*.

13. See Byrne, *Mecca of Revolution*; El Guabli, "Refiguring Pan-Africanism through Algerian-Moroccan Competitive Festivals"; and Lydon, "Writing Trans-Saharan History."

14. Researchers who work on racial dynamics in the Sahara are doing important work. Indeed, while debates over the grammar of race are omnipresent in the European and American press, it is important to historicize this grammar. As historians of Africa and the Middle East, we demonstrate that the ethnic and racial

categories that European and French audiences conceive of as immutable have a relatively short history and are directly linked to the history of colonialism. When the French Empire declared control of West Africa in 1895, it fought to separate the region from its North African colonies. This is not to say that racial hierarchies did not exist before the arrival of the French. In *A History of Race in Muslim West Africa*, historian Bruce Hall reveals the dense tapestry of religious, ethno-linguistic, and racial hierarchies that existed in the Sahel region well before the arrival of the French colonial power. The Sahel participated in a large cosmopolitan network, Hall explains, connected "by shared literacy in Arabic and faith in Islam. As such, Sahelian racial thought cannot be understood as 'traditional' any more than it can be deemed a Middle Eastern or European construct. Sahelian intellectuals made active choices in reshaping concepts and practices derived from both local and transregional sources" (317). When the French conquered the Sahel, Hall argues, they were unable to grasp the complex hierarchies already present and settled for a simplistic distinction between North, "white," Africa and South, "Black," Africa. As the French gradually took control of the Maghreb and most of West Africa, they unknowingly reinforced a perception of Blackness that was already latent throughout the region. They drew a line between the Arabs and the Blacks but also between "Arab Islam" and "Black Islam."

In a 2005 article titled "Writing Trans-Saharan History: Methods, Sources and Interpretations across the African Divide," UCLA historian Ghislaine Lydon argues that the contemporary North-South division resulted in part from policies that dramatized the differences between "white" and "Black" Africans. "While explorations allowed for a better understanding of the area," writes Lydon, "the Sahara proved a difficult world for the French to grasp" (312). Obsessed with classifying spaces, races, and species, Lydon explains, the French willingly overlooked the nuances in local understandings of ethnicity and race and created taxonomies and nomenclatures of their own. They reified the Sahara as a continental barrier between "white" and "Black" Africa. But, as historian Jean-Louis Triaud explains, the division between "white" and "Black" Africa was not a simple misunderstanding. In *Le crépuscule des affaires musulmanes en AOF* (500–506), Triaud shows how the colonial administration used multiple tools to reinforce these racial divisions. For one, they kept the administrations and armies separate. As early as 1848, Algeria, the jewel of the French Empire, fell under the control of the Ministry of the Interior. The minister of foreign affairs oversaw the Tunisian (1881) and Moroccan (1912) protectorates. The West African colonies, however, among them Senegal, were the Ministry of Colonies' responsibility (1895). By dividing the administrations in this way, the French government made sure that colonial administrators would come from different schools and have minimal contact with the administrators in different ministries. The separation was thus complete; the French built an institutional barrier between these territories whose frontiers had previously been permeable. In 1904, when the French took control of Mauritania, they privileged the Moorish military and intellectual elite, exempting them from military service and certain forms of taxation, among other things. By implementing these kinds of petty privileges, explains Triaud, the colonial authorities reinforced the distinction between Arabs and Blacks, between white Africa and Black Africa. See also Hisham Aïdi's excellent summary of the divisions between Africa and the Middle East in regard to scholarship and intellectual history, "And the Twain Shall Meet."

15. The canonical story of Pan-Africanism starts in 1900 with the First Pan-African Congress and ends in the early 1960s with African nations attaining independence, and includes only a handful of characters, mostly British and American bourgeois Black men. See, among others, Ajala, *Pan-Africanism*; Esedebe, *Pan-Africanism*; Geiss, *The Pan-African Movement*; and Walters, *Pan Africanism in the African Diaspora*. Scholarship on Pan-Africanism has largely ignored intellectual and political movements striving for an African homeland (whether imaginary or institutional) prior to 1880 or post-1960. A few contemporary scholars are now reconstructing early forms of Pan-Africanism and reframing the Pan-Africanist narrative within a wider chronology; one example is Toyin Falola and Kwame Essien's edited volume *Pan-Africanism, and the Politics of African Citizenship and Identity*, published in 2014. Looking at reverse migrations, this collection of essays demonstrates how these migratory patterns "epitomize the power of alliances, the significance of unity, the influence of the memory of a homeland, contradictions, and contestation about the idea of 'return,' and the enduring legacy of Pan-Africanism or lack thereof" (2). In the past couple of decades, some American scholars, including Michael Gomez, Hisham Aïdi, and Sohail Daulatzai, primarily interested in the study of Islam in the United States, have begun to chart the connections between Black Americans and the Middle East, in which they include North Africa. This important work constructs an intellectual history of the African Diaspora and reveals the global networks of ideas in which these communities participated. These works include but are not limited to Aïdi and Marable, *Black Routes to Islam*; Daulatzai, *Black Star, Crescent Moon*; Gomez, *Black Crescent*; Jackson, *Islam and the Blackamerican*; and McAlister, "One Black Allah." Historian Robin D. Kelley has published many excellent books about Black cultural networks that span the Atlantic and include North Africa, including *Africa Speaks, America Answers* and *Freedom Dreams*.

16. In his seminal book *The Black Atlantic: Modernity and Double Consciousness* (1993), Paul Gilroy develops the concept of the Black Atlantic, a "single, complex unit of analysis," which historians must use to restore Black contributions and contributors to the modern world. Gilroy demonstrates the cruciality of "middle -passages" and of the ship—as a political and cultural site, a new chronotype for

the shaping of modern Black identities on both sides of the Atlantic. In the triangle of the Black Atlantic, however, Gilroy examines only two axes, Africa to America and America to Europe, and one language, English. In *The Practice of Diaspora: Literature, Translation, and the Rise of Black Internationalism* (2003), Brent Hayes Edwards expands on Gilroy's Black Atlantic and retraces the encounters between Black intellectuals from both the anglophone and francophone worlds in Paris, arguing that Paris allowed "boundary crossing, conversations, and collaborations that were available nowhere else to the same degree" (4). Edwards's and Gilroy's work, as well the work of historians in the Black Paris or Black London subgenre, have transformed the history of the Atlantic into a story that highlights Black crossings and encounters. Two of the founding works on Pan-African thought in Paris are Michel Fabre's *From Harlem to Paris* and the late Tyler Stovall's excellent *Paris Noir: African Americans in the City of Lights.* Works on these Black Atlantic connections also include, among others, Archer-Straw, *Negrophilia*; Clarke and Thomas, *Globalization and Race*; Goebel, *Anti-imperial Metropolis*; Matera, *Black London*; Mudimbe, *Surreptitious Speech*; Ndiaye, *La condition noire*; Peabody and Stovall, *The Color of Liberty*; and Sharpley-Whiting, *Négritude Women.*

17. Stovall, *Paris Noir.*

18. In William Gardner Smith's 1963 *The Stone Face*, the protagonist, Simeon Brown, a Black man from Philadelphia, moves to Paris in hopes of finding refuge from the unbearable racism in the United States. He quickly realizes, through interactions with French men and women, that he has nothing to fear: "You understand, we like Negroes here, we don't practice racism in France, it's not like the United States" (208). Simeon eventually grasps that instead French racism targets the Algerians living in Paris. He befriends several Algerians and witnesses the October 1961 Maurice Papon massacre. An Algerian man in a café, angered by Simeon's naive conception of race, chides him: "We're the niggers here! Know what the French call us—*bicot, melon, raton, nor'af.* That means *nigger* in French. Ain't you scared we might rob you? Ain't you appalled by our unpressed clothes, our body odor? No, but seriously, I want to ask you a serious question—would you let your daughter marry one of us?" (57). In the end, Simeon returns to the United States and begins to refer to Black Americans as the Algerians of the United States. In this fascinating novel, not only does Smith shed light on the horrific treatment of Algerians in France, but he also turns Black Americans' conception of race on its head—Algerians become the ultimate victims and those who suffer are, thus, Algerian.

19. Baldwin, *No Name in the Street*, 377. This is a crucial anecdote because, as Tyler Stovall explains in his field-defining book *Paris Noir*, France had always seemed like an appealing place for Black Americans fleeing American white supremacy—many Black Americans mistakenly assumed that white French

people were less racist than their white American counterparts. Baldwin realized, however, that the French were no less racist, simply that their racism was directed toward a different other: the Algerian.

20. The Maghreb Generation's articulation of Blackness as political rather than racial predates British cultural theorist Stuart Hall's coinage of the concept "political blackness" in the 1970s. In the Great Britain of the 1980s, the concept of "political blackness" was all the rage; in a society where Britishness was all too often equated with whiteness, the concept was used to create political solidarity between Black Britons and Asian Britons. Stuart Hall's and the Maghreb Generation's goals were similar: to create solidarity drawing on the internationalist tradition of W. E. B Dubois and Malcolm X. As Malcolm X famously said in a 1964 speech to the Militant Labor Forum of the Socialist Workers Party: "When I say Black, I mean nonwhite. Black, brown, red, or yellow.".

21. See Adi and Sherwood, *The 1945 Manchester Pan-African Congress Revisited*; Ashley Farmer, "Black Women Organize for the Future of Pan-Africanism: The Sixth Pan-African Congress" (blog), Black Perspectives, July 3, 2016, https://www.aaihs.org/black-women-organize-for-the-future-of-pan-africanism-the-sixth-pan-african-congress/; and Hodder, "Elusive History of the Pan-African Congress." See also two more recent contributions to the field of Pan-Africanism: Adi, *Pan-Africanism*; and Boukari-Yabara, *Africa Unite!*

22. In 1953, Mário de Andrade and Francisco Tenreiro published the *cuaderno Poesía negra de expressão portuguesa* with the intention of publicizing a specifically Luso-African form of *négritude*.

23. René Depestre, "L'intellectuel révolutionnaire et ses responsabilités envers le Tiers-Monde," *Souffles*, no. 9 (1968): 45.

24. Ted Joans to André Breton, May 5, 1966, Bibliothèque Littéraire Jacques Doucet, Paris.

25. Ibid.

26. Abdellatif Laâbi, "Lisez 'Le petit marocain,'" *Souffles*, no. 2 (1966): 7. See also Ted Joans, "The Negro and the Hippies," box 16:33, BANC MSS 99/244z, Bancroft Library.

27. Mario de Andrade, "Culture et lutte armée," *Souffles*, no. 9 (1968): 54.

28. Abdellatif Laâbi, "Prologue," *Souffles*, no. 1 (1966): 6.

29. Mahler, *From the Tricontinental*, 13.

30. I have chosen to limit my study of the Black Maghreb to Algeria, Morocco, and Tunisia, in order to curb the scope of the book. There is also excellent literature on the role of Cairo in Pan-African networks. The three countries in the western Maghreb have received comparatively limited scholarly inquiry, particularly in anglophone academia. For some titles on Egypt, see Curtis, "'My Heart Is in Cairo'"; Lubin, *Geographies of Liberation*; and Tawfik, "Egypt and the Transfor-

mation of the Pan-African Movement. Another reason for my choice to exclude Cairo from *Maghreb Noir* is that the networks in Cairo were somewhat different from those that evolved in Algiers, Rabat, and Tunis. It seems to me that the Black networks in Cairo were largely dominated by African Americans, whereas the cities of the Maghreb Noir attracted a more diverse range of militant-artists from across the African continent and the African Diaspora. There are probably several explanations for this phenomenon, one of which may be the issue of language: the Maghreb attracted many francophone militant-artists, as well as people for whom learning French would not have been too difficult, for example, the Lusophones. Another reason may be the matter of political news circulation. Gamal Abdel Nasser, who served as president of Egypt between 1954 and 1970, was a charismatic leader who had struck a defiant stance against the colonial powers during the 1956 Suez Canal crisis, thus earning the admiration of many Black radicals in the United States. As Sohail Daulatzai explains, "For Black Muslims in the United States, not only was Egypt the center of African civilization and proof of Black historical greatness, but it was also now a Muslim country. In linking Black greatness and Islam, Nasser and Egypt came to represent a powerful symbol that connected Africa and Asia, a space in which the Muslim Third World and Black Islam forged a defiant anticolonial posture against white supremacy" (*Black Star, Crescent Moon*, 24). Cairo thus became a center for African American expatriates, and in particular for many Muslim Black Americans. The cities of the Black Maghreb did not have a similar religious appeal, or at least not in this period. In fact, the members of the Maghreb Generation showed little interest in religion; rarely did they mention religion or God in their writings, and when they did, it was overwhelmingly in a negative light, as something that restricted their ability to speak or act freely.

31. For extensive descriptions of both men's archival collections, look no further than Alcalay and Tronrud, "Ted Joans: Poet Painter / Former Villager Now / World Traveller"; and Krienke, "Sun under the Weapons."

32. Sarah Maldoror, interview with author.

33. Loi n° 2005-158 du 23 février 2005 portant reconnaissance de la Nation et contribution nationale en faveur des Français rapatriés, Article 4.

Chapter One: Revolt Respects No Borders

1. Noureddine Djoudi, interview with author.

2. State Department to US embassy in Lagos, telegram, November 6, 1970, box 2039, folder Pol ALG-UAR, 1/1/70, WHCF, State Department Telegrams, RG 59, entry 1613; cited in Guettas, *Algeria and the Cold War*, 95.

3. Noureddine Djoudi, interview with author.

4. Ibid.

5. The 1963 War of the Sands started with a series of desert skirmishes along the Algerian-Moroccan desert border—skirmishes that escalated into full-blown conflict between the two young nations at the end of September 1963. The war was a result of the absence of clear delineation between the two countries and of the discovery of important natural resources in the disputed area. The war ended in November 1963, but the rivalry between the two countries continued long after the war, influencing Algeria's policy vis-à-vis the western Sahara. See Vermeren, *Histoire du Maroc depuis l'indépendance*, 36–37.

6. See Byrne, *Mecca of Revolution*; Meghelli, "'A Weapon in Our Struggle for Liberation'" and "From Harlem to Algiers; Mokhtefi, *Algiers, Third World Capital*; Salama, *Alger, la Mecque des révolutionnaires (1962–1974)*; and Westad, *The Global Cold War*. This is not to forget, of course, Matthew Connelly's *A Diplomatic Revolution*, which first demonstrated the international nature of the FLN's fight against the French. Before the postcolonial Algerian state served as a home base for liberation groups from across Africa and the rest of the world, the FLN had already harnessed the nascent forces of globalization to lead a struggle for international public opinion rather than confronting France in a purely military struggle.

7. Leftists from around the world were dubbed the *pieds-rouges* in reference to the French *pieds-noirs*, colonial Algeria's European inhabitants. See Byrne, *Mecca of Revolution*, 5.

8. Scholarship on Morocco's role in assisting the liberation struggles in Africa is sparse compared to the work that lauds Algeria's active participation in training and hosting liberation movements from the Lusophone world and South Africa. Perhaps this is because Morocco's support was more discreet than Algeria's and was a point of contention within the Moroccan administration. It may also be a consequence of a lack of source material: the Moroccan National Archives have kept no records of the government's' financial or administrative assistance to African liberation movements, or at least no archives that are accessible to the public. When I visited the archives in January 2018, the archivists assured me that I would find nothing about the postcolonial period and recommended searching the French Diplomatic Archives in Nantes. Traces of Morocco's involvement are visible within the collection of the Nantes diplomatic archives. Most of the documents were issued by the French embassies in Morocco and were intended for the French foreign services. They carry a strong French bias, of course, and tend to underestimate Morocco's anti-Western tendencies, as it seems France was determined to think of Morocco as an ally in contrast to its bellicose neighbor, Algeria. Other information comes from the offices of the CONPC, established in Casablanca in April 1961, but very few of their pamphlets have been conserved. Together with the testimonies of some of the leaders of the liberation movements (or their family members), these sources provide a glimpse into the rich history of the network of

militants from the Portuguese colonies that used Rabat as a home base to plan and preach decolonization and African liberation.

9. *Présence africaine* is a quarterly cultural, political, and literary journal published in Paris. It was founded in 1947 by Alioune Diop and expanded in 1949 to include a publishing house and was a powerful tribune for the *négritude* and Pan-African movements in the 1940s, 1950s, and 1960s. *Présence africaine* organized the First International Congress of Black Writers and Artists in Paris in 1956. For more on *Présence africaine*, see Bennetta, *Black Paris*; and Mudimbe, *Surreptitious Speech*; see also Reis, "África imaginada."

10. See Comitini and Cabral, *Amílcar Cabral*, 23. The Luso-African militant-poets claimed to be one with the masses: "It did not suffice to keep up a purely intellectual attitude, to sing the distress and the alienation of the people, but one must merge with the masses in their roots and everyday life," explained Mozambican poet Virgilio de Lemos in an issue of *Présence africaine* dedicated to African poetry in 1966 ("Poesia africana de expressão portuguesa," 434).

11. Reza, "African Anti-colonialism," 38. Reza explains that scholars have tended to express some confusion concerning this apparent ambiguity. Cemil Aydin talks of a puzzle ("Pan-Nationalism of Pan-Islamic, Pan-Asian, and Pan-African Thought"), while Vijay Prashad talks of "internationalist nationalism" (*Darker Nations*) and Rahual Rao of a "space between cosmopolitanism and nationalism" (*Third World Protest*, 118–119).

12. The young king Hassan II was convinced that he needed to reestablish the exterior policy balance in favor of the Western bloc and restore a certain level of economic and social conservatism domestically. Strongly supported by the conservative and nationalist branch of the Istiqlal, the government's main concern was to stave off the UNFP, a syndicalist and Third-Worldist break-off from the Istiqlal, whose allegiances were more with the Eastern bloc. See Vermeren, *Histoire du Maroc*, 30–32. Breaking with his father's policies, Hassan II turned toward anti-communist countries, dispatching Moroccan troops to support Mobutu in the 1977–1978 Shaba crisis, thus undermining the very MPLA that his father had fed and boarded in Rabat in the late 1950s. See Boussaid, "Brothers in Arms." Hassan also attempted to become commander of the African faithful, turning toward majority Muslim countries, sending money to build mosques in Dakar, strengthening Tijani connections with West Africa, and building a gigantic mosque in Casablanca. For more on Hassan II's relationship to Islam, the Levant, and the African continent, see Aboulouz, *Al-Harakāt Al-Salafya fi-l Maghreb*; Alaoui, "Morocco, Commander of the (African) Faithful?"; Baylocq and Hlaoua, "Diffuser un 'islam du juste milieu'?"; Belhaj, *La dimension islamique*; Gil Benumeya, "Oriente Medio y nuevo Islam"; Daadaoui, "Islamism and the State in Morocco"; and Roberson, *The Changing Face of Morocco*.

13. For more information on the history of the CEI, see Castelo and Jerónimo, *Casa dos Estudantes do Império*; Faria, *Linha Estreita de Liberdade*; Helder, *Casa dos Estudantes do Império*; and *Mensagem: Cinquentenário da Fundação da Casa dos Estudantes do Império 1944–1994*. For an anthology of poetry from the CEI, see Rosinha, *Antologias de poesia da Casa dos Estudantes do Império.*

14. Daniel dos Santos, *Amílcar Cabral*, 79.

15. For more on Mario de Andrade, see the excellent collection of essays and primary sources compiled by Inocência Mata and Laura Padilha, *Mario Pinto de Andrade*; and his daughter Henda de Andrade's homage to him, *Mario Pinto de Andrade*; as well as Amaral, *Em torno dos nacionalismos africanos.*

16. For more on Cabral, see Peter Karibe Mendy's recent book in Ohio University Press's Short Histories series, *Amílcar Cabral: A Nationalist and Pan-Africanist Revolutionary.* Mario de Andrade wrote a political biography of Cabral that is intimate and rigorous: *Amílcar Cabral: Essai de biographie politique.* For a collection of essays on Cabral and his political and economic legacy in Cape Verde and the rest of the world, see Fonseca, Pired, and Martins, *Por Cabral, Sempre.* For an in-depth analysis of Cabral's political philosophy, see Reiland, *Concepts of Cabralism.* To learn more about Cabral the poet, see Moser, "Poet Amílcar Cabral."

17. Andrade, "Mémoires d'une aventure intellectuelle," March 19, 1984, Fundo Mario de Andrade, Fundação Mário Soares, http://casacomum.org/cc/visualizador?pasta=10195.001.001, 49.

18. Very little scholarship engages with Marcelino dos Santos, even though he produced a lot of poetry and many political pamphlets and interviews. See Adjali and dos Santos. *Frelimo: Interview with Marcelino dos Santos*; and Marcelino dos Santos, *Canto do amor natural* and *Escrever é criar.* When scholars have written about dos Santos, it seems to be mostly in the context of an anthology or a collection of testimonies about FRELIMO. See Sellström, *Liberation in Southern Africa*; Williams, *Poets of Mozambique.*

19. Messiant, "Sur la première génération du MPLA" (interview with Mario de Andrade), 194. For Andrade's own take on Lusophone Africanity and *négritude*, see the preface to his 1953 *cuaderno* of Luso-African poetry (Andrade and Tenreiro, *Poesía negra de expressão portuguesa*). For more on Andrade's later opinions concerning the Luso-African poet's role in leading the people, see Andrade, *Négritude africana de lingua portuguesa.*

20. Ibid.

21. Andrade, *Uma entrevista*, 65.

22. Messiant, "Sur la première génération du MPLA," 196.

23. Ibid., 199.

24. Andrade, "Mémoires d'une aventure intellectuelle," 82.

25. Ibid., 85.

26. Andrade and Tenreiro, *Poesía negra de expressão portuguesa*.

27. Messiant, "Sur la première génération du MPLA," 199.

28. Andrade, *Uma entrevista*, 108–109.

29. Helgesson, *Transnationalism in Southern African Literature*, 2.

30. Ibid.

31. Salama, *1954, la fin d'un monde colonial*.

32. Bragança, *Battles Waged, Lasting Dreams* (interview with Mario de Andrade), 95.

33. Tyler Stovall's published dissertation, *Paris Noir: African Americans in the City of Lights*, is dedicated to retracing the lives of Black people from across the globe in Paris. In 2008, when Pap Ndiaye published *La condition noire*, his goal was to initiate a Black studies *à la française*. Citing Stovall and Brent Hayes Edwards at length, Ndiaye delineated a field of study that would trace the history of the Black community in France but also shed light on ways in which the myth of French colorblindness has obfuscated the daily discrimination that Black people in France endure. He was certainly not the first to call for an in-depth study of the French Black community, but his work, mingling historical enquiry and ethnographic research, has already been hailed as the founding text of French Black studies. Ndiaye has since become the minister of education in Emmanuel Macron's second term. More recently, Michael's Goebel's *Anti-imperial Metropolis: Interwar Paris and the Seeds of Third World Nationalism* centers on the daily lives of Asian, African, and Latin American migrants to Paris. It was in Paris, Goebels argues, through contact with other Third World Nationalists, that these men and women dreamed up a postimperial world order.

34. Abdellatif Laâbi, *L'écorché vif*, 59.

35. Andrade, in Messiant, "Sur la première génération du MPLA," 203.

36. Ibid., 208. Aimé Césaire himself had a difficult time with the French Communist Party, where, he claimed, it was difficult to be "nègre" and "Martiniquais."

37. Andrade, "Mémoires d'une aventure intellectuelle," 99. For more on this, see Chaps. 2 and 4.

38. Andrade, in Messiant, "Sur la première génération du MPLA," 205.

39. Mehdi Ben Barka was a Moroccan anticolonial activist and member of the Istiqlal party. He participated in the negotiations that led to the return of King Mohamed V and was president of the Moroccan assembly from 1956 to 1959. In 1959, he broke from the Istiqlal, arguing that the party was too conservative, and established the UNFP. Ben Barka had studied in Algiers and was always committed to intra-Maghrebi cooperation. In 1963, when the War of the Sands broke out, he denounced the conflict and was sentenced to death by King Hassan II. Forced into exile, he continued to work as a Third-Worldist organizer, responsible for the Tricontinental Conference of Havana in 1966. Just a few months before the conference was due to

begin, Ben Barka was kidnapped by members of the French police in Paris and disappeared. See Bachir Ben Barka, *Mehdi Ben Barka en héritage*; Bouamama, *Figures de la révolution africaine*; and Gallissot and Kergoat, *Mehdi Ben Barka*.

40. Andrade, "Mémoires d'une aventure intellectuelle," 91–92.

41. Bragança, *Battles Waged, Lasting Dreams*, 119.

42. Ibid., 120.

43. Marcelino dos Santos, in Bragança, *Battles Waged, Lasting Dreams*, 120; Mario de Andrade, in ibid., 98.

44. Manifesto of the MAC, Department of Information, Propaganda and Culture of the Central Committee of the PAIGC, document no. 4 of the Serie Documentos Orientadores; cited in ibid., 133.

45. Andrade, "Mémoires d'une aventure intellectuelle," 118.

46. See Stora, *Histoire de la guerre d'Algérie*; and Horne, *Savage War of Peace*.

47. Andrade, *Uma entrevista*, 150–151.

48. Andrade, "Literatura e nacionalismo em Angola," in Imata and Padhila, *Mario Pinto de Andrade*, 22.

49. Andrade, "Mémoires d'une aventure intellectuelle," 123.

50. Traditionally, scholars have thought of the Middle Passage as the physical crossing of the Atlantic, but this obscures the "middle passages" that slaves who crossed the Sahara or stayed on the African continent had to endure. The "middle passage" refers to a series of passages leading the slave further and further from home, further and further from the familiar. The middle passages are a journey through space but also a psychological, physical, and social journey from captivity to enslavement; it is a sickening but meaningful journey from the familiar to the strange to the magical. "Through their dramatic and varying languages of travel and alienation," writes Pier M. Larson, "captives remembered their horrid journeying as both painful and meaningful. By vividly and richly describing estrangement, they simultaneously imagined their specific continental homes and confirmed their sense of precaptive placement" ("Horrid Journeying," 434). It is through the process of progressive estrangement that slaves construct a narrative about their free selves and their original habitat. This estrangement makes them slaves, but it also makes them Africans. Here Andrade uses the term "middle passage" in a figurative sense, not only as a physical crossing but also as a painful process of creating his identity.

51. Andrade, in Messiant, "Sur la première génération du MPLA," 214.

52. Not to be confused with the better-known Casablanca Conference that took place in 1943. In January 1961, the first king of independent Morocco, Mohammed V, inspired by his encounter with Patrice Lumumba, brought together the hard-liners and stars of the nascent institutional Pan-Africanist ideology (Algerian Ferhat Abbas, Malian Modibo Keita, Egyptian Gamal Abdel Nasser,

Ghanaian Kwame Nkrumah, and Guinean Ahmed Sékou Touré) for the Conference of the Casablanca Group. The stated goal of the conference was to eliminate racial segregation as well as to eradicate the colonial regimes throughout Africa. The participants stood firmly behind Algeria and the Congo in their struggles for independence and called for inter-African cooperation. See Balafrej, "La charte de Casablanca et l'unité africaine"; El Guabli, "Refiguring Pan-Africanism"; and Zerbo, "La problématique de l'unité africaine."

53. Anouchka de Andrade, interview with author; Henda de Andrade, interview with author.

54. Marcelino dos Santos to Aristides Pereira, September 1961, Fundo Amílcar Cabral, Fundação Mário Soares, http://casacomum.org/cc/visualizador?pasta=04604.023.039.

55. Maria Amália Lopes Fonseca appears at the margins of much of the CONCP's archive. I have found very little biographical information about her. Historian Ângela Sofia Benoliel Coutinho argues that many of the women who were active in the Cape Verdean independence struggle were erased from the archive and from collective memory, through the construction of a national memory of the independence struggle that occluded the role of women and glorified that of men. In her article "Militantes invisíveis," she retraces the journeys of a number of these women, including Fonseca.

56. Maria Amália Lopes Fonseca, interview with Paulo Lara, March 2, 2011, Luanda, Angola, Fundo ATD, https://www.tchiweka.org/video/9067001002.

57. Andrade, in Bragança, *Battles Waged, Lasting Dreams*, 99. One reason to choose Morocco over Tunisia was the Bourguiba government's show of support for Robert Holden's party, the FLNA. The MPLA and FLNA were battling for control of the anticolonialist movement. Based in eastern Angola, Robert Holden's party drew support from the United States and Israel. The MPLA's allegiances were communist, on the other hand, and they received support from the Soviet Union. See Arslan Humbaraci, "Le Plan Khatib," *Jeune afrique*, January 23, 1962.

58. "Le Mouvement de Libération Nationale dans les Colonies Portugaises," Conferência das Organizações Nacionalistas das Colónias Portuguesas, 1965, Arquivo Mário Pinto de Andrade, Fundação Mário Soares, 2, http://casacomum.org/cc/visualizador?pasta=04322.005.005#!1.

59. Amílcar Cabral, "Mensagem ao II Congresso da UGEAN," August 1963, Rabat, Fundo Amílcar Cabral, Fundação Mário Soares, 3, http://casacomum.org/cc/visualizador?pasta=04602.029#!1.

60. Mohammed Darbani, speech, CONCP, Rabat, 1961, 49, http://casacomum.org/cc/visualizador?pasta=04357.009.001#!1.

61. Adelino Gwambe, speech, CONCP, Rabat, 1961, 29, http://casacomum.org/cc/visualizador?pasta=04357.009.001#!1.

62. Photo of Mario de Andrade, Rabat, 1964, Fundo Mario Pinto de Andrade, Fundação Mário Soares, http://casacomum.org/cc/visualizador?pasta=07223.002.038; photo of Iva Cabral, Rabat, n.d., Documentos Amílcar Cabral, Fundação Mário Soares, http://casacomum.org/cc/visualizador?pasta=05221.000.026#!1.

63. Jocelyne Laâbi, *La liqueur d'aloès*, 123.

64. "Mohammed V et L'Afrique—Témoignage," Testemunho de Mario Pinto de Andrade sobre Mohamed V, November 5, 1987, Fundo Mário Pinto de Andrade, Fundação Mário Soares, http://casacomum.org/cc/visualizador?pasta=04357.009.002#!3.

65. Marcelino dos Santos, "Letter to his Majesty Hassan II," April 27, 1961, Rabat, Fundo Amílcar Cabral, Fundação Mário Soares, http://casacomum.org/cc/visualizador?pasta=04623.158.004#!1.

66. Marcelino dos Santos, "Letter to Joao Cabral," June 11, 1961, Rabat, Fundo Amílcar Cabral, Fundação Mário Soares, http://casacomum.org/cc/visualizador?pasta=04604.023.011. For information on Joao Cabral, see Sellström, *Sweden and National Liberation in Southern Africa*, 385.

67. Ibid. In his 1958 *Antología da poesía de expressão portuguesa*, Andrade concluded his introductory remarks with a similar usage of the phrase "Incha Allah," demonstrating that even before moving to Rabat, his contact with Moroccans and Algerians at the Paris Cité Universitaire influenced his language.

68. Marcelino dos Santos to Mario de Andrade, May 17, 1961, Fundo Amílcar Cabral, Fundação Mário Soares, http://casacomum.org/cc/visualizador?pasta=04604.023.002#!2.

69. Lucio Lara to Abel Djassi, February 21, 1960, Fundo Amílcar Cabral, Fundação Mário Soares, http://casacomum.org/cc/visualizador?pasta=07196.154.026#!1.

70. Marc Ollivier, Interview with author.

71. Luis Cabral to Abel Djassi (Amílcar Cabral), February 7, 1960, Casablanca, Fundo Amílcar Cabral, Fundação Mário Soares, http://casacomum.org/cc/visualizador?pasta=07196.154.023.

72. Zakya Daoud, email interview; and Boubker Mongachi, interview with author.

73. Bulletin d'Informations du Secrétariat Permanent de la Conférence des Organisations Nationalistes des Colonies Portugaises, no. 1, Rabat, December 30, 1961, Fundação Mário Soares, http://casacomum.org/cc/visualizador?pasta=02603.016#!1.

74. Minervina Celeste Fortunato, "Assises Maroc-Afrique, February 18–19, 2018, Rabat, Morocco," transcript of speech in author's posesssion.

75. Programa da formação técnica e militar dos estagiários do PAIGC em Marrocos, March 10, 1962, Fundo Amílcar Cabral, Fundação Mário Soares, http://casacomum.org/cc/visualizador?pasta=07068.098.017#!3.

76. Marcelino dos Santos to Amílcar Cabral, March 16, 1962, Rabat, Fundo Amílcar Cabral, Fundação Mário Soares, http://casacomum.org/cc/visualizador?pasta=07068.098.017#!3.

77. Aristides Pereira to the Director of the Port of Conakry, April 1963, Fundo Amílcar Cabral, Fundação Mário Soares, http://casacomum.org/cc/visualizador?pasta=07073.130.005#!2.

78. Jacques Tiné to the Minister of Foreign Affairs in Paris, July 6, 1963, Rabat, 558/PO/1, Archives Diplomatiques de Nantes, Nantes, France.

79. Ibid.

80. Bragança, *Battles Waged, Lasting Dream*, 164; Helder, *Porque Sakrani?*

81. Pierre de Leusse to the Minister of Foreign Affairs in Paris, 1963, Rabat, 7, 558/PO/1, Archives Diplomatiques de Nantes, Nantes, France.

82. Albert Roux to the Minister Conseiller Chargé d'Affaires in Rabat, August 2, 1962, 558/PO/1, Archives Diplomatiques de Nantes, Nantes, France.

83. Jacques Tiné to Colonel Duprez, Rabat, September 8, 1962, 558/PO/1, Archives Diplomatiques de Nantes, Nantes, France.

84. French embassy to Portuguese embassy, September 21, 1962, Rabat, 558/PO/1, Archives Diplomatiques de Nantes, Nantes, France.

85. A. Deschamps, Chargé d'Affaires of Tanganyika, to the French Minister of Foreign Affairs, January 12, 1963, Dar Es Salaam, 558/PO/1, Archives Diplomatiques de Nantes, Nantes, France.

86. See note 5 above for more on the War of the Sands.

87. Andrade, *Uma entrevista*, 186.

88. Amílcar Cabral to Hassan II, telegram, 1963, Fundo Amílcar Cabral, Fundação Mário Soares, http://casacomum.org/cc/visualizador?pasta=07075.144.050.

89. Marcelino dos Santos to Aristides Pereira, August 2, 1961, Fundo Amílcar Cabral, Fundação Mário Soares, http://casacomum.org/cc/visualizador?pasta=04604.039.024#!1.

90. The "July plot" was a largely fabricated attempted coup supposedly instigated by the UNFP against the Moroccan king Hassan II. One hundred or so people were put on trial, eleven of whom were sentenced to death, among them Mehdi Ben Barka. For more, see Maâti Monjib, "Le complot de Juillet 1963" and *La monarchie marocaine*.

91. Mehdi Ben Barka to Amílcar Cabral, December 14, 1963, Fundo Amílcar Cabral, Fundação Mário Soares, 3, http://casacomum.org/cc/visualizador?pasta=04621.115.028#!3

92. In 1955, representatives from across Africa, Asia, and Latin America gathered in Bandung, Indonesia, to debate the role of the Third World in the Cold War. At the heart of the discussion was the principle of self-determination. In fact, of the

twenty-nine countries represented in Bandung, many had recently emerged from difficult anticolonial struggles and were determined to protect their sovereignty. The Bandung Conference's final resolution laid the groundwork for the nonaligned movement, whose goal was for Third World countries to avoid being pulled into one side or another of the Cold War. See the final communiqué of the Bandung Conference: https://www.cvce.eu/en/obj/final_communique_of_the_asian_african_conference_of_bandung_24_april_1955-en-676237bd-72f7-471f-949a-88b6ae513585.html. See also Lee, *Making a World after Empire*.

93. Resolução de 12 de Setembro de 1963 do Comité Executivo do Movimento de Solidariedade dos Povos Afro-Asiáticos, Fundo Amílcar Cabral, Fundação Mário Soares, http://casacomum.org/cc/visualizador?pasta=04621.115.024#!2.

94. For more on this, see Chap. 3.

95. Mario Pinto de Andrade's passport, Arquivo Mário Pinto de Andrade, Fundação Mário Soares, http://casacomum.org/cc/visualizador?pasta=04359.006.006; Zakya Daoud, email interview with author.

96. See Senghor, "Négritude et civilisation de l'universel."

Chapter Two: A Continent in Its Totality

1. Abdellatif Laâbi, "Cellule de prisonnier," in *Sous le bâillon*, 139.

2. El Guabli, "Refiguring Pan-Africanism"; Hammoudi, *Master and Disciple*; Valensi, "Le roi chronophage.

3. For more on Mehdi Ben Barka and his assassination, see Bachir Ben Barka, *Mehdi Ben Barka en héritage*; Bouamama, *Figures de la révolution africaine*; and Gallissot and Kergoat, *Mehdi Ben Barka*.

4. See El Guabli, "Moroccan Society's Educational and Cultural Losses."

5. Hassan II, cited in Lindsey, "Restoring Morocco's Past."

6. Rollinde, *Le mouvement marocain des droits de l'Homme*; Sefraoui, *La revue Souffles*, 53–56; Vermeren, *Histoire du Maroc*.

7. For more on the Years of Lead, see Daoud, *Les années Lamalif*; El Guabli, "Testimony and Journalism" and "Theorizing Intergenerational Trauma"; Hachad, *Revisionary Narratives*; Rollinde, *Le mouvement marocain des droits de l'Homme*; Slyomovics, *Performance of Human Rights in Morocco*; and Vermeren, *Histoire du Maroc depuis l'indépendance*.

8. *Summary of the Final Report*, IER Committee, https://www.cndh.ma/sites/default/files/documents/rapport_final_mar_eng-3.pdf. At the time of writing, the full report was not available, as the Arabic website was "under maintenance." The English translation, unfortunately, is only a summary.

9. El Guabli, "Reading for Theory."

10. See El Guabli's introduction to Alalou and El Guabli, *Lamalif*.

11. Excellent articles about *Souffles/Anfas* include Babana-Hampton, "Translat-

ing the Postcolonial Condition; Lyamlahy, "'A Boundless Creative Ferocity'"; Osten, "Aesthetics of Decolonization"; Pitman and Stafford, "Introduction: Transatlanticism and Tricontinentalism"; Stafford, "Tricontinentalism in Recent Moroccan Intellectual History"; and Villa-Ignacio, "Decolonizing Violence." See also Harrison and Villa-Ignacio's excellent anthology, *Souffles-Anfas.*

12. I use the term "militant-poet" to designate political activists who came to activism through poetry. After being agitated by poetry, these militant-poets continued to write literature and to do the work of political activists, whether it was distributing pamphlets, organizing meetings, or even taking up the gun. See the Introduction for a more thorough definition of militant-poet and it's accompanying term militant-artist.

13. Mohamed Melehi, cited in Jaggi, "Casablanca's Gift to Marrakech."

14. Maraini, "Black Sun of Renewal."

15. Tahar Ben Jelloun, interview with Kenza Sefraoui, September 13, 2004, Paris, in Sefraoui, *La revue Souffles,* 322.

16. Toni Maraini, email exchange with author, January 30, 2018.

17. Toni Maraini, cited in Sefraoui, *La revue Souffles,* 372.

18. Ibid., p. 40.

19. Abdellatif Laâbi, "Réalités et dilemmes de la culture nationale (II)," *Souffles,* no. 6 (1967): 33.

20. See Ngũgĩ wa Thiong'o, *Decolonising the Mind.*

21. Mehdi Ben Barka, "L'Afrique au delà de l'indépendance," published posthumously.

22. Ibid.

23. Ibid.

24. Ibid.

25. Ibid.

26. Though at first Laâbi meant "extremism" as literary or linguistic extremism, he did condone other types of violent extremism as well, arguing, much like Fanon, that violence was the only way to topple colonialism and neocolonialism.

27. Abdellatif Laâbi, "Prologue," *Souffles,* no. 1 (1966): 6.

28. Karakayali, in Laâbi, *Une saison ardente.*

29. Abdellatif Laâbi, "Les singes électroniques," *Souffles,* nos. 16–17 (1969): 40.

30. Abdallah Stouky, "Le festival mondial des arts nègres ou les nostalgiques de la négritude," *Souffles,* no. 2 (1966): 41. On April 1, 1966, a mere six years after Senegalese independence, André Malraux, the French minister of culture, inaugurated the First World Festival of Black Arts in Dakar with this now-famous statement: "Here we enter history. For the first time a head of state holds in his perishable hands the destiny of an entire continent" (https://malraux.org/discours-de-dakar-30-mars-1966/). Funded primarily by UNESCO and the French government, the

Dakar festival attracted political and cultural personalities from around the globe, among whom were George Pompidou (French prime minister), René Maheu (director of UNESCO), Aimé Césaire, Duke Ellington, and Langston Hughes. The twenty-four days of dance shows, music, exhibitions, plays, speeches, and symposiums were intended to prove to the world that Black culture was alive, well, and ready to join the *civilization de l'universel* (universal civilization). Using the festival as a platform, Senghor made numerous speeches on *négritude*, Art Nègre, *francophonie*, and Senegal's relationship to France. He did not, however, invite North African artists to participate in certain events, such as the contemporary art exhibition—only Black artists could present their work—which created numerous tensions. Senegal had asked the OAU to fund and participate in the organization of the festival, but they decided to abstain because of the exclusive nature of the event. Many African countries, such as Algeria and Guinea-Conakry, deplored Senghor's championing of an ideology that excluded a large segment of the continent. Other countries, however, such as Tunisia, were sympathetic to Senegal's vision of Africa. For more on this, see Samuel Anderson, "'Négritude Is Dead'"; Ficquet and Gallimardet, "'On ne peut nier longtemps l'art nègre'"; and Tolan-Szkilnik, "Flickering Fault Lines."

31. Stouky, "Le festival mondial des arts nègres," 43.

32. See Chap. 1.

33. Stouky, "Le festival mondial des arts nègres," 43.

34. Ibid., 45.

35. Mostapha Nissaboury, interview with author.

36. According to a document supplied by Kenza Sefraoui in the author's possession ("Les auteurs cités par *Souffles*"), Césaire was cited by ten writers over the course of *Souffles'* tenure.

37. André Laude, "Préface à un Procès de la Négritude," *Souffles*, no. 3 (1966): 33.

38. Ibid.

39. For more on Frantz Fanon's worldwide reception, see Batchelor and Harding, *Translating Frantz Fanon*; Edmund Burke, "Frantz Fanon's 'The Wretched of the Earth,'" and Guimarães, "Frantz Fanon's reception in Brazil."

40. Abdellatif Laâbi and Alessandra, *La brûlure des interrogations*, 32.

41. Khatibi, *Maghreb pluriel*.

42. Sefraoui, *La revue Souffles*, 67.

43. Kenza Sefraoui, "Les auteurs cités par *Souffles*" (document in author's possession). See also Sefraoui's excellent article "Encore un qui a tout dit!'"

44. Abdellatif Laâbi, "Littérature maghrébine actuelle et francophonie," *Souffles*, no. 18 (1970): 37.

45. I use the male pronoun, despite my initial instinct to utilize the gender-neutral "they," because in Fanon's and Depestre's minds the "colonized writer" is a

man, as demonstrated by their usage of *lui* and *il*. Using "they" would thus hide these men's own erasure of colonized women writers. This is a policy I have adopted throughout the book.

46. Depestre, "Face à la nuit"; cited in Fanon, *Wretched of the Earth*, 156.

47. Ibid., 159.

48. Abdellatif Laâbi, "Réalités et Dilemmes de la culture nationale," *Souffles*, no. 4 (1966): 7.

49. Ibid.

50. Abdellatif Laâbi, "Intervention à la rencontre des poètes arabes," *Souffles*, nos. 20–21 (1971): 55.

51. Alessandra, *Abdellatif Laâbi*, 44.

52. Moroccan writer Abdelkebir Khatibi's French-language novel *Amour bilingue* retraces the journey of a bilingual character from diglossia to plurilingualism. Khatibi forgoes all narrative techniques, character descriptions, and plotlines, weaving his stream-of-consciousness monologue around certain dramatized thematic elements that function as fictional and symbolic supports for the evolution of the language question.

53. When, as a young student and novelist, Ngũgĩ wa Thiong'o participated in the 1962 Conference of African Writers of English Expression in Uganda, he noted that the role of language as a determinant of both national and class audiences was not even broached. All the attendees assumed the fatalistic logic of relegating their native tongue to orality and accepting the gift of a European language that had been forced upon them. Ngũgĩ warned of the dangers of accepting this logic: how can we create a literature that addresses itself to the lives of the people when we write in language they do not understand and cannot read? The Kenyan writer thus broke from what he scathingly called a petty-bourgeois–Afro-European tradition, and after the publication of *Decolonizing the Mind*, he decided to write exclusively in his native Gikuyu. "The future of the African novel," he said, "is then dependent on a willing writer, a willing translator, a willing publisher, or a progressive state which would overhaul the current of neo-colonial linguistic policies and finally, and most important, a willing and widening readership" (85). The writer, he argued, was best placed to break the vicious cycle of neocolonial linguistics and root themselves in the rich oral tradition of the peasantry.

54. Bender, *Africa under the Portuguese*, 222; Hamilton, "Language and Literature in Portuguese-Writing Africa," 203; "Lusofonia, Africa, and Matters of Languages and Letters".

55. Albert Memmi (1920–2020), a Tunisian intellectual, is best known for his 1957 *Portrait of the Colonized Preceded by the Portrait of the Colonizer*. Malek Haddad (1927–1978) was a francophone Algerian poet. Though they were francophone writers, both believed that Maghrebi literature in French was bound to die.

56. Abdellatif Laâbi, "Réalités et dilemmes de la culture nationale," *Souffles*, no. 4 (1966): 7.

57. Lyamlahy, " 'A Boundless Creative Ferocity.' "

58. Abdellatif Laâbi, "Prologue," *Souffles*, no. 1 (1966): 5.

59. Mustapha Nissaboury, *Souffles*, no. 1 (1966): 8.

60. Abdellatif Laâbi, "Littérature maghrébine actuelle et francophonie," *Souffles*, no. 18 (1970): 36.

61. Ibid.

62. See Lyamlahi's introduction to Khaïr-Eddine's *Agadir.*

63. Abdellatif Laâbi, "Au sujet d'un certain procès de la littérature maghrébine écrite en français," *Souffles*, no. 18 (1970): 64.

64. Abdellatif Laâbi, "Avant-Propos," *Souffles*, no. 22 (1971): 4.

65. Ibid.

66. Ibid., 5.

67. El Guabli, "Reading for Theory"; Koumiya, "Post-68 Uprisings."

68. llā al-Amām, *Al-wathā'iq al-asāsya*, http://www.30aout. info/media/00/01/359899644.pdf.

69. Babana-Hampton, "Translating the Postcolonial Condition," 177.

70. *Area Handbook for Morocco*, 153.

71. Sefraoui, *La revue Souffles*, 40.

72. *Souffles*, no. 22 (1972): 1.

73. Abdellatif Laâbi, *Le livre imprévu.*

74. "Sahara Occidental," *Souffles*, no. 19 (1970): 48.

75. See Abraham Serfaty, "Le judaïsme marocain et le sionisme" and "L'État d'Israël est-il une nation?" *Souffles*, no. 15 (1968): 46–49.

76. El Amrani, "In the Beginning There Was *Souffles*; Serfaty, "Decidedly Marxist."

77. More on this in Chap. 3.

78. Daure-Serfaty and Serfaty, *La mémoire de l'autre*, 106.

79. Abraham Serfaty, "Révolution en Afrique et direction du prolétariat," *Souffles*, nos. 20–21 (1971): 46–49.

80. "Falisṭyn jadyda fy al-ṣaḥrā' " *Anfas*, no. 8 (1971–1972): 66–77.

81. Laâbi, *La liqueur d'aloès.*

82. *Souffles*, no. 9 (1968): 31.

83. Andrade and Tenreiro, *Poesía negra de expressão portuguesa.*

84. Mario de Andrade, "Réflexions autour du congrès culturel de la Havane," *Souffles*, no. 9 (1968): 37.

85. René Depestre, "L'intellectuel révolutionnaire et ses responsabilités envers le Tiers-Monde," *Souffles*, no. 9 (1968): 45. For more on the history of Black Zionism and its intellectual roots in the Jewish Zionist movement, see Neuberger,

"Black Zionism" and "Early African Nationalism, Judaism and Zionism,"; and Michael W. Williams, "Pan-Africanism and Zionism."

86. Condetto Nenekhali Camara, "Conscience révolutionnaire, ideologie et culture," *Souffles*, no. 9 (1968): 50.

87. Mario de Andrade, "Culture et Lutte Armée," *Souffles*, no. 9 (1968): 51–54.

88. Stafford, "Tricontinentalism," 223.

89. "Présence impérialiste et perspectives de lutte en Africe" (editorial), *Souffles*, no. 19 (1970): 5.

90. Chabâa, "Angola 10 MPLA vaincra," in Laâbi, *Une saison ardente*, 402.

91. See the Abu Dhabi Cultural Foundation's exhibition on Mohammed Chabâa and the Casablanca school, "Mohammed Chabaa: Visual Consciousness," for an interactive 3D tour: https://culturalfoundation.ae/en/exhibitions/mohammed-chabaa-visual-consciousness.

92. "Fiche Erythrée," *Souffles*, no. 19 (1970): 49

93. Ibid.

94. Agostinho Neto, "Nous devons nous battre jusqu'à la victoire," *Souffles*, no. 19 (1970): 34.

95. Thanks to Khalid Lyamlahy for helping me identify the second caricaturist. Jamal Bellakhdar was also arrested and spent time in jail as part of the Marxist-Leninist movement.

96. "Bulletin du FRELIMO, July 1969," *Souffles*, no. 19 (1970): 83.

97. Ibid.

98. Ibid., 91.

99. Fanon, *Wretched of the Earth*, 159.

100. For notable exceptions to this statement, see Askew, *Performing the Nation*; Turino, *Nationalists, Cosmopolitans, and Popular Music*; and Vail and White, *Power and the Praise Poem*.

101. As Marissa Moorman, a historian of Angola, explains in her monograph *Intonation*, after historians had identified writers as the precursors of nationalist politics, they left "culture to the literary critics and return[ed] to their analysis of former nationalist politics." According to Moorman, "above all, culture inflamed political imagination" (12).

102. Andrade to Abdellatif Laâbi, July 25, 1970, Algiers, Arquivo Mario Pinto de Andrade, Fundação Mário Soares, http://casacomum.org/cc/visualizador?pasta=04311.003.058.

103. Abdellatif Laâbi to Mario de Andrade, February 5, 1971, Rabat, Arquivo Mario Pinto de Andrade, Fundação Mário Soares, http://casacomum.org/cc/visualizador?pasta=07559.001.015#!2.

104. Ibid.

105. El Amrani, "In the Beginning There Was *Souffles*"; Daure-Serfaty and Serfaty, *La mémoire de l'autre*, 121–124.

106. Laâbi, *La liqueur d'aloès,* 128.

107. Ibid., 174.

108. Since the publication of Kenza Sefraoui's excellent dissertation, *La revue Souffles (1966–1973),* the scholarship on *Souffles* has grown rapidly. Scholars have delineated the theoretical and political underpinnings of the *Souffles* editorial board, interviewed its members, and conducted in-depth analyses of the journal's content. Scholars such as Teresa Villa-Ignacio have explored the group's ties to the Black American community; others such as Andy Stafford have analyzed the Third-Worldist tendencies of the journal. See Osten, "Aesthetics of Decolonization"; Pitman and Stafford, "Introduction"; Stafford, "Tricontinentalism"; and Villa-Ignacio, "Decolonizing Violence."

109. El Amrani, "In the Beginning There Was *Souffles*"; Daure-Serfaty and Serfaty, *La mémoire de l'autre.*

110. Abdellatif Laâbi, "Cellule de prisonnier," in *Sous le bâillon,* 88.

111. Abdellatif Laâbi, "Lettre à un ami angolais," in *Sous le bâillon,* 139.

112. Ibid.

113. Ibid., 140.

114. Ibid.

115. Ibid., 141.

116. Ibid.

117. "Mario Pinto de Andrade: Obituary," *Times* (London), August 28, 1990.

118. Albellatif Laâbi, invitation for a publication launch, November 18, 1985, Paris, Arquivo Mario Pinto de Andrade, Fundação Mário Soares, http://casacomum.org/cc/visualizador?pasta=10189.004.004.

Chapter Three: Poetry on All Fronts

1. William Klein filmed a 1969 documentary titled *Festival Panafricain d'Alger 1969;* long difficult to find, it has now been reissued and shown at many film festivals worldwide. At the time, though, many Maghrebi and Black filmmakers resented the fact that the Algerian government had commissioned a European director to make the film.

2. Participants at the PANAF did not hesitate to compare the festival to the French-funded First World Festival of Black Arts celebrated in Dakar in 1966, highlighting the change in rhetoric. Where the First World Festival of Black Arts championed *négritude* and Black universalism, the PANAF supposedly espoused revolutionary art. For more on this festival, see note 30 in Chap. 2.

3. Jacques Dupuy to the Minister of Foreign Affairs, August 4, 1969, Algiers, 4, N_3_3_1, dossier Festival Panafricain, Archives Diplomatiques de Nantes, Nantes, France.

4. Hocine Tandjaoui, interview with author.

5. Hocine Tandjaoui, "Feuille de route," in Laâbi, *Une saison ardente,* 30–32.

6. Boussad Ouadi, interview with PANAFEST archives, May 13, 2014, Algiers, http://webdocs-sciences-sociales.science/panafest/#00-Menu-Inroduction_PANAFEST___une_archive_en_devenir.

7. Sénac, diary, July 1969, box S10, Jean Sénac Archives, Algerian National Library, Algiers.

8. Ibid.

9. Denis Martinez, interview with author.

10. The Tifinagh alphabet is used to write the Berber languages.

11. See the Aouchem manifesto, which was signed by Algerian painters Hamid Abdoun, Mustafa Adane, Baya (Fatma Haddad-Mahiedine), Mohamed Ben Baghdad, Mahfoud Dahmani, Denis Martinez, Choukri Mesli, Said Saidani, and Arezki Zerarti (Greenspan, "Manifesto of the Aouchem Group," 189).

12. "Algiers, A Haven for Exile Groups," *New York Times*, March 7, 1965, 13.

13. Salama, *Alger, la Mecque des révolutionnaires (1962–1974)*. In his 2016 monograph *Mecca of Revolution: Algeria, Decolonization, and the Third World Order*, Jeffrey James Byrne explores how Algiers became so appealing a place for rebels from such places as Angola, Mozambique, Palestine, South Africa, Argentina, and Vietnam. In Algiers, he reveals, these rebels "lived together, conspired together, and vowed to die together" (3).

14. Vermeren, *Histoire du Maroc*, 36; Zartman, "Politics of Boundaries in North and West Africa," 163.

15. In fact, Ben Bella maintained strong ties with the two men who were the biggest threats to Hassan II's and Bourguiba's regimes—Mehdi Ben Barka in Morocco and Salah Ben Youssef in Tunisia; both were assassinated by their respective governments (see Byrne, *Mecca of Revolution*, 83).

16. Byrne claims that Ben Bella would have told Tito that once he had "pointed out the links between Moroccans and the [Kabyle leader] Hocine Aït Ahmed," the Algerian people had shown his government extraordinary support, "so that now, neither Aït Ahmed nor the defense of borders represents a problem for us." Ben Bella thus used the 1963 War of the Sands to splinter and marginalize Kabyle rebels (ibid., 222).

17. Vermeren argues that Hassan II immediately distanced himself from the nonalignment of the Casablanca Group, and that his ascension was a relief for the Europeans, a sure sign that Morocco would be joining the Western camp in the Cold War (*Histoire du Maroc*, 31).

18. See Rahal, *Algérie 1962*. For more on the Algerian War of Independence, see, in particular, Horne, *Savage War of Peace*; Shepard, *Invention of Decolonization*; and Thénault, *Histoire de la guerre d'indépendance algérienne*.

19. Interview with Chief Mandela.

20. Byrne, *Mecca of Revolution*, 196. Created in 1963 in Addis-Ababa, the OAU

consisted of thirty-two independent African states; there are now fifty-three. The OAU charter declared that the organization's functions were to "promote unity and solidarity between African states; coordinate and intensify cooperation and attempts to ameliorate the lives of the peoples of Africa; defend the sovereignty, the territorial integrity, and the independence of the OAU's member states; eradicate all forms of colonialism in Africa; promote international cooperation all the while respecting the United Nations Charter and the Universal Declaration of Human Rights" (Organization of African Unity, http://actrav.itcilo.org/actrav-english/telearn/global/ilo/law/oau.htm). The first meeting was tense, however, divided between two groups with very different visions for the future of Africa. The first group, consisting of Kwame Nkrumah's Ghana and Abdel Nasser's Egypt, advocated for a United States of Africa. The second group, including the Ivory Coast of Félix Houphouët-Boigny, the Nigeria of Tafana Balewa, the Tunisia of Habib Bourguiba, and the Senegal of Léopold Sédar Senghor, consisted of countries that were attached to their national sovereignty and favored a more gradual process of unification. As one can tell from reading the guiding principles in the OAU charter, the second group prevailed. For more on this, see Cervenka, *Organization of African Unity*; and Mfoulou, *L'O.U.A., triomphe de l'unité ou des nationalités?*

21. Algeria was not just playing a rhetorical game. As Byrne explains in *Mecca of Revolution*, the archives of the Algerian Foreign Ministry "reveal not only the construction of a newly independent country's diplomatic apparatus but also a largely successful effort to translate lofty Third-Worldist rhetoric into a practicable foreign policy doctrine" (189). Byrne ends the book with Houari Boumédiène's successful 1965 coup against the beloved president Ahmed Ben Bella. While Third Worldism remained strong in Algeria, Byrne argues that the coup meant the end of decolonization's "most idealistic and optimistic phase. Out of the diversity of political imaginings and spirit of limitless possibility that had brightened the twilight of empire, a surprisingly homogenous, constrictive, and even conservative postcolonial order had emerged" (286). The Third-Worldism that followed Boumédiène's coup, Byrne contends, was entirely directed by the postcolonial state—a state that managed all interactions between the domestic space and the outside world. "In that sense, the profusion of Third Worldist–themed events such as Afro-Asian writers' conferences and Pan-African music festivals reflected a desire to filter every kind of cross-border contact through official international channels, whereas transnational activities that the authorities did not supervise were treated as inherently suspicious" (291). Byrne benefited from unprecedented access to FLN archives and has been instrumental in illuminating the diplomatic contacts between the Algerian state and the rest of the Third World before 1965. His story, however, remains a top-down history, a diplomatic history that does not investigate the cul-

tural underbelly of the activity in Algiers. Though Byrne points to the fact that revolutionaries from the Third World tended to recognize each other through their shared manner and lifestyle, he does not investigate the consequences of this shared lifestyle, the culture that emerged from that "cosmopolitan fauna" in Algiers.

22. Ibid., 189.

23. Ibid.

24. For more on the coup, see ibid.; Byrne, "Beyond Continents, Colours, and the Cold War"; McDougall, *History of Algeria*; and St. John, "Independent Algeria from Ben Bella to Boumédiène."

25. Denis Martinez, interview with author.

26. Cleaver, "Back to Africa," 218.

27. Khellas, *Le premier festival culturel panafricain*, 47.

28. Pamphlet published by the Algerian government for the PANAF, in Ted Joans, "Black Man's Guide to Africa," p. 64, BANC MSS 99/244, box 5:16–17, Bancroft Library.

29. Ibid., 65.

30. Ratcliff, "Liberation at the End of a Pen."

31. For more information on the organization of the PANAF, see Anderson, "'Négritude Is Dead"; Khellas, *Le premier festival culturel panafricain*; Meghelli, "From Harlem to Algiers" and "'A Weapon in Our Struggle for Liberation'"; and Tolan-Szkilnik, "Flickering Fault Lines" and "Quest for a Pan-African Groove."

32. The *pieds-noirs* are the people of French, Italian, Maltese, and other European descent who were born in Algeria during the period of European colonialism, from about 1830 to 1962. The majority of *pieds-noirs* moved to France immediately following Algerian independence. Some, like Jean Sénac and Denis Martinez, chose to stay, claiming that they were Algerian, no matter their origins. For more, see Eldridge, *From Empire to Exile*; Hubbell, *Remembering French Algeria*; and Shepard, *The Invention of Decolonization*. See also Sénac, "La Patrie," March 1954, Algiers, box 7, Jean Sénac Archives, Marseille. For biographical information on Sénac, see Bencheikh and Chaulet-Achour, *Jean Sénac*; Mazo, *Jean Sénac*; and Temime and Tuccelli, *Jean Sénac, l'Algérien*. In particular, see Kai Krienke's excellent dissertation, "Jean Sénac, Poet of the Algerian Revolution," which he generously made available online.

33. Sénac, "La Patrie," March 1954, Algiers, box 7, Jean Sénac Archives, Marseille.

34. Sarner, "Jean Sénac, poète assassiné," *Revue Ballast*, November 12, 2014.

35. Krienke, *Jean Sénac*, 26. For more on Camus and Sénac's friendship, see the compilation of letters put together by Sénac's friend Hamid Nacer-Khodja: *Albert Camus, Jean Sénac, or The Rebel Son*.

36. Krienke, *Jean Sénac*, 26; and Sénac, diary 1962, box S10, Jean Sénac Archives, Algerian National Library, Algiers.

37. Sénac, "Poème-programme," *La république* (December 1963).

38. The OAS was a secret terrorist organization created by a group of *pieds-noirs* who were determined to maintain the French presence in Algeria. The organization committed targeted assassinations and terrorist attacks in both Algeria and France until Algerian independence. For more, see Harrison, *Challenging de Gaulle*; and Robin, *Escadrons de la mort*.

39. Sénac, "Citoyens de beauté," in *Œuvres poétiques*.

40. Letter to the President from the Executive Bureau of the Union of Algerian Writers, n.d., box 18, Jean Sénac Archives, Marseille.

41. Charter of the National Union of Algerian Writers, box S2, Jean Sénac Archives, Algerian National Library, Algiers.

42. Sénac to the Union of Algerian Writers, Algiers, April 2, 1967, box 18, Jean Sénac Archives, Marseille.

43. "Poésie sur tous les fronts," *El-Moudjahid*, August 1971.

44. Khodja Mohammed to Jean Sénac, June 24, 1969, Algiers, box S4, Jean Sénac Archives, Algerian National Library, Algiers.

45. Djaffar Ait and Kaci Djerbit to Jean Sénac, January 14, 1968, Tizi Ouzou, box S14, Jean Sénac Archives, Algerian National Library, Algiers.

46. Gauthier, *Entre deux rives*, 29.

47. Hocine Tandjaoui, interview with author.

48. Ibid.

49. Ibid.

50. Jean Sénac to Jean Breton, June 9, 1970, Algiers, box S7, Jean Sénac Archives, Algerian National Library, Algiers.

51. Mazo, *Jean Sénac*. Kateb Yacine (1929–1989) was a prominent Algerian writer, known for his plays and novels (such as *Nedjma*, published in 1956) in French and Algerian Arabic, and for his political activism on behalf of the Berber cause in Algeria.

52. Sénac, "Cette ville," in *Œuvres complètes*, 709–713.

53. Patrick MacAvoy to Jean Sénac, December 5, 1968, Algiers, box S9, Jean Sénac Archives, Algerian National Library, Algiers.

54. Jean Sénac to Jean Breton, June 9, 1970, Algiers, box S7, Jean Sénac Archives, Algerian National Library, Algiers.

55. Gauthier, *Entre deux rives*, 28.

56. "L'émission poétique de Jean Sénac en Algérie est interdite." Newspaper clipping, June 3, 1972, box 19, Jean Sénac Archives, Marseille.

57. Sénac, notes on the meeting of young Algerian poets, in Krienke, "Sun under the Weapons."

58. Sénac, "Testament," May 2, 1973, Algiers, box 19, Jean Sénac Archives, Marseille.

59. Tahar Ben Jelloun to Jean-Pierre Peroncel Hugoz, September 15, 1973, box 15, Jean Sénac Archives, Marseille.

60. Krienke, *Jean Sénac*, 14. Another man was later arrested in September 1973, according to a short article in *El-Moudjahid*, resolving "a mystery which had caused much emotion in the intellectual world because of the personality of this poet." "Arrestation du meurtrier du poète Jean Sénac," *El-Moudjahid*, September 21, 1973, box 19, Jean Sénac Archives, Marseille.

61. "Ba'ḍ mā qālahu 'anhu," *Al-Sh'b al-Thaqāfy*, October 5, 1973, file 4, box 19, Jean Sénac Archives, Marseille.

62. Sainson, "'Entre Deux Feux.'" Boudjedra was not the only one to make this assessment; in *Le blanc de l'Algérie*, Algerian writer Assia Djebar memorialized him as the first victim in Algeria's long list of assassinated artists during the 1990s, the "décennie noire" (black decade) (137–138).

63. Sarah Maldoror, interview with author.

64. Sénac, "Quand je serai mort, jeunes gens," box 21, Jean Sénac Archives, Marseille.

65. Unfortunately, the Algerian National Radio destroyed these recordings when they fired Jean Sénac from his position in 1972. A few old reels did make it into Sénac's archives at the National Library, but they were tangled, and nowhere could anyone find the machine necessary to read them.

66. Sénac, opening for *Poésie sur tous les fronts*, box S2, Jean Sénac Archives, Algerian National Library, Algiers.

67. Sarah Maldoror, interview with author.

68. Anouchka de Andrade, interview with author.

69. "Algérie," September 23, 1973, Mario de Andrade Archives, Fundação Mário Soares, http://hdl.handle.net/11002/fms_dc_85919 (2019-1-8).

70. Henda de Andrade, interview with author.

71. Andrade, *Uma entrevista*, 119.

72. Sénac, "Salut aux écrivains et artistes noirs," 1956, René Depestre Archives, Limoges, France.

73. Krienke, *Jean Sénac*, 84.

74. In his 1949 introduction to Léopold Sédar Senghor's *Anthologie de la poésie nègre et malgache*, Jean-Paul Sartre took the entire poetry of *négritude* under his wing, acting as a self-proclaimed doyen to those he simply called "les poètes nègres." In "Orphée noir," Sartre's preface to Senghor's *Anthologie de la nouvelle poésie nègre et malgache*, the white French writer explained to his French audience that European society was hopelessly rotten, that Europe had become a mere geographic accident, "une presqu'île que l'Asie pousse jusqu'à l'Atlantique," and that

the future lay on the tongues and lips of the colonized of the world, the wretched of the earth, the *négritude* poets (x). Sartre proclaimed *négritude* a form of antiracist racism, a middle passage between oppression and Marxist revolution. Eventually, he claimed, the "Blacks" (as he called them) would have to sacrifice their newfound racial pride on the altar of the proletarian revolution.

75. Andrade, *Uma entrevista*, 131.

76. Sénac, "Angola," *Matinales de mon peuple*, 1961, box S6, Jean Sénac Archives, Algerian National Library, Algiers.

77. Ibid.

78. Mario de Andrade, "Intervention commune des mouvements de libération des colonies portugaises," *Souffles*, nos. 16–17 (1969): 23–25.

79. Sénac, "Dans le cadre du PANAF: De Lumumba aux Maquis de l'Angola; Le chant armé du peuple," *Poésie sur tous les fronts*, August 4, 1969, Algiers, box S2, Jean Sénac Archives, Algerian National Library, Algiers.

80. Ibid.

81. Sénac, "Poète à Cuba," *Poésie sur tous les fronts*, August 4, 1969, Algiers, box S6, Jean Sénac Archives, Algerian National Library, Algiers.

82. René Depestre, interview with author. See Chap. 4 for more.

83. *Marronage* refers to the process of extricating oneself from slavery. It usually refers to those slaves who escaped the plantations in the southern United States and the Caribbean.

84. René Depestre, "Fondements socio-culturels de notre identité," *Souffles*, nos. 16–17 (1969): 30.

85. René Depestre, interview with author.

86. René Depestre, "Fondements socio-culturels de notre identité," *Souffles*, nos. 16–17 (1969): 31.

87. Sénac, "Poète à Cuba," *Poésie sur tous les fronts*, August 4, 1969, Algiers, box S2, Jean Sénac Archives, Algerian National Library, Algiers.

88. René Depestre, "L'âge du Vietnam," *Poésie sur tous les fronts*, August 4, 1969, Algiers, box S2, Jean Sénac Archives, Algerian National Library, Algiers.

89. Hamid Nacer Khodja to Jean Sénac, September 23, 1969, Algiers, box S14, Jean Sénac Archives, Algerian National Library, Algiers.

90. Sénac, diaries, box S10, Jean Sénac Archives, Algerian National Library, Algiers.

91. Mario de Andrade, "Réflexions autour du Congrès Culturel de la Havane" and "Culture et Lutte Armée," *Souffles*, no. 9 (1968).

92. Hocine Tandjaoui, interview with author; and Hocine Benkheira, interview with author.

93. Toni Maraini, email interview with author.

94. *Souffles*, nos. 16–17 (1969).

95. Mohamed Melehi, phone interview with author.

96. Tahar Ben Jelloun, "Entretien avec Sembène Ousmane," *Souffles*, nos. 16–17 (1969): 51.

97. Abdellatif Laâbi to Hocine Tandjaoui, January 1, 1970, Rabat, in author's possession; Abdellatif Laâbi, interview, May 10, 2012, PANAFEST archives, Paris.

98. Serfaty and Daure-Serfaty, *La mémoire de l'autre*; Serfaty, "Salut aux Afro-Américains," *Souffles*, nos. 16–17 (1969): 33

99. Ibid.

100. Ibid.

101. Sénac, "La grande protestation des poètes américains de descendance africaine: La misère," *Poésie sur tous les fronts*, September 11, 1979, Algiers, box S6, Jean Sénac Archives, Algerian National Library, Algiers.

102. Sénac, "Jadis l'instituteur," in *Œuvres poétiques*, 277.

103. Stokely Carmichael, cited in Joseph, *Stokely*, 216.

104. Stokely Carmichael, in Sénac, "La grande protestation des poètes américains de descendance africaine: La révolte," *Poésie sur tous les fronts*, September 11, 1979, Algiers, box S6, Jean Sénac Archives, Algerian National Library, Algiers.

105. Quotation from Ted Joans in ibid.

106. Mouloud Feraoun, an Algerian writer, was assassinated by the OAS on March 15, 1962, in Algiers; see Lenzini, *Mouloud Feraoun*. Ali la Pointe, an Algerian fighter in the FLN, was killed by the French army during the Battle of Algiers, a scene made famous by Gillo Pontecorvo's *The Battle of Algiers*.

107. Léopold Sédar Senghor, "Assassinats," in Sénac, "La grande protestation des poètes américains de descendance africaine: La révolte," *Poésie sur tous les fronts*, September 11, 1979, Algiers, box S6, Jean Sénac Archives, Algerian National Library, Algiers.

108. Jean Sénac to Mohamed Bejdaoui, November 30, 1969, Algiers, box S7, Jean Sénac Archives, Algerian National Library, Algiers.

109. Ted Joans to Jean Sénac, January 1972, Marrakech, box S15, Jean Sénac Archives, Algerian National Library, Algiers.

110. Ibid.

111. Jean Sénac, interview with Jean Peroncel-Hugoz, *L'Afrique littéraire et artistique*; cited in Nacer-Khodja, *Jean Sénac*, 528.

112. Sénac, "Ode à l'Amérique africaine," in *Œuvres poétiques*, 293–294.

113. Ibid.

114. Ibid.

115. Hocine Tandjaoui, interview.

116. Krienke, *Jean Sénac*, 62. Krienke argues that the silencing of voices of dissent in poetry was a worldwide phenomenon linked to the cultural Cold War between the United States and the Soviet Union.

117. See Chap. 5.

Chapter Four: Nothing to Fear from the Poet

1. For more on the 1969 PANAF, see Chap. 3.

2. For more on the Black Panthers' presence in Algiers, see Khellas, *Le premier festival culturel panafricain*; Klein, *Eldridge Cleaver*; Meghelli, "From Harlem to Algiers" and "'Weapon in Our Struggle for Liberation'"; and Tolan-Szkilnik, "Flickering Fault Lines."

3. According to Elaine Mokhtefi, the Panthers refused to acknowledge the power imbalance between themselves and the Algerian political hierarchy, repeatedly underestimating their hosts and measuring their power against the authority of the Algerian government. They barely spoke French (and even less Arabic) and did not venture beyond the boundaries of the city, nor did they read the Algerian press or listen to the local radio. Their knowledge of Algeria, a country they had idealized from afar, was almost exclusively based on Gillo Pontecorvo's 1966 film *The Battle of Algiers*, Frantz Fanon's texts, and Malcolm X's speeches. "They had no perspective on the colonial past in Algeria," said Mokhtefi, " not the ravages of the war or the profound underdevelopment that the regime was attempting to tackle" (*Algiers, Third World Capital*, 167).

4. Ibid., 105.

5. Charlotte Hill, in "American Exiles in East Africa (Part 2)," New Yorker Radio Hour, March 8, 2019, https://www.wnycstudios.org/podcasts/tnyradiohour/segments/american-exiles-east-africa-part-2-seg.

6. Ouadi, interview with PANAFEST archives.

7. Hill, in "American Exiles in East Africa (Part 2)."

8. Denis Martinez, interview with author.

9. To disclose these accounts is by no means to discredit the project of creating a Pan-African union; rather, I seek to explore the many struggles that any group of individuals from radically different backgrounds had to face and how these miscomprehensions sometimes limited the potential of their Pan-African community. In *The Practice of Diaspora: Literature, Translation and the Rise of Black Internationalism*, Brent Hayes Edwards argues that it is only through the haunting gaps produced by misunderstandings, or what he calls "décalage," that we can articulate such concepts as diaspora (15), or, I would add, such networks as the Maghreb Generation. For more scholarship that explores solidarity across the Black Atlantic, see Daulatzai, *Black Star, Crescent Moon*; Gilroy, *Black Atlantic* (of course); Kelley, *Africa Speaks, American Answers*; Makalani, *In the Cause of Freedom*; Meriwether, *Proudly We Can Be Africans*; Plummer, *Rising Wind*; and Von Eschen, *Race against Empire*.

10. This revolutionary masculinity had many commonalities with the Black notions of masculinity that emerged after World War II among followers of Islam and jazz musicians as well as among zoot-suiters. See Kelley, *Race Rebels*; and Turner, *Soundtrack to a Movement*. For more on Black masculinities in the Black Panther

Party, see Bloom and Martin, *Black against Empire*, 95. See also this exchange between Alice Walker and Panther Elaine Brown published in the *New York Times* on May 5, 1993: https://www.nytimes.com/1993/05/05/opinion/black-panthers-of-black-punks-they-ran-on-empty.html.

11. "L'Algérie au carrefour de la culture africaine," *Algérie Actualité*, July 27–August 2, 1969, 1; "On a découvert l'Afrique," *El-Moudjahid*, July 22, 1969, 4; Martine Perrin, "L'Afrique fête ses retrouvailles" and "Le festival est une entreprise lucide et enthousiaste de l'affirmation de notre personnalité," *El-Moudjahid*, July 22, 1969, 1. All newspaper clippings from the Matt Schaffer Collection, Emory University, Atlanta, Georgia.

12. Abdelmadjid M., "Lettre ouverte à l'Afrique retrouvée," *El-Moudjahid*, July 22, 1969, 2.

13. Mustapha Ait Khaled, "Accueil et hébergement des artistes: Un motif de satisfaction," *El-Moudjahid*, July 30, 1969, 4.

14. Ibid.

15. Jacques Dupuy to the Ministère des Affaires Étrangères, telegram, August 3, 1969, Algiers, 2, dossier Festival Pan-Africain, N_3_3_1, Archives Diplomatiques de Nantes, Nantes, France.

16. Of course, the image that the Algerian government wanted to project may very well have differed significantly from Algerian officials' actual sentiments toward African governments and peoples. Unfortunately, as I did not have access to government archives, all I can offer is this façade of entente and statements acquired secondhand. The Algerian government touted its Africanity, its brotherly relationship with Africans, when that benefited its international relations. In 1964, in a conversation with Yugoslavian president Tito, Algerian president Ben Bella, intent on proving that Algeria had much in common with Yugoslavia, admitted that yes, "Algeria wants to focus on Africa in its policies. Not because of skin color—we are white like you, maybe a little browner—but because we have problems identical to problems of other nations on the continent and because our problems are intertwined" (Byrne, *Mecca of Revolution*, 201). Algerian officials, eager to get support from whomever they could, used their country's racial ambiguity to claim to belong in turn to either Eastern Europe or Africa.

17. Salah Guemriche, interview with author.

18. I use "Black Africa" here because it is what the Algerians use in the newspapers and interviews. It is important to note, however, that when Algerians thought of their nation as "white," as opposed to a "Black" Africa, they willfully ignored the fact that many Algerians were in fact Black. Scholars such as Muriam Haleh Davis, Chouki El Hamel, John Hunwick, Bruce Hall, Bernard Lewis, and Eve Troutt Powell have examined the construction and fluctuation of racial categories in the Sahara and the Sahel, that is, in the spaces of intersection between Black, White,

Arab, and more. Some titles include but are not limited to Davis, *Markets of Civilization*; Hall, *History of Race in Muslim West Africa*; El Hamel, *Black Morocco*; Hunwick and Troutt Powell, *Same but Different*; Lewis, *Race and Slavery in the Middle East*; and Troutt Powell, *Different Shade of Colonialism*.

19. Boussad Ouadi, interview with PANAFEST archives.

20. Ibid.

21. Houari Niati, cited in "Flashback: 21 July 1969; Pan African Cultural Festival Rocks Algiers," Carinya Sharples (blog), September 24, 2012: https://carinyasharplesjournalist.wordpress.com/2012/09/24/flashback-21-july-1969-Pan-African-culture-Festival-rocks-algiers/.

22. Ibid.

23. These comments are reminiscent of Ibn Battuta's descriptions of the Black women of Mali, who "appeared naked before people, exposing their genitals" (in Mackintosh-Smith, *Travels of Ibn Battutah*, 290). Ibn Battuta's manuscripts were widely circulated throughout northern Africa and likely contributed to the formation of stereotyped images of Black women's bodies for generations of Maghrebis.

24. Denis Martinez, interview with author.

25. Decades of scholarship on sex and sexualities have given us an intricate understanding of the political, social, and economic implications of sexual inequality. Particularly revealing are the works of Ann Stoler and Anne McClintock, who have elucidated how sex and race intertwined to create complex systems of power and desire in the colonial contexts. Such works include Ballhatchet, *Race, Sex, and Class under the Raj*; Hodges, *Contraception, Colonialism and Commerce*; McClintock, *Imperial Leather*; and Stoler, *Carnal Knowledge and Imperial Power* and "Educating Desire in Colonial South-East Asia." Very little has been written, however, on sex between the colonizer and the colonized. Studies of sex and its power remain centered on the colonizer/colonized dichotomy. Medievalists such as David Nirenberg offer one perspective of what sexual relationships look like in communities that have different levels of power but are not in a colonizer/colonized hierarchy. See, for instance, Nirenberg, *Communities of Violence* and *Neighboring Faiths*.

26. As Tsitsi Jaji notes in her article "Bingo Magazine in the Age of Pan-African Festivals," festivals such as the PANAF and the JCC, as we will see in Chapter 5, "necessarily privileged artists and cultural workers with the means and/or support for travel from governmental, United Nations, or nongovernmental organizations and were often dominated by male participants and planners." Thus, explains Jaji, the festival history of Pan-Africanism and Third-Worldism is subject to much of the same criticism scholars have leveled against scholars of globalization, transnationalism, and cosmopolitanism. "A history of global black thought that privileges such events will inevitably tend to gloss over the ways gender, class, education

level, and plain old cultural capital shut out certain participants and thus obscure many local iterations of black internationalist impulses. It will also emphasize the role of the state and its male-dominated structures of governance and cultural planning" (113).

27. The government-sponsored newspapers included some cursory articles about Miriam Makeba's and Nina Simone's performances but did not often engage with them as political actors in the Pan-African community.

28. Kathleen Cleaver, interview with author.

29. Hill, "American Exiles in East Africa (Part 2)."

30. Kathleen Cleaver, interview with author

31. Kathleen Cleaver, interview with PANAFEST archives, June 2015, New York City, http://webdocs-sciences-sociales.science/panafest/#PANAF_69-Kathleen_Neal_Cleaver.

32. Ibid.

33. Elaine Mokhtefi, interview with author.

34. For many Black American men throughout the twentieth century, the experience of traveling to North Africa seems to have been a liberating one; this was certainly the case for Ted Joans but also for other Black American men such as jazz musician Randy Weston, boxer Muhammed Ali, noir novelist Chester Himes, and before any of them, novelist Claude McKay. Indeed, as early as 1928, McKay, who was sick of Paris and its group of despondent White American expats, traveled to Tangiers and Tetouan on his first visit to the African continent. In his autobiography, *A Long Way from Home*, McKay writes that it was only in Morocco that he felt himself free of his "condition as a black man." In Morocco, McKay "experienced a feeling that must be akin to the physical well-being of a dumb animal among kindred animals, who lives instinctively and by sensations, without thinking." He felt at home among these people that he called "magical and barbaric" (300, 338). Little has been written on Black Americans' experiences in Algeria, Morocco, and Tunisia compared to the wealth of scholarship on Cairo as a center for the African American expatriate community. For work on Cairo, see Beckett, "Why 1964 Cairo Mattered in 1975 Oakland"; Kosba, "*. . . And Bid Him Sing*"; and Lubin, *Geographies of Liberation*. In the 1970s and 1980s, North Africa gradually became a less appealing place for many Black Americans, who argued that Islam was racist and that Arabs were colonizers of Africa. For more on this, see Aïdi, "Egypt and the Afrocentrists" and "Slavery, Genocide, and the Politics of Outrage."

35. To some Africans the meeting in Algiers was the unraveling of an ideal, proof that Africa was too fragmented to pull off continental unity, be it political or cultural. For more on the tension between Black Americans and Black Africans at the PANAF, see Tolan-Szkilnik, "Quest for a Pan-African Groove."

36. William Klein, *Festival Panafricain d'Alger*; Shepp, *Live at the Pan-African Festival*.

37. Very few scholars have tackled the complex figure of Ted Joans. This is not for lack of an archive: his papers, housed in the Bancroft Library at the University of California, Berkeley, comprise twenty linear feet of collages, correspondence, prose, poetry, film scripts, travel logs, pamphlets, posters, and more. Excluded from most of the major literary anthologies of the second half of the twentieth century, when Joans *is* included, for example, in works on the Beat generation, he is a lone Black face in a sea of white faces, along with Bob Kaufman. For a discussion on Joans's exclusion from the African American literary canon, see Elliot Fox, "Ted Joans and the (B)reach of the African American Literary Canon"; and Gerald Nicosia's preface to Joans's *Teducation: Selected Poems 1949–1999*, iv.

38. For more biographical elements, see Lawlor, *Beat Culture*; and Tronrud and Alcalay, "Poet Painter / Former Villager Now / World Traveler." For an example of an invitation to Ted Joans's birthday party in Greenwich Village, see McDarrah and McDarrah, *Beat Generation*, 94. Ted Joans is credited with scrawling the phrase "Bird Lives" around Greenwich Village when Charlie Parker died in 1955.

39. Ted Joans, "Going Home," BANC MSS 99/244, box 1:10, Bancroft Library.

40. Ted Joans "Africa," BANC MSS 99/244, box 1:36, Bancroft Library.

41. Ted Joans "Onboard the *Lyautey*," BANC MSS 99/244, box 17:23, Bancroft Library.

42. Ibid.

43. "Ted Joans expose à la Librairie des Colonnes," *Journal de Tanger*, Saturday, January 19, 1963, BANC MSS 99/244, box 3:71, Bancroft Library.

44. Ted Joans collage, BANC MSS 99/244, box: Oversize 1, Bancroft Library.

45. Ibid.

46. Ted Joans "Twin Sounds," March 24, 1965, BANC MSS 99/244, box 2:2, Bancroft Library.

47. Ted Joans, scrawl on PANAF program, BANC MSS 99/244, box 4:9, Bancroft Library.

48. Ted Joans, *The Black Man's Guide to Africa*, BANC MSS 99/244, box 12:14, Bancroft Library.

49. In many ways, Joans's trip to North Africa emulated Malcolm X's 1964 hajj to the Middle East and North Africa. During his trip to the Maghreb, Malcolm had also visited the Moroccan and Algerian casbahs and identified with the anticolonial struggle of the Maghrebi people. In the Middle East and North Africa, Malcolm made a surprising discovery, as he expressed in a letter to his assistants in Harlem: "[Islam] is the one religion that erases from its society the race problem. Throughout my travels in the Muslim world, I have met, talked to, and even eaten with people who in America would have been considered 'white'—but the 'white' attitude was removed from their minds by the religion of Islam" (Haley, *Autobiography of Malcolm X*, 347). Malcolm X, unlike Ted Joans, understood that colorism existed throughout Africa. For more, see the excellent list of primary and second-

ary sources on Malcolm X and the Afro-Arab connection, put together by the American Institute of Beirut: https://aub.edu.lb.libguides.com/c.php?g=975600&p=7789907. See also Aïdi, "Du Bois, Ghana, and Cairo Jazz." The discourse on Islam as race blind was not uncommon in the Black American community; see Jackson, *Islam and the Blackamerican*. It was while he was living in Morocco that Joans learned of Malcolm X's assassination. After reading the news in a French Moroccan newspaper, Joans wrote: "I raised my head toward the African sky so that I wouldn't cry / I thought not of good food / I thought not of good sex / I thought not of great art / I just stood with my head raised toward the East / and in peace I thought of you and now I confess / that you spoke for me and thus died for me / Yes I confess / I loved you Malcolm X" (Ted Joans, February 1965, Goulimine, Morocco, BANC MSS 99/244, box 2:1, Bancroft Library).

50. Ted Joans, *The Black Man's Guide to Afric*a, BANC MSS 99/244, box 12:14, Bancroft Library. During his time in Africa, Ted Joans set off to write *The Black Man's Guide to Africa* in "Black English," a tongue that, according to Joans, "has a rhythm that causes statements to swing loosely and of course un-academic. . . . This language is a living force, a freedom thing." The guide, which is funny and informative much of the time, is a revealing window onto one Black American man's struggle to make sense of Africa and its people.

51. In a 1975 interview, Joans referred to this collection of poems as his "hand-grenade poems: poems you pulled the pin out of, threw and BOOM that was it" ("Ted Joans: Tri-continental Poet," 8).

52. Ted Joans "The Pieds Noirs," in *Afrodisia*, 33.

53. Ted Joans, "Home," BANC MSS 99/244, box 4:26, Bancroft Library.

54. Ted Joans "We, Don and Me," BANC MSS 99/244, box 4:27, Bancroft Library.

55. Ted Joans, *The Black Man's Guide to Africa*, BANC MSS 99/244, box 12:14, Bancroft Library.

56. Ibid.

57. Ted Joans to Hy Shore, December 4, 1969, BANC MSS 99/224, box 23:18, Bancroft Library.

58. Ted Joans, *The Black Man's Guide to Africa,* BANC MSS 99/244, box 12:14, Bancroft Library.

59. Ibid.

60. Document published by the Senegalese government, 186 PO/1, box 832, Archives Diplomatiques de Nantes, Nantes, France.

61. Bitty Moro, interview with PANAFEST archives, May 8, 2014, Abidjan, Ivory Coast, http://webdocs-sciences-sociales.science/panafest/#PANAF_69-Bitty_Moro.

62. Houphouët-Boigny, the "father" of the Ivory Coast's independence, was op-

posed to Pan-African unity as proposed by Kwame Nkrumah. Houphouët-Boigny considered himself a moderate and opposed the revolutionary regimes of Algeria and the Guinea of Sekou Touré. A partisan of Francophonie, he maintained strong relationships with the French government and with French cultural and economic interests well after the Ivory Coast's independence. For more, see Nandjui, *Houphouët-Boigny*. Houphouët-Boigny also developed a strong relationship with American president John F. Kennedy. In fact, the JFK Presidential Library and Museum in Boston includes a whole room dedicated to the relationship between the two presidents and their first ladies (who featured on an August 1962 cover of *Ebony* magazine together) that includes gifts, pictures, and menus from state dinners that the Houphouët-Boignys attended at the White House.

63. Bitty Moro, interview with PANAFEST archives.

64. See Tolan-Szkilnik, "Quest for a Pan-African Groove."

65. Bitty Moro, interview with PANAFEST archives.

66. For more on the links between race, slavery, and sex in northern Africa and the Sahara, see Beshir, *Terramedia*; Ennaji, *Soldats, domestiques et concubines*; Gaudio, "Trans-Saharan Trade"; Goodman, "Demystifying 'Islamic Slavery'"; Chouki El Hamel, "'Race,' Slavery and Islam" and "Surviving Slavery"; Hunwick and Troutt Powell, *African Diaspora*; McDougall, "Concubinage as Forced Marriage" and "'To Marry One's Slave'"; and Silverstein, "Racial Politics of the Amazigh Revival."

67. Bitty Moro, interview with PANAFEST archives.

68. Tahar Ben Jelloun, "Entretien avec Sembène Ousmane," *Souffles*, nos. 16–17 (1969): 51.

69. Historian David Nirenberg, in a discussion of restrictions around prostitution in the Middle Ages, asks, "Why would a community invest its honor with women whom the community itself defined as without honor?" (*Communities of Violence*, 152). In fourteenth-century Iberia, Nirenberg argues, prostitutes functioned symbolically as the skin and body that bound the Christian community together, "hence the danger of a miscegenation that could achieve, at least symbolically, the clandestine admittance of the non-Christian into the Christian community through the body of the prostitute" (156). In "French Regulation of Prostitution in Nineteenth-Century Colonial Algeria," Bruce Dunne argues that in precolonial Algeria, sex workers were seen as a communal good: they functioned as a public service for adolescent sexual initiation in a society that was sexually segregated. In the colonial period, European and "Indigenous" sex workers were separated, and each serviced their own community. By excluding sex workers from the streets and cafés of Algiers for the PANAF, the Algerian government was perhaps demonstrating its fear that Blackness could "contaminate" Algerian youth through the bodies of sex workers, a common concern for colonial administrations throughout the

world. It was a form of social control over poor, single women on the part of an Algerian state that did not care what happened to these women per se but did care how these women's actions affected the sexual lives of adolescent Algerian men.

70. René Depestre, interview with author.

71. Ted Joans, "My Trip," in *Afrodisia*, 64.

72. Another example: "Black Caper," BANC MSS 99/244, box 6:23, Bancroft Library.

73. In *Imperial Leather*, historian Anne McClintock discusses the "gendering of empire," the process by which unconquered, "virgin" land was feminized: "Women are the earth that is to be discovered, entered, named, inseminated and, above all, owned. Linked symbolically to the land, women are relegated to a realm beyond history and thus bear a particularly vexed relation to narratives of historical change and political effect" (31).

74. Depestre and Joans were part of a culture that sexualized Arab women. Influenced perhaps by their extensive sojourns in France, these men internalized the white, male French gaze toward Algerian women. In *The Colonial Harem* (1986), Algerian poet and literary critic Malek Alloula followed the gaze of the colonial photographer as he tried to capture the Algerian woman, frustrated by her veil, mentally stripping her of her clothing, staging his crimped fantasies, and creating, through his postcards, an anthology of "Moorish bosoms." Alloula demonstrated that photographs of Algerian women represented the colonial regimes' "booty," the plunder of war, and the colonizer's fantasies of creating a bordello on the conquered land. For a more recent and extensive discussion of sex, race, and colonialism as seen by the French, look no further than the volume edited by Boëtsch et al., *Sexualités, identités et corps colonisés*.

75. Ted Joans, "Pretty Far-a-Way," BANC MSS 99/244, box 7:30, Bancroft Library. Black women also fetishized Algerian women behind their veils. Black American Jesse Fauset, who visited Algiers from Marseille in 1925, was entranced "by the mysterious figures of women clothed in white and numerous garments, a white face veil covering mouth and nose, cheeks and hair, all but two dark impenetrable eyes and a triangle of creamy forehead" ("Dark Algiers," 384). See also Garcia, "For a Few Days."

76. René Depestre, interview with author.

77. Ted Joans, "As Don Took Off at Dawn," in *Afrodisia*, 54.

78. Ibid., 52.

79. Sex was, as historian Marc Matera argues, "an ongoing revision of self-presentation" for the Pan-African revolutionary (*Black London*, 223).

80. René Depestre, interview with author.

81. Tunisian journalist Jelila Hafsia, in a 1988 letter to René Depestre, had already identified Depestre's tendency to use women as symbols rather than as his-

torical, political actors in their own right: "Women in all your books are the main character. Symbol? Dream?" (Jelila Hafsia to René Depestre, March 23, 1988, Tunis, René Depestre Archives, Limoges, France).

82. Depestre, "Éros et révolution," in *Rage de vivre*, 285–286.

83. In *Black London*, Marc Matera explores the tensions at play in the London-based Black community of the 1920s and 1930s. By looking at the journals of many of the young Black intellectuals who lived in London (including South African novelist Peter Abrahams and Trinidadian historian C. L. R. James) and analyzing the way these men talked about their sexual relationships, particularly with white women, Matera concludes that sexuality was "central to the reconstitution of gendered selves in opposition to empire, and Black masculinity was the presumptive staging ground of anticolonial political subjectivity" (236).

84. The men were participating in a global movement of revolutionary love, and a very prevalent one in the 1960s. In *El socialismo y el hombre en Cuba*, Che Guevara famously said, "Let me say, at the risk of seeming ridiculous, that the true revolutionary is guided by great feelings of love."

85. Ted Joans, "Cuntinent," in *Afrodisia*, 72.

86. bell hooks, *Killing Rage*, 64.

87. But why, asks Black American poet Audre Lorde in "Sexism: An American Disease in Black Face," must Black women, or in this case, Algerian women, pay the price for the wounds inflicted by white supremacy and imperialism upon Black men?

Chapter Five: The Red in Red-Carpet

1. As Morgan Corriou noted in a recent email to the author, this is even more of a myth because Cheriaa knew Egyptian film well and was attempting to rehabilitate Egyptian films in Tunisian cinemas by showcasing movies by Egyptian director Youssef Chahine, among others.

2. Sembène, *La noire de . . . .*

3. Challouf, *Tahar Cheriaa*; Gadjigo, *Sembène!*

4. Twenty-sixth edition of the JCC, poster, November 2018, Tunis.

5. Férid Boughedir, interview with author.

6. Vermeren, "Misère de l'historiographie du 'Maghreb' postcolonial."

7. Dakhlia, *Tunisie, le pays sans bruit*, 39.

8. Historian Charles Micaud introduces his *Tunisia: The Politics of Modernization* (1964) by lauding Tunisia for its painless adaptation to the modern world. Unlike most other new countries, Micaud argues, Tunisia "offers patterns of social development and a set of political institutions that, so far, seem to be meeting the task for modernization without sacrificing basic human values for totalitarian 'short cuts.'" This observation, coming from a Franco-American historian just

eight years after Tunisian independence, demonstrates quite clearly the European desire to single out Tunisia as a model for African and Middle Eastern development. Until now, much scholarship on postindependence Tunisia, such as Micaud's book, has participated in circulating the image of an exceptionally moderate country—one with a European mindset and just a touch of Orientalist exoticism. For a more recent example of scholars portraying Tunisia as a liberal oasis, see Marsis, *Tunisia: An Arab Anomaly*.

9. A report titled *La politique culturelle de la Tunisie* (1970), destined for UNESCO and written by Rafik Saïd, director of cultural affairs in Tunisia in the 1960s and Tunisian ambassador to Canada, perfectly illustrates the rhetoric of the Tunisian government in the 1960s. Throughout the report, Saïd strives to show that Tunisia is the country with the richest culture in the world. Its strategic geographical position, he argues, gave Tunisia a modern and Western culture with an authentic Tunisian touch. Tunisia "should attain a sublime level of civilization . . . [and] the people living in this pacific land, inheritors of so many different races, are they not one of the most cultured in the world?"

10. Habib Bourguiba, cited in Kasmi, *Tunisie*, 34.

11. "L'humanisme de Bourguiba," *Le Monde*, June 26, 1972, http://www.lemonde.fr/archives/article/1972/06/26/temoignage-l-humanisme-de-m-bourguiba_2390957_1819218.html#pQgPvjHEvooLmQ79.99.

12. Sirius, "Unité et diversité," *Le Monde*, April 27, 1964, http://www.lemonde.fr/archives/article/1963/04/27/unite-et-diversite_2206197_1819218.html#QlojTwO1MjSeOR5G.99. As late as 2006, the notable French political scientist Béatrice Hibou would not use the word "dictatorship" to designate Tunisia. While the government could be coercive at times, she wrote, "most Tunisians just adapt, and find concrete and material advantages to these rules." Maya Lenoir, interview with Béatrice Hibou, "La Tunisie sous la loupe de Béatrice Hibou," *Nawaat*, September 9, 2006, http://nawaat.org/portail/2006/09/09/la-tunisie-sous-la-loupe-de-beatrice-hibou/.

13. Habib Bourguiba, "Unité dans la Diversité," speech at the Conference of Independent African States, May 23, 1963, Addis Ababa, collected in *Bourguiba-Discours*, available at the Bibliothèque Nationale de France (BNF), 12–13.

14. Lajili, *Bourguiba-Senghor*, 147; Toumi "La politique africaine de la Tunisie," 120.

15. Petrucci and Fois, "Attitudes towards Israel in Tunisian Political Debate."

16. Scholarly accounts differ in their interpretation of Bourguiba's feelings about Africa. In their biography of Bourguiba, historian Sophie Bessis and journalist Souhayr Belhassen imply that Bourguiba had little admiration for the cultures of the African continent south of the Sahara; throughout his trip he simply followed the program, "acted like a tourist, in Cameroon, demanded to be shown

Pygmies, and asked all of his hosts to gift him wild beasts for the Tunis zoo" (Bessis and Blehassen, *Bourguiba*, 312). Scholar Mohsen Toumi, however, argues that Bourguiba turned toward Africa after his notorious speech in Jericho in March 1965, to find a new and compensating field in which Tunisia might deploy its power (Toumi, "La politique africaine de la Tunisie," 120). In any case, Bourguiba's special rapport with Africa came up again and again in interviews, particularly his relationship with Senghor, which according to newspapers of the time and many interviewees remembering now, was particularly intimate.

17. "Francophonie" designates the group of people, organizations, and institutions who use French. "La Francophonie" is also often used as shorthand to designate the Organisation Internationale de la Francophonie, created in 1970 with the backing of Léopold Sédar Senghor, Habib Bourguiba, Hamani Diori of Niger, and Norodom Sihanouk of Cambodia. La Francophonie's goal is to encourage cultural and technological cooperation among francophone countries throughout the world. Though the organization signed its charter in 1970, the seeds of the project were planted during Bourguiba's visit to Senegal in 1965. For more on *francophonie*, see Glasze, "Discursive Constitution"; Middell, "Francophonia as a World Region?"; and Parker, "Francophonie et universalité."

18. "Bourguiba aux Sénégalais: J'ai l'impression de m'adresser à des Tunisiens," *La Presse* (Tunis), November 27, 1965, 6.

19. Abdellatif Ben Amar, interview with author.

20. Ibid.

21. Tahar Cheriaa, "Les cinémas maghrébins: Presentation," Kaiser Cheriaa, personal archives, Tunis.

22. Hassan Daldoul, interview with author.

23. Recently, scholars of the 1970s across the world have attempted to refute the narrative of the 1970s as an era of decline. Titles such as the *The Shock of the Global: The 1970s in Perspective*, edited by Niall Ferguson, Charles S. Maier, Erez Manela, and Daniel J. Sargent, point to the many ways in which the 1970s were a "transformative" decade—as indeed they were. And though, as Alan Taylor argues in his contribution to the volume, they may have been a hopeful decade for the United States, which managed to spread its message of globalization and neoliberalism throughout the world, for many countries in Africa the 1970s were synonymous with increasing economic and political dependence on international monetary institutions and Western companies. As Stephen Ellis explains in "Writing Histories of Contemporary Africa," the 1970s were a major point of rupture in African history, even more so than the decade of independence. "If one seeks to identify points of discontinuity in Africa's history since independence or, to be more precise, in the history of Africa's insertion in the world," writes Ellis, "it becomes apparent that many ruptures first became visible in the 1970s, when oil crises,

currency instability and a series of related events and trends combined to create a comprehensive change in the prospects for African states and societies, and in the forms of their political life" (9).

24. Laude, *Joyeuse apocalypse*, 144–145.

25. The Senegalese Tirailleurs were a corps of the French army that comprised subjects of the French Empire. Though they were called the Senegalese Tirailleurs (*tirailleurs sénégalais*), they came from across western, central, and eastern Africa. Ousmane Sembène made an excellent film, *Camp de Thiaroye* (1988), which tells the story of a group of Senegalese Tirailleurs (who had fought for the French in World War II) who were massacred by the French army as they were demanding their veteran's benefits in Thiaroye, on the outskirts of Dakar. The film was banned in France for ten years, and the French government has yet to issue an official apology. For more on this, see the recently published graphic novel by Patrice Perna and Nicolas Otéro, *Morts par la France: Thiaroye 1944*.

26. For more on African filmmakers' experiences studying film in the Soviet Union, see Chomentwoski, "L'expérience soviétique des cinemas africains," 111; and Pierre-Bouthier, "Founding Transnational Experience."

27. See Diawara, *African Cinema: Politics and Culture*; and Ukadike, *Black African Cinema*. In "Francophone West African Cinema, 1955–1969," David Murphy explains that it is no coincidence that neorealism became the go-to style of many filmmakers of the 1960s and 1970s: its do-it-yourself ethic allowed filmmakers who had little money to make socially committed films (54). The neorealist style focused on the difficult conditions of the working class, were usually filmed on location, and frequently used nonprofessional actors.

28. Med Hondo, in Signaté, *Med Hondo*, 19–20.

29. For more on France's "Fond Sud," the country's anti-American-globalization cinema politics, see Lecler, *Une contre-mondisalisation audiovisuelle*.

30. Hondo, "What Is Cinema for Us?" (Mauritania, 1979), 302.

31. Ibid.

32. Hondo, in Signaté, *Med Hondo*, 28.

33. Ousmane Sembène, in "1er Festival International des Journées Cinématographiques de Carthage," *Nawadi*, publication of the Fédération Tunisienne des Ciné-Clubs, September 1968, Archives Nationales de Tunisie, Tunis.

34. Ousmane Sembène, "Quatre Africains à Cannes," round table organized by Jean-Claude Morellet, correspondant of *Jeune afrique*, in "Tahar Cheriaa's Cannes Journal," Hassan Daldoul, personal archives, Tunis.

35. Ukadike, *Black African Cinema*. For more on the Third Cinema, see the founding text: Getino and Solanas, "Towards a Third Cinema." Like many members of the Maghreb Generation, Fernando Solanas was inspired by Frantz Fanon's writings. In an interview during the PANAF in Algiers, Solanas explained that his

goal in film was primarily to put Frantz Fanon's revolutionary ideals into practice: "Our work is indexed on a continuous fight for liberation, and our thinking is always to follow the masses and to fight against all intellectual hierarchy, which is clearly a reflection of a so-called universal culture." He argued that Fanon was just as important in Argentina as he had been in Algeria and Cuba. "Interview de Fernando E. Solanas," *El-Moudjahid*, August 1, 1969, 3AA.94, Quai Branly Archives, Paris. For more on the circulation of the Third Cinema's manifesto in the Arab world and its translation, see Farine, *Naḥwa Sīnīmā Thawriyya*.

36. Nouri Bouzid, "On Inspiration," 49.

37. Hassan Daldoul, interview with author.

38. Kaiser Cheriaa, interview with author.

39. Cheriaa, *Écrans d'abondance*.

40. Férid Boughedir, interview with author.

41. Tahar Cheriaa, "Perspective d'action cinématographiques en Tunisie," April 1956, 3, Hassan Daldoul, personal archives, Tunis.

42. Conversation with Kmar Bendana, Institut de Recherche sur le Maghreb Contemporain (IRMC), November 5, 2018, Tunis.

43. Férid Boughedir (interview), in Challouf, *À l'ombre du baobab*.

44. Cheriaa, "Les responsabilités de l'artiste créateur dans une société violente," in "Colloque sur l'impact de la violence dans les moyens d'information," UNESCO, Paris, 1970, 1, Hassan Daldoul, personal archives, Tunis.

45. Kaiser Cheriaa, interview with author.

46. Ousmane Sembène, in "Quatre Africains à Cannes."

47. Walid Shmit, "Al-film al-sawdā' yarbaḥ jā'izat qarṭāj," *Al-Nahār Al-Lubnānī*, December 14, 1966.

48. Corriou and Oualdi, "Les Journées Cinématographiques de Carthage."

49. Press clipping from *Al-'amal*, December 4, 1966, Centre de Documentation Nationale, Tunis.

50. Mary Azoury, "Les Journées Cinématographiques de Carthage seront désormais une référence," *La Revue du Liban*, November 9, 1968, 13.

51. Christine Gouze-Rénal, *Jeune afrique* 3, no. 2 (January 1967): 58.

52. Ibid.

53. Ousmane Sembène (interview with Hechmi Trabelsi), "Un état fort est celui qui accorde à ses artistes la liberté de critique," *L'Action*, October 16, 1968.

54. Hassan Daldoul, interview with author.

55. Corriou, "Cinéphilie et engagement estudiantin."

56. Néjib Ayed, interview with author.

57. Corriou and Oualdi, "Les Journées Cinématographiques de Carthage."

58. *Perspectives Tunisiennes*, April 12, 1967; cited in Hendrickson, "Finding Tunisia in the Global 1960s," 72.

59. For more about March 1968 in Tunisia, see Hendrickson "March 1968." Hendrickson argues, compellingly, that Tunisia figures very little in the history of 1968, even though the protests in Tunis occurred before the infamous French May 1968. Even with the plethora of studies on the global 1960s, Hendrickson explains, very few scholars have looked at student movements in the Third World, and even less so in Tunisia.

60. Corriou, "Cinéphilie et engagement estudiantin."

61. For more on the Third Cinema, see note 35 above.

62. Tahar Cheriaa, interview with Samira Dami; cited in "En passant par les écoles et les lycées," Kaiser Cheriaa, personal archives, Tunis. For an excellent article on the influence of Pan-Africanism, Third-Worldism, and the idea of militant film on the members of the FTCC, see Corriou, "À quoi rêvent les cinéphiles Tunisiens?"

63. George Gaucher, Ambassador of France in Tunisia, to the Minister of Foreign Affairs, November 6, 1970, Tunis, 7, Nantes Diplomatic Archives, Nantes, France.

64. Ahmed Ben Salah was a Tunisian socialist who did not hesitate to criticize the emerging Tunisian bourgeoisie. Bourguiba appointed Ben Salah minister of finance and planning, sensing the enthusiasm for socialism in the Tunisian population. At the end of the 1960s, however, when Ben Salah's ten-year plan to collectivize the Tunisian agricultural sector had failed, Bourguiba put Ben Salah on trial. The Tunisian regime ostracized him; he fled Tunisia and received asylum in Algeria. For more, see Astrow, "Interview with Ahmed Ben Salah," 56; Borsali, *Livre d'entretiens avec Ahmed ben* Salah; and Braun, "À quoi servent les partis tunisiens?"

65. George Gaucher, Ambassador of France in Tunisia, to the Minister of Foreign Affairs, Tunis, November 6, 1970, 7, Nantes Diplomatic Archives, Nantes, France.

66. Corriou, "Cinéphilie et engagement estudiantin en Tunisie."

67. Abdellatif Ben Amar, interview with author.

68. Ibid.

69. Tahar Cheriaa, interview with Samira Dami; cited in "En passant par les écoles et les lycées," Kaiser Cheriaa, personal archives, Tunis.

70. Hassan Daldoul, interview with author.

71. Férid Boughedir, interview with author.

72. Ibid.

73. Mohammed Challouf, interview with author.

74. Ahmed Bedjaoui, interview with author.

75. Ousmane Sembène, "Témoignages sur les JCC: Réstrospective Carthage 1966–76," *Écrans de Tunisie*, October 1986, 3.

76. Mahmoud Ben Salama, in ibid.

77. Victor Bachy, in "Les Vème journées cinématographiques de Carthage à travers la presse internationale: Un éventail savoureux de commentaires" (réaction de "*La Libre Belgique*"), *Dialogue*, December 1974.

78. Though Maldoror was born in France of Guadeloupean parents, she is widely considered an African filmmaker owing to her lifelong dedication to the liberation struggles of multiple countries in Africa and her close ties to the MPLA (through her partner Mario de Andrade). As David Murphy writes in his introduction to *Africa's Lost Classics*: "Her [Maldoror] films display a deep commitment to the history of the liberation struggles of African peoples, which has earned her honorary status as an African filmmaker" (Bisschoff and Murphy, *Africa's Lost Classics*, 10).

79. Cheriaa, "Ousmane Sembène."

80. *Journées Cinématographiques de Carthage, Quatre Décennies* (Tunis: Ministère de la Culture, de la Jeunesse et des Loisirs de Tunisie, 2004).

81. Néjib Ayad, interview with author.

82. Hassan Daldoul, interview with author.

83. Jelila Hafsia, *Instants de vie*, 94.

84. Ibid.

85. David Murphy explains that this perception has been dominant in most studies of African cinema until recently, when a few scholars have challenged this narrative and revived the works of the African "mavericks," such as Djibril Diop Mambéty (Bisschoff and Murphy, *Africa's Lost Classics*, 1–24). For more, see Diawara, *African Film*; Harrow, *Trash*; and Tcheuyap, *Postcolonialist African Cinema*. Social realism refers to work by artists who are concerned with portraying the actual labor and living conditions of the working class.

86. Murphy, "Francophone West African Cinema," in Bisschoff and Murphy, *Africa's Lost Classics*, 56.

87. Ousmane Sembène, interview with Noureddine Ghali, in Downing, *Film and Politics in the Third World*, 41–53.

88. Celluloid Liberation Front, "Mother of African Cinema."

89. Cummings, "Films of Sarah Maldoror."

90. Maldoror, *Sambizanga*.

91. Ellerson, *Sisters of the Screen*; Maldoror, "On Sambizanga," 308.

92. Maldoror, "On Sambizanga."

93. *Sarah Maldoror: Cinema Tricontinental*, Palais de Tokyo, Paris, 5 (free publication accompanying the exhibit).

94. Hafsia, *Instants de vie*, 69.

95. Hassan Daldoul, interview with author.

96. In an October 1972 interview for *La Presse*, the reporter describes Maldoror thus: "Tall, dark-haired, beautiful, always dynamic, and never taking herself too

seriously, Sarah Maldoror remains in any case a model of femininity itself. She rebels against any questions that regard her personal life and categorically refuses to answer. She still responded to some of our questions, laughing raucously at intervals. "Sarah Maldoror: Ce festival est très important pour nous," *La Presse*, October 5, 1972, 10. Maldoror similarly refused to discuss her private life with me during our interview.

97. Camau, *Tunisie au présent*; Ridha Kefi, "Et Bourguiba libéra la femme," *Jeune afrique*, August 28, 2009, http://www.jeuneafrique.com/Article/LIN27086etbouemmefao/; Kraïem, *État et société*, 292–298.

98. Charlotte Naccache, interview with author.

99. Ynousse N'Diaye, *TAP*, October 14, 1968. Echoes of European admiration for Bourguiba's emancipation of Tunisian women also appeared in the Western press. A 1969 article in *Le Monde* reads: "If not for the few women walking by, draped in the traditional white veil . . . it is difficult to walk around the streets of Tunis without believing that we are in Italy, or in the South of France. At hotels, at the post office, in the shops and offices, young polite, joyous, and efficient women act with more ease than on the other side of the Mediterranean" (Nicole Bernheim, "L'expérience sans complexes de la Tunisie," *Le Monde*, January 6, 1969, http://www.lemonde.fr/archives/article/1969/01/06/iii-l-experience-sans-complexes-de-la-tunisie_2421597_1819218.html#XEoXbHEdEXIMJE3U.99.

100. Ukadike, *Black African Cinema*, 80.

101. Hondo, "Cinema of Exile."

102. Laude, *Joyeuse apocalypse*, 140.

103. Ibid.

104. Sénac's poem "Citizens of Beauty" depicts a man still basking in the glow of a new spring: "And now we will sing love / For there is no Revolution without Love." It ends somewhat ominously, however, warning that Algeria's leaders were squandering away the country's future: "At the cafés' terraces our swollen monkeys / nibble at the future in between their peanuts ("Citoyens de Beauté," 9). Comparing turncoat African leaders to monkeys was common among the militant-artists of this period. These leaders were accused of imitating [*singeant* in French] European leaders, mere copycats who preferred the comforts of collaboration to the unknowns of nonalignment. Abdellatif Laâbi wrote a poem titled "Les singes électroniques," comparing postcolonial African leaders to wind-up toys (*Souffles*, nos. 16–17 [1969]: 40).

105. Med Hondo, in Boughedir, *Caméra d'Afrique*.

106. David Murphy (introduction to Bisschoff and Murphy, *Africa's Lost Classics*) and others have recently argued that the common representation of Sembène as the "father of African cinema" has skewed scholars' vision of African cinema: scholars who focus on Sembène's work tend to perceive African cinema as purely ideologically motivated and less concerned with aesthetic experimentation than

European cinema. While Murphy's argument is valid for African film in general, the African filmmakers who traveled to Carthage in the 1970s were committed to revolutionary cinema as a way to mobilize the African masses against colonialism and imperialism.

107. As Mantha Diawara has argued, African filmmakers benefited from the experience of their North African neighbors, who had already nationalized their film industries and defined policies of distribution, production, and exhibition. Diawara, "The Artist as the Leader," 99.

108. Férid Boughedir, "Connaissance du cinéma africain," *ACECOP Liaison* (1975): 16.

109. Diawara, "The Artist as the Leader," 99.

110. Férid Boughedir, interview with author.

111. Bakari and Cham, *African Experiences of Cinema*, 25.

112. Diawara, "The Artist as the Leader," 102.

113. Ibid.

114. Deuxième congrès de la FEPACI in Algiers, January 15–19, 1975, 17, Kaiser Cheriaa, personal archives, Tunis.

115. Diawara, "The Artist as the Leader," 100.

116. Cheriaa, "African Cinema and the Headshrinkers," 43.

117. Sarah Maldoror, in Mourad Bourboune, "Nos mutuelles différences," *Les nouvelles littéraires* 2, no. 353 (1972).

118. Boughedir, "A Cinema Fighting for Its Liberation" and "Le nouveau credo des cineastes Africains," 168; Diawara, "The Artist as the Leader," 103.

119. Hassan Daldoul, interview with author.

120. Cheriaa, "African Cinema and the Headshrinkers," 44.

121. Such texts include Bakari and Cham, *African Experiences of Cinema*; Diawara, *African Cinema*; Downing, *Film and Politics in the Third World*; Martin, *Cinemas of the Black Diaspora*; Nwachukwu, *Black African Cinema*; and Sherzer, *Cinema, Colonialism, Postcolonialism*. There is one dissertation that delves into the intricacies of the JCC: see Bourguiba, "Finalités culturelles et esthétiques d'un cinéma arabo-africain en devenir." Morgan Corriou has also written a couple of excellent articles that explore the political tensions surrounding the JCC and the world of film in Tunisia: "Cinéphilie et engagement estudiantin" and "Les Journées Cinématographiques de Carthage."

122. Néjib Ayed, interview with author.

Conclusion

1. Hollein and Morris, Foreword to *Surrealism beyond Borders*, 7.

2. Ousmane Sembène, "Entretien avec Ousmane Sembène," *Souffles*, nos. 16–17 (1970): 50.

3. Di-Capua, *No Exit*.

4. In the 2021–2022 academic year, there were five jobs advertised as professorships in sub-Saharan African history. For examples, see the Wikipage for academic jobs in history: https://academicjobs.fandom.com/wiki/African/Middle_Eastern_History_2021–22.

5. See Bernabé, Chamoiseau, and Confiant, *Éloge de la créolité*; and Glissant, *Le discours antillais* and *Poétique de la relation.*

6. For more on the civil wars in Angola and Mozambique, see Chabal, *History of Postcolonial Lusophone Africa*; Emerson, *Battle for Mozambique*; Finnegan, *Complicated War*; Funada-Classen, *Origins of War in Mozambique*; Koppel and Waters, *Cuba and Angola*; Liebenberg et al., *Far-Away War*; Marques, *Segredos da descolonização de Angola*; Mbunga, *Angola e a crise pós-independência*; and Messiant, *L'Angola postcolonial.*

7. See Aggoun and Rivoire, *Françalgérie*; Dakhlia, *Tunisie*; Samraoui, *Chroniques des années de sang*; Habib Souaïdia, *La sale guerre*; and Benjamin Stora, *La guerre invisible.*

8. Klein, *Eldridge Cleaver* and *Festival Panafricain d'Alger.*

9. El Mostafa El Ktiri, "Allocution d'ouverture Colloque Maroc-Afrique," Rabat, February 19, 2018, notes in author's possession. Thank you to Claire Marynower for helping me access the speeches and notes for these meetings.

10. This becomes clear at the end of El Ktiri's speech, when he begins talking about developing relationships with African countries only if they respect Morocco's claims on the Sahara.

11. *Sarah Maldoror: Cinéma tricontinental*, Palais de Tokyo, Paris, November 2021–March 2022.

BIBLIOGRAPHY

Archives

Archives in Morocco

Institute of African Studies, Mohammed V University, Rabat
Moroccan National Archives, Rabat
National Library of the Kingdom of Morocco, Rabat

Archives in Algeria

Frantz Fanon Archives, Musée Nationale du Bardo, Algiers
Jean Sénac Archives, Bibliothèque Nationale d'Algérie, Algiers

Archives in Tunisia

Center of National Documentation, Tunis
Hassan Daldoul, personal archives, Tunis
Kaiser Cheriaa, personal archives, Tunis
Salah Al Dhaoui, personal archives, La Marsa
Tunisian National Archives, Tunis
Tunisian National Library, Tunis

Archives in France

Archives Audiovisuelles, Bibliothèque Nationale de France, Paris
Archives Diplomatiques, Nantes
Archives Nationales d'Outre-Mer, Aix-en-Provence
Archives of the Centre Culturel Algérien, Paris

Archives of the Musée du Quai Branly, Paris
Bibliothèque Jacques Doucet, Paris
Collection René Depestre, Bibliothèque Francophone Multimédia, Limoges
Fond Sénac, Bibliothèque de Marseille

Archives in the United States
Bran Duncan, personal archives, Philadelphia
Matt Schaffer Collection, Emory University, Atlanta
Ted Joans Papers, Bancroft Library, University of California, Berkeley
Ted Joans Papers, Schomburg Center for Research in Black Culture, NYC

Online Archives
Casa Comum Archives, http://casacomum.org/cc/arquivos
PANAFEST video archives, http://webdocs-sciences-sociales.science/panafest/

Newspapers, Magazines, and Journals
Al-ʿamal
Algérie actualité
Black Panther Journal
Cinémaction
Cinéma Québec
Dialogue
Écrans de Tunisie
Freedomways
Al-Ḥayā al-Thaqāfya
Jeune afrique
Journal de Tanger
Lamalif
Les nouvelles littéraires
Mensagem
Le Monde
Le Monde Diplomatique
El-Moudjahid
Al-Nahār al-Lubnānī
Nation africaine
Nawadi
New York Times
Présence africaine
La Presse
La Revue du Liban
Al-Sabāḥ

Al-Sh'b al-Thaqāfy
Souffles/Anfas
Tricontinental

Interviews

Hassan Akrout—Interviewed June 6, 2018, La Goulette, Tunisia
Anouchka de Andrade—Interviewed July 17, 2018, Saint-Denis, France
Néjib Ayed—Interviewed June 6, 2018, Tunis
Ahmed Bedjaoui—Interviewed March 13, 2018, Algiers
Abdellatif Ben Amar—Interviewed May 30, 2018, Tunis
Kmar Bendana—Interviewed November 5, 2018, Tunis
Béchir Ben Salama—Interviewed March 8, 2014, Tunis
Férid Boughedir—Interviewed June 12, 2018, Paris
Mohammed Challouf—Interviewed November 6, 2018, Tunis
Kaiser Cheriaa—Interviewed June 7, 2018, Tunis
Kathleen Cleaver—Interviewed September 26, 2015, Atlanta, Georgia
Hassan Daldoul—Interviewed June 8, 2018, Tunis
René Depestre—Interviewed December 13, 2017, Lézignan-Corbières, France
Salah Al Dhaoui—Interviewed May 25, 2018, La Marsa, Tunisia
Nourredine Djoudi—Interviewed March 27, 2018, Algiers
Henda Ducados—Interviewed August 28, 2018, in Saint-Denis, France
Abdelkrim Gabous—Interviewed May 29, 2018, Tunis
Salah Guemriche—Interviewed June 18, 2018, Angers, France
Jelila Hafsia—Interviewed March 3, 2014, Tunis
Henri Lopes—Interviewed June 22, 2015, Paris
Sarah Maldoror—Interviewed August 28, 2018, Saint-Denis, France
Chief Mandela—Interviewed March 29, 2018, Zeralda, Algeria
Toni Maraini—Email interview, February 4, 2018.
Denis Martinez—Interviewed March 28, 2018, Blida, Algeria
Mohamed Melehi—Phone interview, January 31, 2018
Elaine Mokhtefi—Interviewed September 3, 2018, New York City
Boubker Mongachi—Interviewed February 12, 2018, Casablanca, Morocco
Maati Monjib—Interviewed February 7, 2018, Rabat, Morocco
Charlotte Naccache—Interviewed March 26, 2014, Paris
Mostafa Nissabouri—Interviewed February 13, 2018, Casablanca, Morocco
Marc Ollivier—Interviewed May 3, 2018, Paris
Hocine Tandjaoui—Interviewed December 18, 2017, Paris
Ikbal Zalila—Interviewed June 9, 2018, Tunis

Books, Articles, and Films

Adi, Hakim. *Pan-Africanism: A History*. London: Bloomsbury Academic, 2018.

Adi, Hakim, and Marika Sherwood. *The 1945 Manchester Pan-African Congress Revisited*. London: New Beacon Books, 1995.

Adimi, Kaouther. *Nos richesses*. Algiers: Barzakh, 2017.

Adjali, Boubaker, and Marcelino dos Santos. *Frelimo: Interview with Marcelino dos Santos*. Richmond, BC: Liberation Support Movement Information Center, 1971.

Adotevi, Stanislas. *Négritude et négrologues*. Paris: Union Générale d'Éditions, 1972.

Aggoun, Lounis, and Jean-Baptiste Rivoire. *Françalgérie, crimes et mensonges d'états: Histoire secrète, de la guerre d'indépendance à la "troisième guerre" d'Algérie*. Paris: La Découverte, 2004.

Agnaou, Fatima. *Gender, Literacy, and Empowerment in Morocco*. New York: Routledge, 2004.

Ahmida, Ali Abdullatif, ed. *Bridges across the Sahara: Social, Economic and Cultural Impact of the Trans-Sahara Trade during the 19th and 20th Centuries*. Newcastle, UK: Cambridge Scholars, 2009.

Aïdi, Hisham. *And the Twain Shall Meet: Connecting Africa and the Middle East*. POMEPS (Project on Middle East Political Science). https://pomeps.org/and-the-twain-shall-meet-connecting-africa-and-the-middle-east.

———. "Du Bois, Ghana, and Cairo Jazz: The Geopolitics of Malcolm X." In *Routledge Handbook of Postcolonial Politics*, ed. Olivia U. Rutazibwa and Robbie Shilliam, 413–431. New York: Routledge, 2018.

———. "Egypt and the Afrocentrists: The Latest Round." In *Africa Is a Country*. https://africasacountry.com/2022/03/egypt-and-the-afrocentrists-the-latest-round.

———. "Slavery, Genocide, and the Politics of Outrage: Understanding the New Racial Olympics." MERIP (Middle East Information and Research Project) 234 (2005). https://merip.org/2005/03/slavery-genocide-and-the-politics-of-outrage/.

Ajala, Adekunle. *Pan-Africanism: Evolution, Progress and Prospects*. London: A. Deutsch, 1973.

Alalou, Ali, and Brahim El Guabli, eds. *Lamalif: A Critical Anthology of Societal Debates in Morocco during the "Years of Lead" (1966–1988)*. Liverpool, UK: Liverpool University Press, 2023.

Alaoui, Sarah. "Morocco, Commander of the (African) Faithful?" *Brookings* (blog), April 8, 2019. https://www.brookings.edu/blog/order-from-chaos/2019/04/08/morocco-commander-of-the-african-faithful/.

Alessandra, Jacques. *Abdellatif Laâbi: Traversée de l'œuvre*. Paris: La Différence, 2008.

Alfredo, Margarido. *Poetas Angolanos: Antologia da Casa dos Estudantes do Imperio*. Lisbon: CEI, 1962.

Allison, Robert. *The Crescent Obscured: The United States and the Muslim World, 1776–1815*. Chicago: University of Chicago Press, 2014.

Alloula, Malek. *The Colonial Harem*. Minneapolis: University of Minnesota Press, 1986.

Amaral, Ilidio do. *Em torno dos nacionalismos africanos: Memorias e reflexoes em homenagem a Mario Pinto de Andrade*. Porto, Portugal: Granito Editores, 2000.

Amine, Laila. *Postcolonial Paris: Fictions of Intimacy in the City of Light*. Madison: University of Wisconsin Press, 2018.

El Amrani, Issandr. "In the Beginning There Was *Souffles*: Reconsidering Morocco's Most Radical Literary Quarterly." *Bidoun*, no. 13 (Winter 2018). https://www.bidoun.org/articles/in-the-beginning-there-was-souffles.

Amselle, Jean-Loup. *Littératures et cultures en Afrique: Spécificités et partages*. Rabat: CCLMC, 2010.

———. *Rétrovolutions: Essais sur les primitivismes contemporains*. Paris: Stock, 2010.

Anderson, Benedict. *Imagined Communities: Reflections on the Origin and Spread of Nationalism*. London: Verso, 1983.

Anderson, Jon Lee, and Jose Hernandez. *Che: A Revolutionary Life*. New York: Penguin, 2018.

Anderson, Samuel D. "'Negritude Is Dead': Performing the African Revolution at the First Pan-African Cultural Festival (Algiers, 1969)." In *The First World Festival of Negro Arts, Dakar 1966: Contexts and Legacies*, ed. David Murphy, 143–160. Liverpool, UK: Liverpool University Press, 2016.

Andrade, Henda de. *Mario Pinto de Andrade: Um olhar intimo*. Luanda, Angola: Caxinde, 2009.

Andrade, Mário de. *Amílcar Cabral: Essai de biographie politique*. Paris: Maspero, 1980.

———. *Antologia da poesia negra de expressão portuguesa*. New York: Kraus Reprint, 1970.

———. *Antologia temática de poesia africana: Na noite grávida de punhais*. Lisbon: Sá da Costa, 1975.

———. *La poesie africaine d'expression portugaise*. Paris: Pierre Jean Oswald, 1969.

———. *Liberté pour l'Angola*. Paris: Maspero, 1962.

———. *Négritude africana de lingua portuguesa*. Braga, Portugal: Angelus Novus, 2000.

———. *Origens do nacionalismo africano: Continuidade e ruptura nos movimentos unitários emergentes da luta contra a dominação colonial portuguesa, 1911–1961*. Lisbon: Publicaçãoes Dom Quixote, 1997.

———. "Sur la première génération du MPLA: 1948–1960." Interview with Christiane Messant. *Lusotopie* 6 (1999): 185–221.

———. *Uma entrevista dada a Michel Laban.* Lisbon: Edições João Sá da Costa, 1997.

Andrade, Mário de, and Marc Ollivier. *A guerra em Angola.* Lisbon: Seara Nova, 1974.

Andrade, Mario de, and Francisco Tenreiro. *Poesía negra de expressão portuguesa.* Lisbon: Livraria Escolar Editora, 1953.

Angrist, Joshua D., and Victor Lavy. "The Effect of a Change in Language of Instruction on the Returns to Schooling in Morocco." *Journal of Labor Economics* 15, no. 1 (1997): S48–76.

Antologias de poesia da Casa dos Estudantes do Imperio, 1951–1963. Vols. 1 and 2. Lisbon: ACEI, 1994.

Appiah, Kwame Anthony. *In My Father's House: Africa in the Philosophy of Culture.* Oxford: Oxford University Press, 1993.

Apter, Andrew. *The Pan-African Nation: Oil and the Spectacle of Culture in Nigeria.* Chicago: University of Chicago Press, 2005.

Archer-Straw, Petrine. *Negrophilia: Avant-Garde Paris and Black Culture in the 1920s.* London: Thames and Hudson, 2000.

Area Handbook for Morocco. Washington, DC: US Government Printing Office, 1966.

Arnaud, Robert. *L'Islam et la politique musulmane française en Afrique occidentale française.* Paris: Comité de l'Afrique Française, 1912.

Aseraf, Arthur. *Sur les traces de Messaoud Djebari: Algérien dans un monde colonial.* Paris: Éditions Fayard, 2022.

Askew, Kelly. *Performing the Nation: Swahili Music and Cultural Politics in Tanzania.* Chicago: University of Chicago Press, 2002.

Astrow, Andre. "Interview with Ahmed Ben Salah." *Africa Report* 33, no. 3 (1988): 56–59.

Austen, Ralph. *Trans-Saharan Africa in World History.* Oxford: Oxford University Press, 2010.

Aydin, Cemil. "Pan-Nationalism of Pan-Islamic, Pan-Asian, and Pan-African Thought." In *The Oxford Handbook of the History of Nationalism*, ed. John Breuilly, 672–693. Oxford: Oxford University Press, 2013.

Babana-Hampton, Safoi. "Translating the Postcolonial Condition in *Souffles-Anfas.*" *Expressions maghrébines* 15, no. 1 (2016): 169–185.

Babas, Latifa. "When Morocco Helped Nelson Mandela during His Fight against the Apartheid Regime." *Yabiladi*, December 5, 2017. https://en.yabiladi.com/articles/details/59903/history-when-morocco-helped-nelson.html.

Bahloul, Abdelkrim, dir. *Le soleil assassiné.* Liège: Les Films du Fleuve, 2003.

Baier, Stephen. "Trans-Saharan Trade and the Sahel: Damergu 1870–1930." *Journal of African History* 18, no. 1 (1977): 37–60.

Bakari, Imruh, and Mbye B. Cham, eds. *African Experiences of Cinema*. London: British Film Institute, 1996.

Balandier, George. "La situation coloniale: Approche théorique." *Cahiers internationaux de sociologie* 11 (1951): 44–79.

Baldwin, James. *Nobody Knows My Name*. New York: Vintage International, 1961.

———. *No Name in the Street*. New York: Vintage International, 1972.

Balibar, Étienne, and Immanuel Wallerstein. *Race, Nation, Class: Ambiguous Identities*. London: Verso, 1991.

Ballhatchet, Kenneth. *Race Sex and Class under the Raj: Imperial Attitudes and Policies and Their Critics 1793–1905*. New York: Palgrave Macmillan, 1980.

Bambara, Toni Cade, ed. *The Black Woman: An Anthology*. New York: Penguin, 1970.

Batchelor, Kathryn, and Sue-Ann Harding. *Translating Frantz Fanon across Continents and Languages*. New York: Routledge, 2017.

Bayart, Jean-François. *The State in Africa: The Politics of the Belly*. Harlow, UK: Longman, 1993.

Baylocq, Cédric, and Aziz Hlaoua. "Diffuser un 'islam du juste milieu'? Les nouvelles ambitions de la diplomatie religieuse africaine du Maroc." *Afrique contemporaine* 257, no. 1 (2016): 113–128.

Beckett, Balthazar Ishmael. "Why 1964 Cairo Mattered in 1975 Oakland." *Callaloo* 39, no. 4 (2016): 919–935.

Belhaj, Abdessamad. *La dimension islamique dans la politique étrangère du Maroc: Déterminants, acteurs, orientations*. Louvain: Presses Universitaires de Louvain, 2009.

Ben Barka, Bachir, ed. *Mehdi Ben Barka en héritage: De la Tricontinentale à l'altermondialisme*. Paris: Éditions Syllepse, 2007.

Ben Barka, Mehdi. "L'Afrique au delà de l'indépendance." In *Option révolutionnaire au Maroc: Suivi des écrits politiques, 1960–1965*. Paris: La Découverte, 1966.

Bencheikh, Jamel-Eddine, and Christiane Chaulet-Achour. *Jean Sénac: Clandestin des deux rives*. Paris: Séguier, 1999.

Ben Jelloun, Tahar. *Moha le fou, Moha le sage*. Paris: Éditions du Seuil, 1978.

Bender, Gerald J. *Angola under the Portuguese: The Myth and the Reality*. Berkeley: University of California Press, 1978.

Ben Slama, Béchir. *Les courants littéraires dans la Tunisie contemporaine*. Tunis: Atlas Éditions, 1998.

Bensmaïa, Réda. *Experimental Nations: Or, the Invention of the Maghreb*. Princeton, NJ: Princeton University Press, 2003.

Bentahar, Ziad. "Continental Drift: The Disjunction of the North and Sub-Saharan Africa." *Research in African Literatures* 42, no. 1 (Spring 2011): 1–13.

Bernabé, Jean, Patrick Chamoiseau, and Raphaël Confiant. *Éloge de la créolité*. Paris: Gallimard, 1989.

Beshir, Mohamed Omer. *Terramedia: Themes in Afro-Arab Relations*. London: Ithaca Press, 1982.

Bessis, Sophie, and Souhayr Belhassen. *Bourguiba*. Tunis: Elyzad, 2012.

Bhabha, Homi. *Location of Culture*. New York: Routledge, 1994.

Bisschoff, Lizelle, and David Murphy, eds. *Africa's Lost Classics: New Histories of African Cinema*. New York: Routledge, 2017.

Bloom, Joshua, and Waldo E. Martin, eds. *Black against Empire: The History and Politics of the Black Panther Party*. Oakland: University of California Press, 2013.

Blum, Françoise, Pierre Guidi, and Ophélie Rillon, eds. *Étudiants africains en mouvement: Contribution à une histoire des années 1968*. Paris: Éditions de la Sorbonne, 2017.

Bocquet, Jean-Louis, and Catel Muller. *Joséphine Baker*. Paris: Casterman, 2016.

Boëtsch, Gilles, et al., eds. *Sexualités, identités et corps colonisés*. Paris: CNRS Éditions, 2019.

Bolton, Jonathan. *Worlds of Dissent: Charter 77, The Plastic People of the Universe, and Czech Culture under Communism*. Cambridge, MA: Harvard University Press, 2012.

Bonnell, Victoria, and Lynn Hunt, eds. *Beyond the Cultural Turn: New Directions in the Study of Society and Culture*. Berkeley: University of California Press, 1999.

Borsali, Noura. *Livre d'entretiens avec Ahmed ben Salah: L'homme fort de la Tunisie des annexes soixante*. Tunis: Self-published, 2008.

Bouamama, Saïd. *Figures de la révolution africaine: De Kenyatta à Sankara*. Paris: La Découverte, 2014.

Boughedir, Férid, dir. *Caméra d'Afrique*. Tunis, 1983.

———. "A Cinema Fighting for Its Liberation." In *Cinemas of the Black Diaspora: Diversity, Dependence, and Oppositionality*, ed. Michael T. Martin, 111–117. Detroit: Wayne State University Press, 1995.

Bouhdiba, Abdelwahab, and Alan Sheridan. *Sexuality in Islam*. London: Saqi Books, 1998.

Boukari-Yabara, Amzat. *Africa Unite! Une histoire du panafricanisme*. Paris: La Découverte, 2017.

Boukman, Daniel. *Chants pour hâter la mort du temps des Orphée*. Paris: L'Harmattan, 1993.

———. *Frantz Fanon: Traces d'une vie exemplaire*. Paris: L'Harmattan, 2016.

Bourguiba, Sayda. "Finalités culturelles et esthétiques d'un cinéma arabo-africain en devenir: Les Journées Cinématographiques de Carthage (JCC)." PhD diss., Université Panthéon-Sorbonne–Paris I, 2013.

Boussaid, Farid. "Brothers in Arms: Morocco's Military Intervention in Support of Mobutu of Zaire during the 1977 and 1978 Shaba Crises." *International History Review* 43, no. 1 (2001): 185–202.

Bracey, John H., August Meier, and Eliott Rudwick, eds. *Black Nationalism in America*. Indianapolis: Bobbs-Merrill, 1970.

Bragança, Silvia de. *Battles Waged, Lasting Dreams: Aquino de Bragança; The Man and His Times*. Saligao, India: Goa 1556, 2011.

Braun, Célina. "À quoi servent les partis tunisiens? Sens et contre-sens d'une 'libéralisation' politique." *Revue des mondes musulmans et de la Méditerranée*, nos. 111–112 (2006): 15–62.

Breuilly, John, ed. *The Oxford Handbook of the History of Nationalism*. Oxford: Oxford University Press, 2016.

Burke, Edmund. "Frantz Fanon's 'The Wretched of the Earth.'" *Daedalus* 105, no. 1 (1976): 127–135.

Byrne, Jeffrey James. "Beyond Continents, Colours, and the Cold War: Yugoslavia, Algeria, and the Struggle for Non-alignment." *International History Review* 37, no. 5 (2015): 912–932.

———. *Mecca of Revolution: Algeria, Decolonization, and the Third World Order*. New York: Oxford University Press, 2016.

Camau, Michel, ed. *Tunisie au présent: Une modernité au-dessus de tout soupçon?* Paris: CNRS, 1987.

Camau, Michel, and Vincent Geisser, eds. *Habib Bourguiba: La trace et l'héritage*. Paris: Karthala, 2004.

Camiscioli, Elisa. *Reproducing the French Race: Immigration, Intimacy, and Embodiment in the Early 20th Century*. Durham, NC: Duke University Press, 2009.

Castelo, Cláudia, and Miguel Bandeira Jerónimo. *Casa dos Estudantes do Império: Dinâmicas coloniais, conexões transnacionais*. Lisbon: Edições 70, 2017.

Caute, David. *Frantz Fanon*. Paris: Éditions Seghers, 1970.

Celluloid Liberation Front. "The Mother of African Cinema: Sarah Maldoror." *Los Angeles Review of Books*, May 21, 2021.

Cervenka, Zdenek. *The Organization of African Unity and Its Charter*. New York: Praeger, 1968.

Césaire, Aimé. *Cahier d'un retour au pays natal*. Paris: Présence Africaine, 1939.

———. *Discours sur la négritude*. Paris: Présence Africaine, 2004.

Chabal, Patrick. *A History of Postcolonial Lusophone Africa*. Bloomington: Indiana University Press, 2002.

Chafer, Tony. *The End of Empire in French West Africa: France's Successful Decolonization?* Oxford, UK: Berg, 2002.

Chakrabarty, Dipesh. *Provincializing Europe: Postcolonial Thought and Historical Difference*. Princeton, NJ: Princeton University Press, 2000.

Challouf, Mohamed, dir. *Tahar Cheriaa: À l'ombre du Baobab*. Tunis: Caravanes Productions, 2014.

Chaplin, Tamara, and Jadwiga E. Pieper Mooney, eds. *The Global 1960s: Convention, Contest, and Counterculture.* New York: Routledge, 2018.

Chatterjee, Partha. *The Nation and Its Fragments: Colonial and Postcolonial Histories.* Princeton, NJ: Princeton University Press, 1994.

Cheikh, Abdel Wedoud Ould. "La caravane et la caravelle: Les deux âges du commerce de l'Ouest saharien." *L'Ouest saharien* [The western Sahara] 2 (2000): 29–70.

Cheriaa, Tahar. *Ayām Qartāj al-Sīnīmā'ya.* Tunis: Éditions Médiacom, 1998.

———. *Écrans d'abondance, ou cinéma de libération en Afrique.* Tunis: SATPEC, 1978.

———. *Naṣībī mina al-Rafḍ Shahādāt.* Tunis: Dar Al-Bousten, 2002.

Chomentowski, Gabrielle. "L'expérience soviétique des cinemas africains au lendemain des indépendances." *Le temps des médias* 26, no. 1 (2016): 111–125.

Chouikha, Larbi, and Éric Gobe. *Histoire de la Tunisie depuis l'indépendance.* Paris: La Découverte, 2015.

Chraïbi, Driss. *Le passé simple.* Paris: Éditions Denoël, 1954.

Clarke, Kamari Maxine, and Deborah A. Thomas, eds. *Globalization and Race: Transformations in the Cultural Production of Blackness.* Durham, NC: Duke University Press, 2006.

Cleaver, Eldridge. *Post-prison Writings and Speeches.* New York: Random House, 1969.

———. *Soul on Ice.* New York: Delta Books, 1992.

Cleaver, Kathleen. "Memories of Love and War." Chapter of unpublished memoirs in author's possession.

College, Nigel C. Gibson, and Roberto Beneduce. *Frantz Fanon: Psychiatry and Politics.* New York: Rowman and Littlefield, 2017.

Comaroff, Jean, and John Comaroff. *Of Revelation and Revolution: Christianity, Colonialism, and Consciousness in South Africa.* Vols. 1 and 2. Chicago: University of Chicago Press, 1991.

Comitini, Carlos, and Amílcar Cabral. *Amílcar Cabral: A arma da teoria.* Rio de Janeiro: CODECRI, 1980.

Connelly, Matthew. *A Diplomatic Revolution: Algeria's Fight for Independence and the Origins of the Post–Cold War Era.* Oxford: Oxford University Press, 2002.

Cooper, Frederick. *Africa since 1940: The Past of the Present.* Cambridge: Cambridge University Press, 2002.

———. "Africa's Past and Africa's Historians." *African Sociological Review* 34, no. 2 (1999): 298–336.

———. *Citizenship between Empire and Nation: Remaking France and French Africa, 1945–1960.* Princeton, NJ: Princeton University Press, 2014.

———. *Colonialism in Question: Theory, Knowledge, History.* Berkeley: University of California Press, 2005.

———. "Possibility and Constraint: African Independence in Historical Perspective." *Journal of African History* 49, no. 2 (2008): 167–196.

Corriou, Morgan, and M'Hamed Oualdi, eds. "Les Journées Cinématographiques de Carthage et la 'guerre de libération cinématographique' (1966–1972)." *Africultures*, nos. 101–102 (2015): 294–317.

———. *Une histoire sociale et culturelle du politique en Algérie*. Paris: Éditions de la Sorbonne, 2018.

Costa Pindo, António, and Stewart Lloyd-Jones, eds. *The Last Empire: Thirty Years of Portuguese Decolonization*. Portland, OR: Intellect Books, 2003.

Courteille, Sophie. *Léopold Sédar Senghor et l'art vivant au Sénégal*. Paris: L'Harmattan, 2006.

Coutinho, Ângela Sofia Benoliel. "Militantes invisíveis: As cabo-verdianas e o movimento independentista (1956–1974)." *Estudos feministas* 28, no. 1 (2020): 1–13.

Crawford, Margo Natalie, and Salah Hassan, eds. "Global Black Consciousness." Special issue, *Nka: Journal of Contemporary African Art*, nos. 42–43 (November 2018).

Cummings, Basia Lewandowska. "The Films of Sarah Maldoror." Africa Is a Country, October 27, 2010. https://africasacountry.com/2011/10/the-films-of-sarah-maldoror.

Cuney, William Waring. "No Images." In *Storefront Church*. London: Paul Breman, 1973.

Curtis, Edward. "'My Heart Is in Cairo': Malcolm X, the Arab Cold War, and the Making of Islamic Liberation Ethics." *Journal of American History* 102, no. 3 (2015): 775–798.

Daadaoui, Mohamed. "Islamism and the State in Morocco." Hudson Institute, April 29, 2016. https://www.hudson.org/research/12286-islamism-and-the-state-in-morocco.

Dakhlia, Jocelyne. *Tunisie, le pays sans bruit*. Paris: Actes Sud, 2011.

D'Alessandro, Stephanie, and Matthew Gale, eds. *Surrealism beyond Borders*. New Haven, CT: Yale University Press, 2021.

Damas, Léon. *Pigments*. Paris: Présence Africaine, 2005.

Daoud, Zakya, ed. *Être marginal au Maghreb*. Paris: CNRS Éditions, 1993.

———. *Les années Lamalif: 1958–1988; Trente ans de journalisme au Maroc*. Casablanca: Tarik Éditions, 2007.

Daulatzai, Sohail. *Black Star, Crescent Moon: The Muslim International and Black Freedom beyond America*. Minneapolis: University of Minnesota Press, 2012.

Daure-Serfaty, Christine, and Abraham Serfaty. *La mémoire de l'autre*. Paris: Stock, 1993.

Davis, Diana K. *Resurrecting the Granary of Rome: Environmental History and*

French Colonial Expansion in North Africa. Athens: Ohio University Press, 2007.

Davis, Muriam Haleh. *Markets of Civilization: Racial Capitalism and Islam in Algeria*. Durham, NC: Duke University Press, 2022.

DeBurke, Randy, and Andrew Helfer. *Malcolm X: A Graphic Biography*. New York: Hill and Wang, 2006.

Depestre, René. *Alléluia pour une femme-jardin*. Paris: Gallimard, 1981.

———. *Bonsoir tendresse: Autobiographie*. Paris: Odile Jacob, 2018.

———. *Hadriana dans tous mes rêves*. Paris: Gallimard, 1988.

Diawara, Manthia. *African Cinema: Politics and Culture*. Bloomington: Indiana University Press, 1992.

———. *African Film: New Forms of Aesthetics and Politics*. New York: Prestel, 2010.

———. "The Artist as the Leader of the Revolution: The History of the Federation Panafricaine des Cineastes." In *Cinemas of the Black Diaspora: Diversity, Dependence, and Oppositionality*, ed. Michael T. Martin, 95–110. Detroit: Wayne State University Press, 1995.

Di-Capua, Yoav. *No Exit: Arab Existentialism, Jean Paul Sartre, and Decolonization*. Chicago: University of Chicago Press, 2018.

Diouf, Mamadou. *Historians and Histories: What For? African Historiographies between the State and the Communities*. Amsterdam: SEPHIS, 2003.

Djebar, Assia. *Le blanc de l'Algérie*. Paris: Albin Michel, 1995.

dos Santos, Daniel. *Amílcar Cabral: Um outro Olhar*. Lisbon: Chiado Editora, 2014.

dos Santos, Marcelino. *Canto do amor natural*. Maputo: Associação dos Escritores Moçambicanos, 1987.

———. *Escrever é criar*. Mozambique: Associação dos Escritores Moçambicanos, 1982.

Downing, John, ed. *Film and Politics in the Third World*. New York: Praeger, 1987.

Dubois, W. E. B. *The Soul of Black Folks*. New York: Dover, 1994.

Dunne, Bruce. "French Regulation of Prostitution in Nineteenth-Century Colonial Algeria." *Arab Studies Journal* 2, no. 1 (1994): 24–30.

Dupré, Colin. *Le Fespaco, une affaire d'État(s)*. Paris: L'Harmattan, 2012.

Durant, Sam. *Black Panther: The Revolutionary Art of Emory Douglas*. New York: Rizzoli International, 2007.

Edwards, Brent Hayes. *The Practice of Diaspora: Literature, Translation, and the Rise of Black Internationalism*. Cambridge, MA: Harvard University Press, 2003.

Eldridge, Claire. *From Empire to Exile: History and Memory within the Pied-Noir and Harki Communities, 1962–2012*. Manchester, UK: Manchester University Press, 2016.

Ellerson, Beti, ed. *Sisters of the Screen: Women of Africa on Film*. Trenton, NJ: Africa World Press, 2000.

Ellis, Stephen. "Writing Histories of Contemporary Africa." *Journal of African History* 43, no. 1 (2002): 1–26.

Emerson, Stephen A. *The Battle for Mozambique: The FRELIMO-RENAMO Struggle, 1977–1992*. Warwick, UK: Helion, 2014.

Ennaji, Mohammed. *Soldats, domestiques et concubines: L'esclavage au Maroc au XIXe siècle*. Casablanca: Éditions Jacob Duvernet, 1994.

Esedebe, P. Olisanwuche. *Pan-Africanism: The Idea and Movement, 1776–1963*. Washington, DC: Howard University Press, 1982.

Fabre, Michel. *From Harlem to Paris: Black American Writers in France (1840–1980)*. Urbana: University of Illinois Press, 1993.

Faik-Nzuji, Clementine, Abbe Paul Mambe, and Kabongo Ilunga. "Au premier festival culturel panafricain: Impressions du Symposium." *Congo-Afrique*, no. 31 (January 1970): 383–399.

Falola, Toyin. *The African Diaspora: Slavery, Modernity, and Globalization*. Rochester, NY: University of Rochester Press, 2013.

Falola, Toyin, and Kwame Essien, eds. *Pan-Africanism, and the Politics of African Citizenship and Identity*. New York: Routledge, 2014.

Fanon, Frantz. *Black Skins, White Masks*. New York: Grove Press, 2008.

———. *A Dying Colonialism*. New York: Grove Press, 1994.

———. *The Wretched of the Earth*. Trans. Richard Philcox. New York: Grove Press, 2004.

Faria, António. *Linha estreita da liberdade: A Casa dos Estudantes do Império*. Lisbon: Edições Colibri, 1997.

Farine, Anaïs. "Naḥwa Sīnīmā Thawriyya." In *Vers un troisième cinéma*, 1–23. Cinémathèque Beirut, 2022. https://www.cinemathequebeirut.com/cinematheque/book/76.

Fauset, Jesse Redmon. "Dark Algiers." In *The Chinaberry Tree: A Novel of American Life and Selected Writings*. Boston: Northeastern University Press, 1995.

Fauvelle, Francois Xavier. *The Golden Rhinoceros: Histories of the African Middle Ages*. Princeton, NJ: Princeton University Press, 2018.

Federici, Silvia, Joseph McLaren, and Cheryl B. Mwaria, eds. *African Visions: Literary Images, Political Change, and Social Struggle in Contemporary Africa*. Westport, CT: Greenwood Press, 2000.

Ferguson, James. *Global Shadows: Africa in the Neoliberal Order*. Durham, NC: Duke University Press, 2006.

Ferguson, Niall, Charles S. Maier, Erez Manela, and Daniel J. Sargent, eds. *The Shock of the Global: The 1970s in Perspective*. Cambridge, MA: Harvard University Press, 2010.

Ficquet, Eloi, and Lorraine Gallimardet. "'On ne peut nier longtemps l'art nègre': Enjeux du colloque et de l'exposition du Premier Festival mondial des arts nègres de Dakar en 1966." *Gradhiva* 10 (2009): 134–155.

Fields, Karen E., and Barbara J. Fields. *Racecraft: The Soul of Inequality in American Life*. London: Verso, 2012.

Finnegan, William. *A Complicated War: The Harrowing of Mozambique*. Berkeley: University of California Press, 1993.

1st Festival Culturel Panafricain Algiers 1969 / *La culture africaine: Le symposium d'Alger, 21 juillet–1er aout 1969*. Algiers: SNED, 1969.

Fonseca, Luis, Rolando Martins, and Olivio Pired, eds. *Por Cabral, Sempre: Comunicações e discursos apresentados no Forum Internacional Amílcar Cabral*. Praia, Cape Verde: Edição da Fundação Amílcar Cabral, 2016.

Forgacs, David, and Eric J. Hobsbawm. *The Antonio Gramsci Reader: Selected Writings 1916–1935*. New York: NYU Press, 2000.

Fox, Robert Elliot. "Ted Joans and the (B)Reach of the African American Literary Canon." *MELUS* 29, nos. 3–4 (2004): 41–58.

Frenz, Margret. *Community, Memory, and Migration in a Globalizing World: The Goan Experience, c. 1890–1980*. New Delhi: OUP India, 2014.

Fuller, Hoyt W. *Journey to Africa*. Chicago: Third World Press, 1971.

Funada-Classen, Sayaka. *The Origins of War in Mozambique: A History of Unity and Division*. Somerset West, South Africa: African Minds, 2013.

Gadjigo, Samba, dir. *Sembène!* Dakar: Galle Ceddo Projects, 2015.

Gallissot, René, and Jacques Kergoat, eds. *Mehdi Ben Barka: De l'indépendance marocaine à la Tricontinentale*. Collection Hommes et Sociétés. Paris: Karthala, 1997.

Garcia, Claire. "'For a Few Days We Would Be Residents in Africa': Jessie Redmon Fauset's 'Dark Algiers the White.'" *Ethnic Studies Review* 30, no. 1 (2007): 103–114.

García, Magaly Rodríguez, Lex Herma van Voss, and Elise van Nederveen Meedkerk, eds. *Selling Sex in the City: A Global History of Prostitution, 1600s–2000s*. New York: Brill, 2017.

Gates, Skip. "Tri-continental Poet: Interview with Ted Joans." *Discourse* 20, nos. 1–2 (1998): 71–90.

Gaudio, Rudolf P. "Trans-Saharan Trade: The Routes of 'African Sexuality.'" *Journal of African History* 55, no. 3 (2014): 317–330.

Gauthier, Gilles. *Entre deux rives: 50 ans de passion pour le monde Arabe*. Paris: Éditions Jean-Claude Lattès, 2018.

Geiss, Imanuel. *The Pan-African Movement: A History of Pan-Africanism in America, Europe, and Africa*. New York: Holmes and Meier, 1974.

Gérard, Albert S. *European-Language Writing in Sub-Saharan Africa*. Amsterdam: John Benjamins, 1986.

Ghazal, Amal N. "The Other Frontiers of Arab Nationalism: Ibadis, Berbers, and the Arabist-Salafi Press in the Interwar Period." *International Journal of Middle East Studies* 42, no. 1 (February 2010): 105–122.

Ghettas, Mohammed Lakhdar. *Algeria and the Cold War: International Relations and the Struggle for Autonomy*. London: I. B. Tauris, 2017.

Gilmore, Glenda Elizabeth. *Defying Dixie: The Radical Roots of Civil Rights, 1919–1950*. New York: W. W. Norton, 2008.

Gilroy, Paul. *The Black Atlantic: Modernity and Double Consciousness*. Cambridge, MA: Harvard University Press, 1995.

Glassman, Jonathan. *War of Words, War of Stones: Racial Thought and Violence in Colonial Zanzibar*. Bloomington: Indiana University Press, 2011.

Glasze, Georg. "The Discursive Constitution of a World-Spanning Region and the Role of Empty Signifiers: The Case of Francophonia." *Geopolitics* 12, no. 4 (2007): 656–679.

Glissant, Édouard. *Le discours antillais*. Paris: Gallimard, 1981.

———. *Poétique de la relation: Poétique III*. Paris: Gallimard, 1990.

Goebel, Michael. *Anti-imperial Metropolis: Interwar Paris and the Seeds of Third World Nationalism*. New York: Cambridge University Press, 2015.

Gomez, Michael. *Black Crescent: The Experience and Legacy of African Muslims in the Americas*. Cambridge: Cambridge University Press, 2005.

———. *Exchanging Our Country Marks: The Transformation of African Identities in the Colonial and Antebellum South*. Chapel Hill: University of North Carolina Press, 1998.

Goodman, R. David. "Demystifying 'Islamic Slavery': Using Legal Practices to Reconstruct the End of Slavery in Fes, Morocco." *History in Africa* 39 (2012): 143–174.

Greenspan, Susan. "Manifesto of the Aouchem Group (1967)." *Critical Interventions* 2, nos. 3–4 (2008): 189.

El Guabli, Brahim. "Moroccan Society's Educational and Cultural Losses during the Years of Lead (1956–1999)." *Journal of Global Initiatives: Policy, Pedagogy, Perspective* 14, no. 2 (2019): 143–161.

———. "Reading for Theory in the Moroccan Marxist-Leninist Testimonial Literature." *African Identities* 18, nos. 1–2 (2020): 145–161.

———. "Refiguring Pan-Africanism through Algerian-Moroccan Competitive Festivals." *International Journal of Postcolonial Studies* 20, no. 7 (2018): 1053–1071.

———. "Tankra Tamazight: The Revival of Amazigh Indigeneity in Literature and Art." *Jadaliyya*, November 1, 2021. https://www.jadaliyya.com/Details/43440/Tankra-Tamazight-The-Amazigh-Revival.

———. "Testimony and Journalism: Moroccan Prison Narratives." In *The Social Life of Memory*, ed. Saadi Nikro and Sonja Hegasy, 113–144. New York: Palgrave Macmillan, 2017.

———. "Theorizing Intergenerational Trauma in Tazmamart Testimonial Literature and 'Docu-testimonies.'" *Middle East Topics and Arguments* 11 (2018): 120–130.

Guemriche, Salah. *Alger la Blanche: Biographies d'une ville*. Paris: Perrin, 2012.

Guettas, Mohamed Lakhdar. *Algeria and the Cold War: International Relations and the Struggle for Autonomy*. London: I. B. Tauris, 2018.

Guevara, Ernesto Che. *El socialismo y el hombre en Cuba*, Havana Cuba: Havana Ediciones, 1965.

Guimarães, Antonio Sérgio Alfredo. "Frantz Fanon's reception in Brazil." *Lusotopie* 16, no. 2 (2009): 157–172.

Guitard, Odette. "Alger ou la désunion Afro-Asiatiques." In *Annuaire de l'Afrique du Nord*, 49–61. Paris: Éditions CNRS, 1966.

Hachad, Naïma. *Revisionary Narratives: Moroccan Women's Auto/Biographical and Testimonial Acts*. Liverpool, UK: Liverpool University Press, 2019.

Haddab, Mustapha, ed. *Actes du Colloque International "Frantz Fanon."* Algiers: CNRPAH, 2011.

Hadouchi, Olivier. "Retour sur 'Festival Panafrican d'Alger' de William Klein." *Mondes du cinéma*, no. 3 (2013) 72–84.

Hafsia, Jelila. *Instants de vie: Chronique familière*. Vol. 2. Tunis: Self-published, 2009.

Haley, Alex. *The Autobiography of Malcolm X*. New York: Ballantine Books, 1999.

Hall, Bruce. *A History of Race in Muslim West Africa*. Cambridge: Cambridge University Press, 2011.

El Hamel, Chouki. *Black Morocco: A History of Slavery, Race, and Islam*. Cambridge: Cambridge University Press, 2013.

———. "'Race,' Slavery and Islam in Maghribi Mediterranean Thought: The Question of the Haratin in Morocco." *Journal of North African Studies* 7, no. 3 (2002): 29–52.

———. "Surviving Slavery: Sexuality and Female Agency in Late 19th Century and Early 20th Century Morocco." *Historical Reflections / Réflexions Historiques* 34, no. 1 (2008): 73–88.

Hamilton, Russell G. "Language and Literature in Portuguese-Writing Africa." *Portuguese Studies* 2 (1986): 196–207.

———. "Lusofonia, Africa, and Matters of Languages and Letters." *Hispania* 74, no. 3 (1991): 610–617.

Hammoudi, Abdellah. *Master and Disciple: The Cultural Foundation of Moroccan Authoritarianism*. Chicago: University of Chicago Press, 1997.

Hare, Nathan. "Algiers 1969: A Report on the Pan-African Cultural Festival." *Black Scholar* (November 1969): 3–10.

Harney, Elizabeth. *In Senghor's Shadow: Art, Politics, and the Avant-Garde in Senegal, 1960–1995*. Durham, NC: Duke University Press, 2004.

Harrison, Alexander. *Challenging de Gaulle: The O.A.S. and the Counterrevolution in Algeria, 1954–1962*. New York: Praeger, 1989.

Harrison, Olivia C., and Teresa Villa-Ignacio. *Souffles-Anfas: A Critical Anthology from the Moroccan Journal of Culture and Politics*. Stanford, CA: Stanford University Press, 2016.

Harrow, Kenneth W. *Postcolonial African Cinema: From Political Engagement to Postmodernism*. Bloomington: Indiana University Press, 2007.

———. *Trash: African Cinema from Below*. Bloomington: Indiana University Press, 2013.

Hayes, Jarrod. *Queer Nations: Marginal Sexualities in the Maghreb*. Chicago: University of Chicago Press, 2000.

Helgesson, Stefan. *Transnationalism in Southern African Literature: Modernists, Realists, and the Inequality of Print Culture*. New York: Routledge, 2009.

Hendrickson, Burleigh. "Finding Tunisia in the Global 1960s." *Monde(s)* 11, no. 1 (2017): 61–78.

———. "Imperial Fragments and Transnational Activism: 1968(s) in Tunisia, France, and Senegal." PhD diss., Northeastern University, 2013.

———. "March 1968: Practicing Transnational Activism from Tunis to Paris." *International Journal of Middle East Studies* 44, no. 4 (2012): 755–774.

Himes, Chester. *My Life of Absurdity: The Autobiography of Chester Himes*. New York: Doubleday, 1976.

Hirschi, Stéphane, and Arnaud Huftier, eds. *Le froid et le chaud, ou Les glaces d'Haïti: Autour de René Depestre, horizons d'un lyrisme francophone?* Amiens: Encrage Édition, 2012.

Hodder, Jake. "The Elusive History of the Pan-African Congress." *History Workshop Journal* 91, no. 1 (2021): 113–131.

Hodges, Sarah. *Contraception, Colonialism and Commerce: Birth Control in South India, 1920–1940*. New York: Routledge, 2008.

Hondo, Med. "The Cinema of Exile." In *Film and Politics in the Third World*, ed. John Downing, 69–76. New York: Praeger, 1987.

———. "What Is Cinema for Us?" In *Film Manifestos and Global Cinema Cultures: A Critical Anthology*, ed. Scott Mackenzie, 300–303. Berkeley: University of California Press, 2014.

hooks, bell. *Killing Rage: Ending Racism*. New York: Holt Paperbacks, 1995.

Horne, Alistair. *A Savage War of Peace: Algeria, 1954–1962*. New York: New York Review Books, 2006.

Howell, Phillip. "Prostitution and Racialized Sexuality: The Regulation of Prostitution in Britain and the British Empire before the Contagious Diseases Acts." *Environment and Planning D: Society and Space* 18, no. 3 (2000): 321–339.

Hubbell, Amy L. *Remembering French Algeria: Pieds-Noirs, Identity, and Exile*. Lincoln: University of Nebraska Press, 2015.

Hughes, Langston. "Afraid." In *The Weary Blues*. New York: Alfred A. Knopf, 1926.

Hunwick, John, and Eve Troutt Powell, eds. *The African Diaspora in the Mediterranean Lands of Islam*. Princeton, NJ: Princeton University Press, 2002.

———, eds. *The Same but Different: Documents on African Slavery in the Islamic Mediterranean (19th–20th Centuries)*. Princeton, NJ: Markus Wiener, 2002.

Ilā al-Amām. *Al-wathā'iq al-asāsya, Mqālāt w nuṣūṣ, 1970–1980*. http://www.30aout.info/media/00/01/359899644.pdf.

Ilkkaracan, Pinar. *Deconstructing Sexuality in the Middle East: Challenges and Discourses*. Abingdon, UK: Routledge, 2008.

Jachec, Nancy. "Léopold Sédar Senghor and the Cultures de l'Afrique Noire et de l'Occident (1960): Eurafricanism, Négritude and the Civilisation of the Universal." *Third Text* 24, no. 2 (2010): 195–204.

Jackson, Sherman. *Islam and the Blackamerican: Looking Towards the Third Resurrection*. New York: Oxford University Press, 2005.

Jaggi, Maya. "Casablanca's Gift to Marrakech and the Birth of Morocco's Modern Art Movement." *New York Review of Books*, August 3, 2019. https://www.nybooks.com/daily/2019/08/03/casablancas-gift-to-marrakech-and-the-birth-of-moroccos-modern-art-movement/.

Jaji, Tsitsi. "Le magazine *Bingo* à l'ère des festivals panafricains: Une archive féministe de la conscience noire mondiale?" *Nka: Journal of Contemporary African Art*, nos. 42–43 (2018): 110–123.

Jian, Chen, Martin Klimke, Masha Kirasirova, Mary Nola, Marilyn Young, and Joanna Waley-Cohen, eds. *The Routledge Handbook of the Global 1960s: Between Protest and Nation-Building*. New York: Routledge, 2018.

Joans, Ted. *Afrodisia*. New York: Hill and Wang, 1970.

———. *Black Pow-Wow: Jazz Poems*. New York: Hill and Wang, 1969.

———. *Our Thang*. Victoria, BC: Ekstasis Editions, 2001.

———. *Teducation: Selected Poems 1949–1999*. Minneapolis: Coffee House Press, 1999.

Jones, Charles Edwin. *The Black Panther Party (Reconsidered)*. Baltimore: Black Classic Press, 1998.

Joqueviel-Bourjea, Marie, and Béatrice Bonhomme. *René Depestre: Le soleil devant*. Paris: Hermann, 2015.

Joseph, Peniel E. *Stokely: A Life*. New York: Civitas, 2014.

Jules-Rosette, Bennetta. *Black Paris: The African Writer's Landscape*. Urbana: University of Illinois Press, 1998.

July, Robert William. *An African Voice: The Role of the Humanities in African Independence*. Durham, NC: Duke University Press, 1987.

Kalter, Christoph. "From Global to Local and Back: The 'Third World' Concept and the New Radical Left in France." *Journal of Global History* 12 (2017): 115–136.

Kamwangamalu, Nkonko M. *Language Policy and Economics: The Language Question in Africa*. Berlin: Springer, 2016.

Kane, Cheikh Hamidou. *L'aventure ambiguë*. Paris: Éditions Julliard, 1961.

Kane, Ousmane Oumar. *Beyond Timbuktu: An Intellectual History of Muslim West Africa*. Cambridge, MA: Harvard University Press, 2016.

Kasmi, Mohamed Salah. *Tunisie: L'Islam local face à l'Islam importé*. Paris: L'Harmattan, 2014.

Kay, Karyn, and Gerald Peary. *Women and the Cinema: A Critical Anthology*. New York: Dutton, 1977.

Kelley, Robin. *Africa Speaks, America Answers: Modern Jazz in Revolutionary Times*. Cambridge, MA: Harvard University Press, 2012.

———. *Freedom Dreams: The Black Radical Imagination*. Boston: Beacon Press, 2002.

———. *Race Rebels: Culture, Politics, and the Black Working Class*. Berkeley: University of California Press, 2008.

Khalfa, Jean, and Robert J. C. Young, eds. *Frantz Fanon: Alienation and Freedom*. London: Bloomsbury Academic, 2018.

Khalil, Andrea Flores. *The Arab Avant-Garde: Experiments in North African Literature and Art*. Westport: Praeger, 2003.

Khatibi, Abdelkebir. *Amour bilingue*. Paris: Fata Morgana, 1983.

———. *Maghreb pluriel*. Paris: Denoël, 1983.

Khellas, Mériem. *Le premier festival culturel panafricain, Alger 1969: Une grande messe populaire*. Paris: L'Harmattan, 2014.

King, Richard H. *Race, Culture, and the Intellectuals, 1940–1970*. Washington, DC: Woodrow Wilson Center Press, 2004.

Klein, William, dir. *Eldridge Cleaver: Black Panther*. Paris: Office National du Commerce et de l'Industrie Cinematographique, 1969.

———, dir. *Festival Panafricain d'Alger*. Paris: Office National du Commerce et de l'Industrie Cinematographique, 1970.

Koppel, Martin, and Mary-Alice Waters, eds. *Cuba and Angola: The War for Freedom*. New York: Pathfinder, 2017.

Kosba, May T. "... *And Bid Him Sing*: Egyptian Race Consciousness in African Diasporic Memory." *Egypte / Monde Arabe* 1, no. 23 (2021): 45–60.

Koumiya, Ghassane. "Post-68 Uprisings and the Rise of the Moroccan Marxist-Leninist Movement" (blog). Verso Books, May 22, 2018. https://www.versobooks.com/blogs/3838-post-68-student-uprisings-and-the-rise-of-the-moroccan-marxist-leninist-movement.

Kraïem, Mustapha. *État et société dans la Tunisie bourguibienne*. Tunis: La Maghrébine, 2011.

Kratli, Graziano, and Ghislaine Lydon, eds. *The Trans-Saharan Book Trade: Manu-*

script Culture, Arabic Literacy and Intellectual History in Muslim Africa. Leiden: Brill, 2011.

Krienke, Kai. "Jean Sénac, Poet of the Algerian Revolution." PhD diss., City University of New York, 2014. https://academicworks.cuny.edu/gc_etds/438/.

———. The Sun under the Weapons: Correspondence and Notes from Algeria, Part II." *Lost and Found* 5, no. 4 (2015): 21–30.

Kumar, Aishwary. *Radical Equality: Ambedkar, Gandhi, and the Risk of Democracy*. Stanford, CA: Stanford University Press, 2015.

Laâbi, Abdellatif. *L'écorché vif: Prosoèmes*. Paris: L'Harmattan, 1986.

———. *Le livre imprévu*. Paris: La Différence, 2010.

———. *L'oeil et la nuit*. Paris: La Différence, 2003.

———. *Sous le bâillon, le poème: Écrits de prison, 1972–1980*. Paris: L'Harmattan, 1981.

———, ed. *Une saison ardente: Souffles, 50 ans après*. Casablanca: Éditions du Sirocco, 2017.

Laâbi, Abdellatif, and Jacques Alessandra. *La brûlure des interrogations*. Paris: L'Harmattan, 2004.

Laâbi, Jocelyne. *La liqueur d'aloès*. Paris: La Différence, 2005.

Lajili, Chaker. *Bourguiba-Senghor: Deux géants de l'Afrique*. Paris: L'Harmattan, 2008.

Langley, Ayodele J. *Pan-Africanism and Nationalism in West Africa, 1900–1945*. Oxford: Clarendon Press, 1973.

Larson, Pier M. "Horrid Journeying: Narratives of Enslavement and the Global African Diaspora." *Journal of World History* 19, no. 4 (December 2008): 431–464.

L'asbī, L'hassan, and Safi al-Nāsirī. *Aqsā al-yasār fil-maghrib: Muqāra 'a nabīlah lil-mustahīl*. Casablanca: al-Markaz al-Thaqāfī al-Arabī, 2002.

Laude, André. *Joyeuse apocalypse*. Paris: Stock, 1973.

Lawlor, William T., ed. *Beat Culture: Lifestyles, Icons, and Impact*. Santa Barbara, CA: ABC-CLIO, 2005.

Lecler, Romain. *Une contre-mondisalisation audiovisuelle, ou Comment la France exporte la diversité culturelle*. Paris: Presses de l'Université Paris–Sorbonne, 2019.

Lee, Christopher J. *Frantz Fanon: Toward a Revolutionary Humanism*. Athens: Ohio University Press, 2015.

———. *Making a World after Empire: The Bandung Moment and Its Political Afterlives*. Athens: Ohio University Press, 2010.

Lefèvre, Raphaël. "Morocco, Algeria and the Maghreb's Cold War." *Journal of North African Studies* 21, no. 5 (2016): 735–740.

Lenoir, Maya. "La Tunisie sous la loupe de Béatrice Hibou." *Nawaat*, September 9,

2006. https://nawaat.org/2006/09/09/la-tunisie-sous-la-loupe-de-beatrice-hibou/.

Lenzini, José. *Mouloud Feraoun: Un écrivain engagé*. Paris: Actes Sud, 2013.

Lewis, Bernard. *Race and Slavery in the Middle East*. Oxford: Oxford University Press, 1990.

Liebenberg, Ian, Jorge Risquet, V. G. Shubin, Gert Van der Westhuizen, Hedelberto López Blanch, and G. V. Shubin, eds. *A Far-Away War: Angola 1975–1989*. Stellenbosch, South Africa: Sun Press, 2015.

Lindberg, Kathryne V. "Mister Joans, to You: Readerly Surreality and Writerly Affiliation in Ted Joans, Tri-Continental Ex-Beatnik." *Discourse* 20, nos. 1–2 (1998): 198–227.

Lindsey, Ursula. "Restoring Morocco's Past." *New York Review of Books*, November 22, 2018. https://www.nybooks.com/articles/2018/11/22/restoring-moroccos-past/.

Lopes, Henri. *Tribaliques*. Yaoundé, Cameroon: Éditions Clé, 2011.

Lopes, Paul. *Art Rebels: Race, Class, and Gender in the Art of Miles Davis and Martin Scorsese*. Princeton, NJ: Princeton University Press, 2019.

Lorde, Audre. "Sexism: An American Disease in Black Face." In *Sister Outsider*, 60–65. Berkeley, CA: Crossing Press, 1984.

Lovejoy, Paul, ed. *Slavery on the Frontiers of Islam*. Princeton, NJ: Markus Wiener, 2004.

Lubin, Alex. *Geographies of Liberation: The Making of an Afro-Arab Political Imaginary*. Chapel Hill: University of North Carolina Press, 2014.

Lyamlahy, Khalid. "'A Boundless Creative Ferocity': The *Souffles/Anfas* Generation, Moroccan Poetry, and Visual Art in Dialogue." In *Multilingual Literature as World Literature*, ed. Jane Hiddleston and Wen-chin Ouyang, 51–68. New York: Bloomsbury, 2021.

———. Introduction to *Agadir*, by Mohammed Khaïr-Eddine. Trans. Pierre Joris and Jake Syersak. New Orleans: Diálogos Books, 2020.

Lydon, Ghislaine. *On Trans-Saharan Trails: Islamic Law, Trade Networks and Cross-Cultural Exchange in Western Africa*. Cambridge: Cambridge University Press, 2009.

———. "Saharan Oceans and Bridges, Barriers and Divides in Africa's Historiographical Landscape." *Journal of African History* 56 (2015): 3–22.

———. "Writing Trans-Saharan History: Methods, Sources and Interpretations across the African Divide." *Journal of North African Studies* 10, nos. 3–4 (2005): 293–324.

Mackenzie, Scott, ed. *Film Manifestos and Global Cinema Cultures: A Critical Anthology*. Berkeley: University of California Press, 2014.

Mackintosh-Smith, Tim, ed. *The Travels of Ibn Battutah*. London: Picador, 2002.

Mahler, Anne Garland. *From the Tricontinental to the Global South: Race, Radicalism, and Transnational Solidarity.* Durham, NC: Duke University Press, 2018.

Makalani, Minkah. *In the Cause of Freedom: Radical Black Internationalism from Harlem to London, 1917–1939.* Chapel Hill: University of North Carolina Press, 2011.

Maldoror, Sarah, dir. *Monogambee.* Algiers: Isabelle Films, 1969.

———, dir. *Sambizanga.* Luanda, Angola: Isabelle Films, 1972. https://www.youtube.com/watch?v=QvoaUprC5bg.

Mamdani, Mahmood. *Citizen and Subject: Contemporary Africa and the Legacy of Late Colonialism.* Princeton, NJ: Princeton University Press, 1996.

Manderson, Lenore, and Margaret Jolly, eds. *Sites of Desire, Economics of Pleasure: Sexualities in Asia and the Pacific.* Chicago: University of Chicago Press, 1997.

Manji, Firoze, and Bill Fletcher Jr. *Claim No Easy Victories: The Legacy of Amílcar Cabral.* Dakar: Conseil pour le Développement de la Recherche Économique et Sociale en Afrique (CODESRIA), 2013.

Maraini, Toni. "Black Sun of Renewal." *Springerin* 12, no. 4 (2006): 32–35.

Margarido, Alfredo. *Poetas Angolanos: Antologia da Casa dos Estudantes do Império.* Lisbon: Secretaría de Estado da Educação e Cultura, Gabinete de Estudos, 1962.

Marques, Alexandra. *Segredos da Descolonização de Angola.* Alfragide, Portugal: Publicações Dom Quixote, 2013.

Marsis, Safwa. *Tunisia: An Arab Anomaly.* New York: Columbia University Press, 2017.

Martin, Michael, ed. *Cinemas of the Black Diaspora: Diversity, Dependence, and Oppositionality.* Detroit: Wayne State University Press, 1995.

Martin, William, Michael West, and Fanon Che Wilkins, eds. *From Toussaint to Tupac: The Black International since the Age of Revolution.* Chapel Hill: University of North Carolina Press, 2009.

Martins, Helder. *Casa dos Estudantes do Império: Subsídios para a história do período mais decisivo da CEI (1953 a 1961).* Maputo: Textos Editores Moçambique, 2017.

———. *Porquê Sakrani? Memórias dum médico duma guerrilha esquecida.* Maputo: Editorial Terceiro Milénio, 2001.

Marynower, Claire. *L'Algérie à gauche, 1900–1962.* Paris: PUF, 2018.

Massad, Joseph A. *Desiring Arabs.* Chicago: University of Chicago Press, 2007.

Mata, Inocência, and Laura Cavalcante Padilha. *Mário Pinto de Andrade: Um intelectual na política.* Lisbon: Edições Colibri, 2000.

Matera, Marc. *Black London: The Imperial Metropolis and Decolonization in the Twentieth Century.* Oakland: University of California Press, 2015.

Mazo, Bernard. *Jean Sénac, poète et martyr.* Paris: Éditions du Seuil, 2013.

Mbembe, Achille. *On the Postcolony*. Berkeley: University of California Press, 2001.

Mbunga, Honoré. *Angola e a crise pós-independência: Cabinda (1975–2006)*. Luanda, Angola: Chá de Caxinde, 2014.

McAlister, Melani. "One Black Allah: The Middle East in the Cultural Politics of African American Liberation, 1955–1970." *American Quarterly* 51, no. 3 (1999): 622–656.

McClintock, Anne. *Imperial Leather: Race, Gender, and Sexuality in the Colonial Contest*. New York: Routledge, 1995.

McDarrah, Fred W., and Gloria S. McDarrah. *Beat Generation: Glory Days in Greenwich Village*. New York: Schirmer Books, 1996.

McDougall, Ann. "Concubinage as Forced Marriage? Colonial *Jawari*, Contemporary *Hartaniyya* and Marriage in the Islamic Republic of Mauritania." In *Marriage by Force?*, ed. Annie Bunting, Benjamin Lawrance, and Richard Roberts, 220–245. Athens: Ohio University Press, 2016.

———. "'To Marry One's Slave Is as Easy as Eating a Meal': The Dynamics of Carnal Relations in Saharan Slavery." In *Sexuality and Slavery: The Dynamics of Carnal Relations*, ed. Gwyn Campbell and Elizabeth Elbourne, 200–238. Athens: Ohio University Press, 2014.

McDougall, James. *A History of Algeria*. Cambridge: Cambridge University Press, 2017.

McDougall, James, and Judith Scheele, eds. *Saharan Frontiers: Space and Mobility in Northwest Africa*. Bloomington: Indiana University Press, 2012.

McKay, Claude. *A Long Way from Home*. New Brunswick, NJ: Rutgers University Press, 2007.

Meghelli, Samir. "From Harlem to Algiers: Transnational Solidarities between the African American Freedom Movement and Algeria, 1962–1978." In *Black Routes to Islam*, ed. Manning Marable and Hisham Aïdi. New York: Palgrave Macmillan, 2009.

———. "'A Weapon in Our Struggle for Liberation': Black Arts, Black Power, and the 1969 Pan-African Cultural Festival." In *The Global Sixties in Sound and Vision: Media, Counterculture, Revolt*, ed. Timothy Scott Brown and Andrew Lison, 167–184. New York: Palgrave Macmillan, 2014.

Memmi, Albert. *L'homme dominé*. Paris: Gallimard, 1968.

———. *Portrait du colonisé, précédé de portrait du colonisateur*. Paris: Gallimard, 2002.

Mémorial International Frantz Fanon. Paris: Présence Africaine, 1984.

Mendy, Peter Karibe. *Amílcar Cabral: A Nationalist and Pan-Africanist Revolutionary*. Athens: Ohio University Press, 2019.

Mensagem: Cinquentenário da Fundação da Casa dos Estudantes do Império 1944–1994. Lisbon: Associação Casa dos Estudantes do Império, 1997.

Meretoja, Hannah. *The Narrative Turn in Fiction and Theory: The Crisis and Return of Storytelling from Robbe-Grillet to Tournier.* New York: Palgrave, 2014.

Meriwether, James H. *Proudly We Can Be Africans: Black Americans and Africa, 1935–1961.* Chapel Hill: University of North Carolina Press, 2002.

Messiant, Christine. *L'Angola postcolonial.* Paris: Karthala, 2008.

Mestaoui, Lobna. "Ousmane Sembène, entre littérature et cinéma." *Babel: Littératures plurielles,* no. 24 (2011): 245–256.

Mfoulou, Jean. *L'O.U.A., triomphe de l'unité ou des nationalités? Essai d'une sociologie politique de l'Organisation de l'Unité Africaine.* Paris: L'Harmattan, 1986.

Micaud, Charles. *Tunisia: The Politics of Modernization.* New York: Frederick A. Praeger, 1964.

Middell, Matthias. "Francophonia as a World Region?" *European Review of History / Revue européenne d'histoire* 10, no. 2 (2003): 203–220.

Mokhtari, Omar. *1er festival culturel panafricain.* Algiers: Éditions Actualité, 1969.

Mokhtefi, Elaine. *Algiers, Third World Capital: Freedom Fighters, Revolutionaries, Black Panthers.* Brooklyn, NY: Verso, 2018.

Mokhtefi, Mokhtar. *J'étais Français-Musulman: Itinéraire d'un soldat de l'ALN.* Algiers: Barzakh, 2016.

Monémbo, Tierno. *Bled.* Algiers: Apic Éditions, 2018.

Monjib, Maâti. *La monarchie marocaine et la lutte pour le pouvoir.* Paris: L'Harmattan, 1992.

———. "Le complot de Juillet 1963." https://maatimonjib.files.wordpress.com/2014/03/complot1963.pdf.

Moorman, Marissa J. *Intonations: A Social History of Music and Nation in Luanda, Angola, from 1945 to Recent Times.* Athens: Ohio University Press, 2008.

Moser, Gerald M. "The Poet Amílcar Cabral." *Research in African Literatures* 9, no. 2 (1978): 176–197.

Mrad Dali, Inès. "Les mobilisations des 'noirs tunisiens' au lendemain de la révolte de 2011: Entre affirmation d'une identité historique et défense d'une 'cause noire.'" *Politique africaine* 40, no. 4 (2015): 61–81.

Mudimbe, Valentin-Yves. *The Invention of Africa: Gnosis, Philosophy, and the Order of Knowledge.* Bloomington: Indiana University Press, 1988.

———. *The Surreptitious Speech: "Presence Africaine" and the Politics of Otherness, 1947–1987.* Chicago: University of Chicago Press, 1992.

Murphy, David. *The First World Festival of Negro Arts, Dakar 1966.* Oxford: Oxford University Press, 2016.

Nacer-Khodja, Hamid, ed. *Albert Camus, Jean Sénac, or the Rebel Son.* East Lansing: Michigan State University Press, 2019.

———. *Jean Sénac: Critique algérien.* Algiers: Éditions El Kalima, 2013.

El Nahas, Hachem. *Al-Sīnima al-Tunisīa fī miṣr.* Cairo: Al-Majlis al-'āly lil-thaqāfa, 2003.

Nandjui, Pierre. *Houphouët-Boigny: L'homme de la France en Afrique*. Paris: L'Harmattan, 1995.

Ndiaye, Pap. *La condition noire: Essai sur une minorité française*. Paris: Folio, 2009.

Neuberger, Benyamin. "Black Zionism: The Return to Africa in Theory and Practice." In *Transnationalism: Diasporas and the Advent of a New (Dis)order*, ed. Eliezer Ben-Rafael and Yitzhak Sternberg, 595–611. Leiden: Brill, 2009.

———. "Early African Nationalism, Judaism and Zionism: Edward Wilmot Blyden." *Jewish Social Studies* 47, no. 2 (Spring 1985): 151–166.

Ngũgĩ wa Thiong'o. *Decolonising the Mind: The Politics of Language in Africa*. Nairobi: East African Publishers, 1994.

Ngwenya, Malangatana, and Paulo Soares. "Artes plásticas e movimento nacionalista em Moçambique." *Portuguese Literary and Cultural Studies* 30–31 (2017): 125–149.

Nirenberg, David. *Communities of Violence: Persecution of Minorities in the Middle Ages*. Princeton, NJ: Princeton University Press, 1996.

———. *Neighboring Faiths: Christianity, Islam, and Judaism in the Middle Ages and Today*. Chicago: University of Chicago Press, 2014.

Nwachukwu, Frank Ukadike. *Black African Cinema*. Berkeley: University of California Press, 1994.

Osten, Marion von. "Aesthetics of Decolonization: The Magazine *Souffles* (1966–1972)." *Asiatische Studien / Études Asiatiques* 70, no. 4 (2016): 1265–1284.

Oualdi, M'hamed. *Esclaves et maîtres: Les mamelouks au service des beys de Tunis du XVIIe siècle aux années 1880*. Paris: Publications de la Sorbonne, 2011.

———. *A Slave between Empires: A Transimperial History of North Africa*. New York: Columbia University Press, 2020.

Paolozzi, Letizia. *Primo festival culturale panafricano di Algeri: Dalla negritudine all' africanismo*. Milan: Giangiacomo Feltrinelli Editore, 1970.

Parker, Gabrielle. "Francophonie et universalité: Évolution de deux idées jumelles." In *Culture post-coloniale, 1961–2006: Traces et mémoires coloniales en France*, ed. Pascal Blanchard, Nicolas Bancel, and Sandrine Lemaire, 228–242. Paris: Autrement, 2006.

Parry, Benita. *Postcolonial Studies: A Materialist Critique*. London: Routledge, 2004.

Pawlik, Joanna. "Ted Joans' Surrealist History Lesson." *International Journal of Francophone Studies* 14, nos. 1–2 (2011): 221–239.

Peabody, Sue, and Tyler Stovall, eds. *The Color of Liberty: Histories of Race in France*. Durham, NC: Duke University Press, 2003.

Perna, Patrice, and Nicolas Otéro. *Morts par la France: Thiaroye 1944*. Paris: Les Arènes, 2018.

Peterson, Derek, and Giacomo Macola, eds. *Recasting the Past: History Writing and Political Work in Modern Africa*. Athens: Ohio University Press, 2009.

Petrucci, Filippo, and Marisa Fois. "Attitudes towards Israel in Tunisian Political Debate: From Bourguiba to the New Constitution." *Journal of North African Studies* 21, no. 3 (2016): 392–410.

Pieprzak, Katarzyna. *Imagined Museums: Art and Modernity in Postcolonial Morocco.* Minneapolis: University of Minnesota Press, 2010.

Pierre-Bouthier, Marie. "A Founding Transnational Experience for the Pioneers of Moroccan National Cinema: Studying in Łódź Film School in the 1960s–70s." *Journal of North African Studies* (February 2022). https://doi.org/10.1080/13629387.2022.2036978.

Pieterse, Jan Nederveen. *White on Black: Images of Africa and Blacks in Western Popular Culture.* New Haven, CT: Yale University Press, 1992.

Pitman, Thea, and Andy Stafford. "Introduction: Transatlanticism and Tricontinentalism." *Journal of Transatlantic Studies* 7, no. 3 (2009): 197–207.

Plummer, Brenda Gayle. *Rising Wind: Black Americans and U.S. Foreign Affairs, 1935–1960.* Chapel Hill: University of North Carolina Press, 1996.

Pontecorvo, Gillo, dir. *The Battle of Algiers.* Igor Film and Casbah Film, 1966.

Pouessel, Stephanie. "Les marges renaissantes: Amazigh, Juif, Noir; Ce que la révolution a changé dans ce 'petit pays homogène par excellence' qu'est la Tunisie." *L'année du Maghreb* 8 (2012): 143–160.

———, ed. *Noirs au Maghreb: Enjeux identitaires.* Paris: Karthala, 2012.

Prashad, Vijay. *The Darker Nations: A People's History of the Third World.* New York: New Press, 2007.

Rahal, Malika. *Algérie 1962: Une histoire populaire.* Paris: La Découverte, 2022.

———. "Comment faire l'histoire de l'Algérie indépendante." *La vie des idées,* March 13, 2012. https://laviedesidees.fr/Comment-faire-l-histoire-de-l-Algerie-independante.

———. "A Local Approach to the UDMA: Local-Level Politics during the Decade of Political Parties, 1946–56." *Journal of North African Studies* 18, no. 5 (December 2013): 703–724.

———. *L'UDMA et les Udmistes: Contribution à l'histoire du nationalisme algérien.* Algiers: Barzakh, 2017.

Rakaba, Reiland. *Concepts of Cabralism: Amilcar Cabral and Africana Critical Theory.* London: Lexington Books, 2015.

Rao, Rahul. *Third World Protest: Between Home and the World.* Oxford: Oxford University Press, 2010.

Ratcliff, Anthony. "Liberation at the End of a Pen: Writing Pan-African Politics of Cultural Struggle." PhD diss., University of Massachusetts, 2009.

———. "When Négritude Was in Vogue: Critical Reflections of the First World Festival of Negro Arts and Culture in 1966." *Journal of Pan African Studies* 6, no. 7 (2014): 167–186.

Reis, Raissa Brescia dos. "África imaginada: História intelectual, Pan-Africanismo, nação e unidade africana na 'Présence Africaine' (1947–1966)." PhD diss., Universidade Federal de Minas Gerais, 2018.

Remaoun, Hassan. "Le regard porté sur l'Afrique par le FLN durant la guerre de libération nationale en Algérie (1954–1962)." In *Entreprises coloniale et luttes de libération en Afrique*, 135–146. Algiers: CNRPH, 2015.

Reza, Alexandra. "African Anti-colonialism and the Ultramarinos of the Casa dos Estudantes do Império." *Journal of Lusophone Studies* 1, no. 1 (2016): 37–56.

Roberson, Jennifer. "The Changing Face of Morocco under King Hassan II." *Mediterranean Studies* 22, no. 1 (2014): 57–87.

Robin, Marie-Monique. *Escadrons de la mort, l'école française*. Paris: La Découverte, 2004.

Robinson, David, and Jean-Louis Triaud, eds. *Le temps des marabouts: Itineraires et strategies islamiques en Afrique occidentale francaise, v. 1880–1960*. Paris: Karthala, 1997.

Rodney, Walter. *How Europe Underdeveloped Africa*. London: Bogle L'Ouverture, 1972.

Rollinde, Marguerite. *Le mouvement marocain des droits de l'Homme*. Paris: Karthala, 2002.

Rose, Peter I., ed. *Americans from Africa: Slavery and Its Aftermath*. New York: Atherton Press, 1970.

Rosinha, Maria do Rosário. *Antologias de poesia da Casa dos Estudantes do Império 1951–1963*. Lisbon: União das citades capitais de lingua portuguesa, 2014.

Russell, Michele. "Algiers Journal." *Freedomways* (Fall 1969): 355–364.

Sadai, Célia. "Racisme anti-Noirs au Maghreb: Dévoilement(s) d'un tabou." *Hérodote* 180, no. 1 (2021): 131–148.

Sahli, Mohamed Chérif. *Décoloniser l'histoire: Introduction à l'histoire du Maghreb*. Paris: François Maspero, 1965.

Saïd, Edward. *Orientalism*. New York: Vintage Books, 1979.

Saïd, Rafik. *La politique culturelle de la Tunisie*. Paris: UNESCO, 1970.

Sainson, Katia. "'Entre Deux Feux': Jean Sénac's Struggle for Self-Determination." *Research in African Literatures* 42, no. 1 (2011): 32–48.

Salama, Ben, dir. *Alger, la Mecque des révolutionnaires (1962–1974)*. Paris: Arte, 2016.

———, dir. *1954, la fin d'un monde colonial*. Paris: Kuiv Productions, 2014.

Samraoui, Mohammed. *Chroniques des années de sang*. Paris: Éditions Denoël, 2003.

Sarner, Éric. "Jean Sénac, poète assassiné." *Revue Ballast*, November 12, 2014. https://www.revue-ballast.fr/jean-Sénac/.

Scaglioni, Marta. "Becoming the 'Abid: Lives and Social Origins in Southern Tunisia." PhD diss., Bayreuth International Graduate School of African Studies (BIGSAS), 2019.

Seesemann, Rudiger, and Benjamin F. Soares. "'Being as Good Muslims as Frenchmen': On Islam and Colonial Modernity in West Africa." *Journal of Religion in Africa* 39, no. 1 (2009): 91–120.

Sefraoui, Kenza. "'Encore un qui a tout dit!': Le groupe de *Souffles*, lecteur des *Damnés de la Terre*." *Politique africaine* 143 (2016): 73–91.

———. *La revue Souffles, 1966–1973: Espoirs de révolution culturelle au Maroc*. Rabat: Éditions du Sirocco, 2013.

Sellström, Tor, ed. *Liberation in Southern Africa: Regional and Swedish Voices; Interviews from Angola, Mozambique, Zimbabwe, Namibia, South Africa, Zimbabwe, the Frontline and Sweden*. Uppsala: Nordic Africa Institute, 1999.

———. *Sweden and National Liberation in Southern Africa: Formation of a Popular Opinion (1950–1970)*. Uppsala: Nordiska Afrikainstitutet, 1999.

Sembène, Ousmane, dir. *Camp de Thiaroye*. Dakar: Filmi Domirev, 1988.

———, dir. *La noire de . . .* Dakar: Filmi Domirev, 1966.

———, dir. *Le docker noir*. Paris: Présence Africaine, 2002.

———, dir. *Les bouts de bois de Dieu*. Paris: Pocket, 1960.

Sénac, Jean. *Œuvres poétiques*. Paris: Actes Sud, 1986.

———. "Poème-programme." *La république* (December 1963).

Senghor, Léopold Sédar, ed. *Anthologie de la nouvelle poésie nègre et malgache de langue française*. Paris: Éditions des PUF, 1948.

———. *Ce que je crois*. Paris: Grasset, 1988.

———. *Œuvre poétique*. Paris: Seuil, 1964.

Serfaty, Abraham. "Decidedly Marxist: An Interview with Abraham Serfaty (1992)." *Viewpoint Magazine*, March 19, 2019. https://viewpointmag.com/2019/03/05/decidedly-marxist-an-interview-with-abraham-serfaty-1992/.

Sharples, Carinya. "Flashback: 21 July 1969; Pan African Cultural Festival Rocks Algiers." *Carinya Sharples* (blog), September 24, 2012. https://carinyasharples.com/2012/09/24/flashback-21-july-1969-pan-african-culture-festival-rocks-algiers/.

Sharpley-Whiting, T. Denean. *Black Venus: Sexualized Savages, Primal Fears, and Primitive Narratives in French*. Durham, NC: Duke University Press, 1999.

———. *Négritude Women*. Minneapolis: University of Minnesota Press, 2002.

Shepard, Todd. *The Invention of Decolonization: The Algerian War and the Remaking of France*. Ithaca, NY: Cornell University Press, 2006.

———. *Sex, France, and Arab Men, 1962–1979*. Chicago: University of Chicago Press, 2018.

Shepp, Archie. *Live at the Panafrican Festival*. 1969. BYG-Actuel 529351.

Sherzer, Dina. *Cinema, Colonialism, Postcolonialism: Perspectives from the French and Francophone World*. Austin: University of Texas Press, 1996.

Signaté, Ibrahima. *Med Hondo: Un cinéaste rebelle*. Paris: Présence Africaine, 1994.

Silverstein, Paul. *The Racial Politics of the Amazigh Revival in North Africa and*

Beyond. POMEPS (Project on Middle East Political Science). https://pomeps.org/the-racial-politics-of-the-amazigh-revival-in-north-africa-and-beyond.

Slyomovics, Susan. *The Performance of Human Rights in Morocco*. Philadelphia: University of Pennsylvania Press, 2005.

Smith, Jennifer B. *An International History of the Black Panther Party*. New York: Garland, 1999.

Smith, William Gardner. *The Stone Face*. New York: Farrar, Straus, 1963.

Snipe, Tracy. *Arts and Politics in Senegal, 1960–1996*. Trenton, NJ: Africa World Press, 1998.

Souaïdia, Habib. *La sale guerre*. Paris: La Découverte, 2001.

Spivak, Gayatri Chakravorty. "Can the Subaltern Speak?" In *Marxism and the Interpretation of Culture*, ed. Cary Nelson, 271–313. Urbana: University of Illinois Press, 1988.

St. John, Peter. "Independent Algeria from Ben Bella to Boumédienne, I: The Counter-revolution and Its Consequences." *World Today* 24, no. 7 (1968): 290–296.

Stafford, Andy. "Tricontinentalism in Recent Moroccan Intellectual History: The Case of *Souffles*." *Journal of Transatlantic Studies* 7, no. 3 (2009): 218–232.

Stoler, Ann L. *Carnal Knowledge and Imperial Power: Gender, Race, and Morality in Colonial Asia*. Berkeley: University of California Press, 2010.

———. "Making Empire Respectable: The Politics of Race and Sexual Morality in 20th-Century Colonial Cultures." *American Ethnologist* 16, no. 4 (1989): 634–660.

Stora, Benjamin. *Histoire de la guerre d'Algérie (1954–1962)*. Paris: La Découverte, 1992.

Stora, Benjamin, and Sébastien Vassant. *Histoire dessinée de la guerre d'Algérie*. Paris: Éditions du Seuil, 2016.

———. *La guerre invisible: Algérie années 90*. Paris: Presses de Sciences Po, 2001.

Stouky, Abdallah. "Témoignage et regard sur la revue *Souffles*." Maroc Diplomatique, September 13, 2016. https://maroc-diplomatique.net/abdallah-stouky-temoignage-regard-revue-souffles/.

Stovall, Tyler. *Paris Noir: African Americans in the City of Lights*. Boston: Houghton Mifflin, 1996.

Suri, Jeremi. *Power and Protest: Global Revolution and the Rise of Détente*. Cambridge, MA: Harvard University Press, 2003.

Sylla, Abdou. *L'esthétique de Senghor*. Dakar: Éditions Feu de Brousse, 2006.

Tandjaoui, Hocine. *Clameur et autres textes*. Paris: 108 Éditions, 2017.

———. *La bande noire dans l'ombre*. Paris: 108 Éditions, 2015.

Tavani, Giuseppe. *Poesia africana di rivolta: Angola, Mozambico, Guinea, Capo Verde, São Tomé*. Bari, Italy: Laterza, 1969.

Tawfik, Rawia. "Egypt and the Transformation of the Pan-African Movement: The Challenges of Adaptation." *African Studies* 75, no. 3 (2016): 297–315.

Taylor, Jodie. *Festivalization of Culture*. Farnham, UK: Ashgate, 2014.

Tcheuyap, Alexie. *Postcolonialist African Cinema*. Manchester, UK: Manchester University Press, 2011.

"Ted Joans: Tri-continental Poet." *Transition*, no. 48 (1975): 4–12.

Temime, Émile, and Nicole Tuccelli. *Jean Sénac, l'Algérien: Le poète des deux rives*. Paris: Autrement, 2003.

Thénault, Sylvie. *Histoire de la guerre d'indépendance algérienne*. Paris: Flammarion, 2005.

Thomas, Dominic. "Culture post-coloniale 1961–2006: Traces et mémoires coloniales en France (review)." *Research in African Literatures* 38 (2007): 234–236.

———. *Nation-Building, Propaganda, and Literature in Francophone Africa*. Bloomington: Indiana University Press, 2002.

Tissières, Hélène Colette. *Transmigrational Writings between the Maghreb and Sub-Saharan Africa: Literature, Orality, Visual Arts*. Translation by Marjolijn de Jager. Charlottesville: University of Virginia Press, 2012.

Tolan-Szkilnik, Paraska. "'Between Their Hands a Fabulous Geography Is Born': The Maghreb Generation and the Fight to Decolonize and Unite Africa's Minds." In *Visions of African Unity*, ed. Frank Gerits and Matteo Grilli, 237–259. London: Palgrave Macmillan, 2022.

———. "'Collecting Bosoms': Sex, Race, and Masculinity at the Pan-African Festival of Algiers, 1969." *Arab Studies Journal* 29, no. 2 (Fall 2021): 96–117.

———. "Flickering Fault Lines: The 1969 Pan-African Festival of Algiers and the Struggle for a Unified Africa." *Monde(s)*, no. 9 (2016): 167–184.

———. "The Quest for a Pan-African Groove: Saxophones and Stories from the Pan-African Festival of Algiers (1969)." *World Art* 9, no. 1 (2019): 67–80.

———. "Run Naked towards the Sun / Raise Your Barricades / Make Your Revolution: Poetic Revolution and Postcolonial Discourse." Roundtable in the *International Journal of Middle East Studies*, ed. Yoav Di-Capua and Cyrus Schayegh, 52, no. 1 (Spring 2020): 161–166.

Toumi, Mohsen. "La politique africaine de la Tunisie." In *Le Maghreb et L'Afrique subsaharienne*, ed. Slimane Chikh, 71–105. Paris: CNRS, 1980.

Triaud, Jean-Louis. "Giving a Name to Islam of the Sahara: An Adventure in Taxonomy." *Journal of African History* 55, no. 1 (2014): 3–15.

———. *Le crépuscule des affaires musulmanes en AOF, 1950–1956*. Paris: Karthala, 1997.

Tronrud, Wendy, and Ammiel Alcalay, eds. "Poet Painter / Former Villager Now / World Traveler." *Lost and Found* 6, no. 4 (2016): pts. 1 and 2.

Troutt Powell, Eve. *A Different Shade of Colonialism: Egyptian Nationalists and the Mastery of the Sudan, 1875–1925*. Berkeley: University of California Press, 2003.

Turino, Thomas. *Nationalists, Cosmopolitans, and Popular Music in Zimbabwe*. Chicago: University of Chicago Press, 2000.

Turner, Richard Brent. *Soundtrack to a Movement: African American Islam, Jazz, and Black Internationalism*. New York: New York University Press, 2021.

Vail, Leroy, and Landeg White. *Power and the Praise Poem: Southern African Voices in History*. London: James Currey, 1992.

Vaillant, Janet G. *Vie de Léopold Sédar Senghor: Noir, français et africain*. Paris: Karthala-Sephis, 2006.

Valensi, Lucette. "Le roi chronophage: La construction d'une conscience historique dans le Maroc poscolonial." *Cahiers d'études africaines* 30, no. 119 (1990): 279–298.

Van Deburg, William L. *New Day in Babylon: The Black Power Movement and American Culture, 1965–1975*. Chicago: University of Chicago Press, 1992.

Vermeren, Pierre. *Histoire du Maroc depuis l'indépendance*. Paris: La Découverte, 2016.

———. *La formation des élites marocaines et tunisiennes: Des nationalistes aux islamistes*. Paris: La Découverte, 2002.

———. "Misère de l'historiographie du 'Maghreb' postcolonial." *Afrique Contemporaine* 245, no. 1 (2013): 149–151.

Villa-Ignacio, Teresa. "Decolonizing Violence: Revolutionary Affinities between the U.S. Black Power Movement and the Moroccan Journal *Souffles*." *Journal of North African Studies* 23, nos. 1–2 (2018): 13–33.

Villegas, Henri. *Cuba and Angola: The War for Freedom*. Atlanta: Pathfinder Press, 2017.

Virmani, K. K. *Angola and the Superpowers*. New Delhi: Department of African Studies, University of New Delhi, 1989.

Von Eschen, Penny. *Race against Empire: Black Americans and Anticolonialism, 1935–1957*. Ithaca, NY: Cornell University Press, 1997.

Wagner, Daniel A. *Literacy, Culture and Development: Becoming Literate in Morocco*. Cambridge: Cambridge University Press, 1993.

Walters, Ronald W. *Pan Africanism in the African Diaspora: An Analysis of Modern Afrocentric Political Movements*. Detroit: Wayne State University Press, 1997.

Westad, Odd Arne. *The Global Cold War: Third World Interventions and the Making of Our Times*. New York: Cambridge University Press, 2011.

White, Luise, Stephan F. Miescher, and David William Cohen, eds. *African Words, African Voices: Critical Practices in Oral History*. Bloomington: Indiana University Press, 2001.

Wilder, Gary. *Freedom Time: Négritude, Decolonization, and the Future of the World*. Durham, NC: Duke University Press, 2015.

Williams, Frederick G. *Poets of Mozambique: A Bilingual Selection*. New York: Luso-Brazilian Books, 2006.

Williams, Michael W. "Pan-Africanism and Zionism: The Delusion of Comparability." *Journal of Black Studies* 21, no. 3 (1991): 348–371.

Wilson-Goldie, Kaelen. "The Revolution Will Be Anthologized." *Bookforum*, April–May 2016.

Wolseley, Roland E. *The Black Press, U.S.A.* Ames: Iowa State University Press, 1971.

Yacine, Kateb. *Le cercle des représailles.* Paris: Seuil, 1959.

———. *Nedjma.* Paris: Seuil, 1956.

Yates, James. *Mississippi to Madrid: Memoir of a Black American in the Abraham Lincoln Brigade.* Greensboro, NC: Open Hand Publishing, 1989.

Young, Crawford. *The Postcolonial State in Africa: Fifty Years of Independence, 1960–2010.* Madison: University of Wisconsin Press, 2012.

Young, Robert J. C. *Colonial Desire: Hybridity in Theory, Culture and Race.* New York: Routledge, 1995.

Zartman, William. "The Politics of Boundaries in North and West Africa." *Journal of Modern African Studies* 3, no. 2 (1965): 155–173.

Zerbo, Yacouba. "La problématique de l'unité africaine." *Guerres mondiales et conflits contemporains* 212, no. 4 (2003): 113–127.

INDEX

Note: Page numbers in *italics* indicate illustrations.

WORLDING THE MIDDLE EAST

Emily Gottreich and Daniel Zoughbie, editors

Jacob Norris, *The Lives and Deaths of Jubrail Dabdoub: Or, How the Bethlehemites Discovered Amerka*
2023

Nadim Bawalsa, *Transnational Palestine: Migration and the Right of Return before 1948*
2022

Carel Bertram, *A House in the Homeland: Armenian Pilgrimages to Places of Ancestral Memory*
2022

Susan Gilson Miller, *Years of Glory: Nelly Benatar and the Pursuit of Justice in Wartime North Africa*
2021

Amélie Le Renard, *Western Privilege: Work, Intimacy, and Postcolonial Hierarchies in Dubai*
2021

The authorized representative in the EU for product safety and compliance is:
Mare Nostrum Group
B.V Doelen 72
4831 GR Breda
The Netherlands

www.ingramcontent.com/pod-product-compliance
Lightning Source LLC
LaVergne TN
LVHW091121080826
845145LV00008B/1998